A Pr[illegible]ct of Anfield

by

Phil Armstrong

This book is published by
Grosvenor House Publishing Ltd
Link House
140 The Broadway, Tolworth, Surrey, KT6 7HT.
www.grosvenorhousepublishing.co.uk

A CIP record for this book
is available from the British Library

ISBN 978-1-83975-461-6

Some names have been changed throughout this book to protect the privacy of the individuals.

For my grandchildren - Andrew, Mikey, Robbie, William, John, Stephen and Katie - Grasp life, it’s wonderful.

CONTENTS

THE EARLY YEARS

I could feel an overwhelming sense of shame and trepidation as I waited for my Father to collect me from a police cell in the Anfield district of Liverpool. Surprisingly I was not subject to the almighty dressing down that I expected, but nevertheless I could sense the disappointment in my Father's voice as he struggled to understand the reasons for my misdemeanours. I was 15years of age and it wasn't the first time I had fallen foul of the law. It was time to change direction. Following a path to Walton jail was somehow far from appealing.

Liverpool in the 1950's and 60's was a colourful place and there is nowhere else on earth I would rather have spent my childhood. However, without being too disparaging to that most magical city, there was certain a 'rogueness' about the place that made sliding onto the wrong side of the law an almost acceptable pastime. That being said, the character of the people living in working class areas such as Anfield was, and undoubtedly still is, exceptional. Their warmth, community spirit, unique sense of humour and uncompromising willingness to help during difficult times, has without a doubt shaped my personality and given me a true and meaningful set of values.

A day at the seaside with Mum and Dad.
Late 1940s.

My early years were spent with my Mother and Father in our three bedroomed (what decadence!) rented terraced house at 12 Mansell Road. No bathroom, no hot water, no inside toilet and would you believe it no television. Saturday nights were special. The small zinc bath was taken off its hook in the cupboard under the stairs, placed in front of the coal fire in the living room and filled up with hot water. The hot water being supplied from numerous pans that had been heated up on the gas cooker in the kitchen. Feeling the heat from the fire whilst listening to 'Journey into Space' on the radio made bath nights something to really look forward to.

Five years old and the first major milestone of my life fast approaching. Before I knew it I found myself clutching my mother's hand as we set off down Boaler Street to, in my eyes, that most foreboding of buildings, Newsham Primary School. It was my first day of school and as we crossed the large concrete based playground, I was finding it increasingly difficult to be brave, especially as some of the children around me had already succumbed, evident by the tears rolling down their cheeks. Determined not to let myself down, and in the process upset my mum, I mustered all my determination and even managed a smile as we parted. And so began my formal education within a colourful and challenging area of working class Liverpool.

Actually, I quite enjoyed myself in primary school and never looked for an excuse not to attend. Mind you after a few years my whole world nearly came crashing down around my head. I was nine years old and quite settled in my class of around thirty pupils. Taking up my position at my desk in the back row of the classroom one Monday morning we were all intrigued as the Headmaster entered the room with an unknown lady at his side. After we had all settled, he introduced our new teacher, Miss Wallace. She had a lovely smile and I instantly and instinctively knew that I was going to like her.

As the weeks progressed, I was proved right, to the extent that I positively looked forward to attending school. One fateful day I was sat at my desk gazing in wonder at my delightful teacher when one of the most unnerving incidents of my life to-date unfolded. Turning to my fellow pupil, Roger, sat nearby I whispered in his ear "You know I'd love to see Miss Wallace's bum". Where on earth did that come from. I was only nine years old for heaven's sake! Anyway, my most inner thoughts had been expressed and matters were about to get worse. To my absolute horror, without hesitation Roger's hand shot up in the air as the words "Miss, Miss" poured out of his mouth. I wanted to run, the shame and humiliation about to come crashing down on me was going to be more than I could stand.

What followed was the first instance of me being looked after by my guardian angel. Just as Roger's hand had shot in the air Miss Wallace turned to write something on the blackboard. At the same time the school bell sounded for the end of lessons. In the commotion that followed Roger failed to gain the attention of Miss Wallace, which gave me the opportunity to bundle him out of the classroom whilst uttering threats of violence into his close by ears. Talk about being 'saved by the bell'.

I was just nine years old and my Mother had been seriously ill with lung cancer for a number of months. She was continually in and out of hospital which meant I was not really seeing much of both my parents. When my Father was not working, he was away visiting my mother. This meant I was spending a lot of time with my Nan. I'm not sure if it was to protect me, but I was not really told much about my Mother's condition. What I was aware of was the worried faces I was surrounded by and the general sombre atmosphere within the household. One afternoon my Father collected me from my Nan's and we took the short walk back to our house in Mansell Road. I could sense I was about to be told some news of my Mother's condition. Opening the front door, my father led me up the 'lobby' to the small lounge area. He sat me down next to the dining table and with tears in his eyes told me the devastating news that my Mother had died.

Initially I didn't really take it in and remember thinking 'how should I react, perhaps I should be crying?' Encouraging tears, I was taken into my father's arms where my false teardrops soon turned to agonising sobs as the reality of it all started to dawn on me. How could my Mother die, she was only young? What were we going to do now? I didn't want to not have a mum. The days following went by in a haze, with lots of aunts, uncles and well-meaning family friends giving me hugs, engulfing me in sympathy. It was thought that I should be spared the ordeal of attending the funeral, which at the time and, in fact to this day, I thought was the wrong decision. I was never given the opportunity to say goodbye to my lovely and loving Mother. Peering through the curtains from my Nan's parlour I watched as the funeral cars pulled up outside 12 Mansell Road. Seeing the coffin being carried to the hearse was heartbreaking.

After my Mother's death my life took on a rather forlorn pattern. My Father's job as a floor layer involved him working away from home on a fairly regular basis. This arrangement had both advantages and disadvantages as far as I was concerned. The advantages came in the form of a certain degree of freedom I was allowed. Freedom to play out late. Freedom to go off exploring into the Wirral and North Wales at the weekends and the freedom to go off camping for long periods during school holidays.

This freedom was exploited to the absolute limit during the school summer holidays of 1956. At the innocent age of 10 years myself and friends Dave Watson and Dickie Davies decided to take off and hitch-hike around the country. With a mere 10 shillings (50p) in our pockets and a minimal amount of clothing we departed the back streets of Liverpool and headed south.

On the evening of the first day, having managed to hitch lifts from a number of cars and lorries, we found ourselves in a rural area of Staffordshire. We weren't carrying any tents, sleeping bags or any form of shelter but had formulated a plan to cover sleeping arrangements. Off we strolled down a country lane until we came upon a large stone farmhouse flanked by numerous sheds and outbuildings. Boldly presenting ourselves at the grand farmhouse door we rattled the solid brass knocker. A plumpish, friendly, motherly looking lady opened the door and was obviously surprised to see three young schoolboys looking up at her. Cheekily we asked if we could sleep in the barn in return for any work she may have wished for us to undertake, pick potatoes, clear up the farmyard etc... She appeared really taken aback as she invited us in. After outlining our adventurous plans to her, she prepared a sustaining, hot and delicious meal. To our amazement she then insisted that she would not allow us to sleep in the barn and that we would spend the night in the comfort of her spare room in which was the biggest and most comfortable bed we had ever come across.

Departing in the morning with an abundant supply of sandwiches and fruit in our bags, we said a fond farewell and left with this wonderful lady's pleas to "take care" ringing in our ears. Of course she would not hear of us undertaking any work as a means of payment for our superb food and lodgings. This unconventional routine was adopted for the remainder of our trip with households the length of the country displaying great kindness to three cheeky youngsters from Scouseland.

Eventually we ended up in Plymouth. Paying for a cup of tea and a scone in a cafe on the Hoe, the proprietor of the establishment, yet another motherly and warm-hearted lady engaged us in conversation. She was incredulous when she heard we had hitch-hiked down from Liverpool and insisted that we accompany her back to her home on the outskirts of the town. Once again, we had landed on our feet and were more than well looked after.

After more than a week away we all agreed to head back up north. Nearing Liverpool, we were all seated in the cab of a large articulated lorry. Speaking to the driver he informed us that his destination was Glasgow. We all looked at each other, smiled and nodded. Liverpool was given a miss as we ventured north of the border. Dropped off in a somewhat rough area of the city, The Gorbals, we started wandering around. The area was quite deprived and although we didn't come from an affluent area ourselves, we felt a little threatened. This feeling turned to reality when a group of youths overheard this strange language emanating from these three young scousers. Menacingly approaching there was no hint of a warm Scotch welcome as one of the group, knife in hand, threatingly said "Giz us what is in yer bags or we'll slit your gizzards". How we got out of that situation I'm not quite sure, but thankfully escape we did.

Heading east we found ourselves on the banks of the River Forth before unanimously agreeing that it was time to head home. After ten amazing and uplifting days we arrived back in Liverpool. We had been keeping in touch with our parents, inclusive of my Dad, by calling from local telephone boxes. All at home had been understandably concerned with our actions, but secretly proud of what we had achieved. This was confirmed a week later when an article appeared in the Liverpool Echo outlining our exploits and praising our adventurous spirit. It turned out that it was my father who had contacted the newspaper and told them of our unconventional summer holiday.

The disadvantages proved to be more sinister. As a young 10-year-old I found myself spending many nights alone in our three bedroomed terrace in Mansell Road. At the time friends and close relations could not understand why I chose to stay by myself when I had loving grandparents only a matter of a few doors away who were more than willing to have me stay with them when my Father was out of town. The truth of the matter was that a dreadful and almost unbelievable incident occurred which left me totally confused, frightened and riddled with a peculiar sense of false guilt. I was sexually abused by someone I loved and respected, my uncle Harry.

Harry was the youngest of my Mother's five siblings and lived with his parents, my grandparents. He was in his early twenties at the time and had served for two years in the Army carrying out his National Service. Eighteen months of that time was spent stationed in Hong Kong out in the Far East. I was mesmerised by his tales of exotic locations and daring adventures in a far-off magical land. I used to so much look forward to spending the night at Nanna's where I would be enthralled by Harry's ongoing tales. I didn't need asking twice when invited to sleep with Harry, it would just mean more great stories. You can imagine my horror and confusion when I awoke in the middle of one night to find I was being sexually abused. In my half asleep state it took me a while to realise and understand exactly what was going on. I just lay there petrified pretending to be asleep. It was truly awful.

Rising early next morning I was filled with a multitude of conflicting emotions, not least disgust. Should I confront uncle Harry? Tell my Grandparents? Tell my Father? In the end I did nothing. I couldn't take a chance on the consequences of revealing such a perverse and squalid event. It had the potential to rip the family apart. I just couldn't do it, especially to my beloved Nanna who I completely adored. So the secret has been mine throughout my life, and although it was the most awful of times I do not regret the extremely difficult and soul searching decision I made at such a young and innocent age.

Spending nights on my own in 12 Mansell Road was at times a daunting prospect. After leaving Nanna's in the early evening with her unable to understand why I would not want to stay in the comfort and security of her house, I would trudge the 100 yards or so to number 12. In the dark I would turn the front door key as my overactive imagination kicked into gear. The front door opened onto a long hallway (lobby), the light switch being positioned at the far end. Walking up that hall in the dark asking myself what I would do if I bumped into an evil, strange looking intruder was never easy. My heart would be pounding as I flicked on the light switch. If a face had appeared at that moment I'm convinced I would have collapsed in fright. That feeling of dread never left me no matter how many times I made that nerve jangling journey down that short dark lobby.

Going upstairs to my bed in the middle back bedroom was another ordeal. I was always convinced there was a mysterious being lying under my bed. As I was lying there, sometimes trembling, in the dark, I awaited this evil creature to start pushing his long, sharp, serrated edged knife up through the mattress and mercilessly into my prone body. Of course I would eventually drop off into a fitful sleep. However, an unfortunate part of this ongoing ordeal was that once under the blankets, if I awoke needing the toilet, I couldn't bring myself to getting out of bed in the dark (the light switch was in the far corner by the bedroom door), making my way downstairs through the parlour and kitchen and down to the bottom of the yard to the outside toilet. As a consequence, I spent many nights sleeping in soiled and foul-smelling sheets.

As with most experiences in life there was a positive development during this unfortunate period of my early years - Dreams. I developed the ability to control my dreams. Looking back, I'm sure it acted as a sort of psychological safety mechanism which stopped me slipping into some sort of juvenile depression. Once asleep I knew I was dreaming. This knowledge fuelled my imagination as I realized I could do almost anything without fear of physical harm or adult chastisement. The adventures I had in this extraordinary dream world were truly wondrous and served to lift my sagging spirits. I recall it got to the stage that I could select what I would like to dream about before I went to sleep.

It was during this magical period that I conceived the ultimate fantasy experience my dreams could open up for me. I wanted to fly. One night asleep in that house of mixed emotions and fears I found myself balanced on the outside ledge of my upstairs bedroom window. My heart was pounding as I was reassuring myself that I was in a dream. Even so there was a fear mixed with excitement and anticipation. "Do it, you are dreaming" I compelled myself. Finally, I fell forward and launched myself into the void. With arms spread wide I hurtled downwards towards the concrete yard below. With only a matter of feet to go before I smashed into the ground my body started to lift as I swooped upward and soared off into the night sky. The feeling of wonder and exhilaration was all consuming as I controlled my flight above the houses and parks of central Liverpool. How uplifting the mind can be. It certainly helped me when I feared I was slipping into an unavoidable period of despair.

Many years later, whilst enjoying a glass of superb malt whisky at the end of the day, I was relaying the above recollections to my married son Paul. Cradling his own glass of fine malt, he sat mesmerised by my account of flying in my fantasy dream world. "Dad" he uttered, "that is truly amazing. Would you believe that I have experienced exactly the same sort of dream you have just so vividly described. Uncanny, especially when you consider that my son is now an experienced commercial airline pilot.

At the tender age of 11 years, I had my first serious encounter with the law. On a warm spring afternoon, cousin Michael and myself decided to go for an adventurous walk around the sprawling countryside of Huyton. After climbing numerous trees and sighting the ideal spot to build a hideaway/den we set off back home. Not far from Mike's house we spotted an abandoned car, a Morris Minor I think, on the large grass verge of the main road into Liverpool. Unable to resist the urge to have one final exciting game we set about scrambling over the car, playing at drivers and cops and robbers. This game of make believe unfortunately turned into reality when out of nowhere a giant and imposing policeman appeared. Identifying an obvious pair of dangerous criminals, he set about his aggressive style of interrogation. What were we doing? What damage had we caused to the vehicle (it was a wreck!) and why did we have one of the orange, pop-out style indicators in our hands? Was the intention to steal it?

After he had just about reduced us to tears, he escorted us the half mile or so back to my uncle Bill's. Presenting us at the front door, he outlined the facts of our heinous crime, adding that we were to be charged with criminal damage and theft. Uncle Bill was really taken aback and asked to be taken to the vehicle in question. On arrival at the crime scene, he could not believe his eyes and almost burst into laughter. "You are obviously joking Officer" he said respectfully. When it dawned upon him that the Police Officer was deadly serious he became somewhat annoyed and almost ended up getting arrested himself.

Mike and I were duly charged and a month or so later were summoned to appear at Prescot Magistrates Court. Standing there in short trousers and school ties with lips quivering we were totally overwhelmed by the occasion. After patiently listening to all the evidence the Magistrate was, thankfully, not overly impressed and after chastising the arresting Officer completely threw out the charges and gave us an absolute discharge.

The whole experience was unnerving and should have put me off upsetting Police Officers for a very long time. Unfortunately, it was not to be, silly old Phil had to learn his lessons in life the hard way.

A favourite pastime when looking for exciting things to do was the reckless pursuit of 'Leggers'. This involved trying to act nonchalantly and indifferent as lorries or suitable vans approached road junctions. As the selected vehicle slowed down the idea was to approach the rear section without being detected, then to find a suitable hand grip to hang on to as the lorry pulled away. The length of Mansell Road was ideal as it led to an exhilarating ride of no more than two or three minutes from top to bottom. Of course I always seemed to be the one who pushed accepted limits.

A coal lorry leaving our street slowed down at the junction with Boaler Street, right opposite my Gran's house. Out I shot from a nearby 'back entry', locally known as 'jiggars', and jumped to find a grip in the middle of the rear tailgate. None of my mates joined me, probably sensing that it represented a challenge too far. Off we went turning right down Boaler Street towards Newsham Park. Boaler Street was considerably longer than Mansell Road and before long the coal lorry was gathering speed as I realized that the grip of my relatively small hands was not nearly as secure as I needed it to be. The top of the tailgate was too wide for my fingers to curl over. To my horror I could feel my fingers slipping as we belted along, passing houses and shops which were now appearing as nothing more than a blur to me. Exhilaration turned to panic as I struggled to hang on. Surely I could make it to the junction with Sheil Road? It was not to be. Well short of salvation, just opposite my school, my hand slipped from the tailgate and I came crashing down onto the tarmac, both my knees absorbing the initial impact before my body tumbled and rolled on along the unforgiving hard road surface. Luckily there was no following traffic, if there had been the resultant outcome could have been far worse than what it was. By the time my astonished and concerned mates arrived on the scene I had managed to pull myself onto the pavement as the lorry disappeared into the distance, the driver completely oblivious to the unfolding drama that was taking place at the rear of his vehicle.

My knees were an absolute mess of cuts, bruises and grazes, as were my elbows and arms. A few cuts on my face completed the look of devastation that my body presented. My poor Gran, once more she opened her front door to the wrecked mess of her adventurous Grandson after my admiring friends had deposited me on the doorstep of 187 Boaler Street. Although still at a fairly young age, the little common sense I had came to the fore as I made a conscious decision to cross 'Leggers' off my list of exciting things to do.

Almost a teenager and a number of memorable adventures behind me, with hopefully many more to come. It was the summer of 1958 and a number of 'our gang', myself, Dave and Ray Watson plus Dickie Davies, had made our way home, having run out of money, from an exciting camping trip in North Wales. What were we going to get up to now? Aimlessly walking down Sheil Road we came to the junction with West Derby Road. On the corner was a three foot or so high stone wall, behind which stood a six to eight foot high green metal junction box construction. Let's see if we can jump from the top of the wall over to the junction box, about four foot away, and scramble up on to its roof. Seemed like a fair challenge, so the four of us hauled ourselves up onto the wall. In preparing to make the leap, I just happened to glance down to the muddy surface below us. My heart started pounding, was that what I thought it was? There lying on the ground was a number of pound notes. Crashing down from the wall I scrambled to collect the ridiculous amount of money spread out before me, my disbelieving friends right alongside. Counting the notes with shaking hands the amount retrieved totalled over £20, a considerable amount in the '50s. It was almost like a dream. How did the money end up where it was? The consensus being that we wouldn't dwell on that mystery for too long. The more burning issue being what we should do with our newly acquired fortune. The suggestion of handing it in to the local police station was instantly discounted, surely this find was meant to be.

It didn't take too long to agree that we should return home, pick up our rucksacks and tents before heading off back to North Wales to resume our camping holiday.

Down at Lime Street Station we excitedly purchased our tickets for Prestatyn, a popular seaside resort we were getting quite familiar with. As we boarded the steam driven train it was noticeable that there were not too many other passengers, which gave us a choice of numerous compartments to occupy. The carriages were of the standard design for the period, having access doors to individual compartments which allowed direct entry from the platform. Once aboard there was another door opposite which allowed access to a corridor running the full length of the carriage.

Piling all our luggage on the overhead racks we settled down on our own and began to make plans for the promising days ahead. Emerging from the tunnel under the River Mersey it wasn't long before we were speeding through The Wirral countryside. The happy frame of mind we were all in resulted in an absolutely hair brained idea being unanimously agreed upon. Having established that the next compartment was empty, the dare was to transit from one compartment to the other via the outside of the train, whilst travelling along at considerable speed.

Of course reckless Phil was first to volunteer. Two guys took up position in the adjoining compartment and wound down the window.

My door nearly blew off as I opened it, the wind created by the speed of the moving train smashing it against the carriage side. Thankfully no serious damage was sustained. Taking a firm grip on a convenient hand rail I stepped out and down onto a narrow footplate which ran the full length of the carriage. Being buffeted by the wind was both frightening and exhilarating. After a short while and welcomed shouts of encouragement I found myself at the door of my sanctuary. Decision time, do I carry on past so the door can be opened thereby allowing me to return and enter, or do I just scramble up through the open window. The latter was deemed the most appropriate as opening the door would restrict the next foolhardy plonker from experiencing such an adrenalin packed adventure. With the help of one of my admiring friends I hauled myself up through the window and collapsed on the compartment floor with a huge silly grin on my face.

Only Dave managed to follow in my foolish footsteps, Ray and Dickie being denied the opportunity because of varying factors, such as a visit from a ticket inspector with a suspicious look on his face and calling at stations where additional passengers embarked. This of course put an end to our fun and games. Mind you what a great start to our unexpected extra holiday. Surely only good times awaited!

I never did quite figure out why most of my friends, affectionately and unthreateningly known as 'Our Gang', went to Butler Street Primary School whilst I attended the nearby Newsham Primary in Boaler Street, after all we all lived within a stone's throw of each other. Anyway, that's the way it was when the first major milestone of our education arrived, the dreaded 'Eleven Plus'. Not wishing to sound boastful, it turned out that of all my friends I was the only one to pass. I suppose I should have been elated, however, circumstances dictated that it was somewhat of a curse that, along with numerous other factors, resulted in me completely wasting my early education.

The policy at the time dictated that the grade of passing the Eleven Plus determined the choice of school you could attend. A high-level pass meant you could opt to attend a Grammar School, inclusive of such prestigious establishments as the Liverpool Collegiate and the Liverpool Institute. Grammar Schools provided an academic and more broadly intellectual education. Middle grade passes offered the opportunity to study at one of the city's Technical Schools, where the emphasis was on preparing students for a trade such as electrician, plumber, carpenter etc. Finally, lower grade passes could attend Commercial Schools who concentrated on preparing pupils for a career in admin, banking etc. Pupils who didn't pass the Eleven Plus went to Secondary Modern schools.

I was awarded a higher-grade pass and therefore presented with the opportunity to attend any secondary school in Liverpool.

Being only 11 years of age, I sought the advice and guidance of my family, who were all of a working class background. Everyone I spoke to, inclusive of uncles, grandparents and my own father, unhesitatingly advised that I should grab the chance to attend a Technical School. 'You get yourself a trade my son,' was their well-meaning viewpoint.

Returning to school, I was somewhat taken aback by the shocked reaction of my primary school teachers when I informed them of my decision. They couldn't understand why I would forego the life changing opportunity to attend the best of Liverpool's most renowned seats of education. But that's the way it was, and I sincerely believe that all my family genuinely had my best interests at heart.

So there I was on my first day at Walton Technical School all decked out in school tie, blazer adorned with school badge and that most hideous and hated item of all, my school cap. The humiliation and verbal abuse I had to suffer from that day on was unrelenting, 'College Pudding' being one of the more gentle terms I had to endure.

This all resulted in me completely wasting my early education, a fact I am not particularly proud of. However, by way of explanation, my priority at the time was to be accepted by my secondary school mates. If this meant gaining their respect by way of bunking off school, rebelling with regard to the wearing of school uniform and generally being a nightmare pupil, then so be it!

My final year of school and absolutely nothing achieved, certainly on the academic front. No, I was still intent on being accepted as 'one of the boys' in my local gang. One of the relatively harmless misdemeanours I drifted into was bunking off school, especially on Friday lunchtimes. There was a place where it all was happening in a backstreet in central Liverpool. That somewhat unremarkable area was called Mathew Street which housed a brick lined cellar called 'The Cavern'. It was the early swinging sixties and the mind-boggling amount of musical talent forming in the city were all anxious to play The Cavern, that was the place to be noticed. Meeting up with my friends at lunchtime we would join the ever-expanding queues that formed whenever there was a session. The crowded atmosphere within the main stage area was electric. In such a small space groups like Gerry and the Pacemakers, The Searchers, Rory Storm and the Hurricanes, The Mersey Beats and many more created such a sound and beat that your body, without prompting, automatically broke into rhythmic motion. Evening outings followed the lunchtime visits and it wasn't long before just about every one of my pals were saying "Have you seen The Beatles yet, they are absolutely fabulous". Thinking to myself "Well they can't be much better than the groups I've already seen" resulted in me not making any great effort to get along and listen to this new phenomenon. However, eventually

I found myself standing no more than 12ft away from John, Paul, George and Ringo as they tuned up on the small, cramped Cavern stage. I was mesmerised as they burst into song. They were so talented, so different and their humour was so natural and unique. My ultimate session when The Beatles were playing was when I found myself under one of the arches right next to the side of the stage, virtually no more than 2ft from John Lennon as he belted out 'Twist and Shout', an unforgettable experience.

A couple of months later as The Beatles' fame was spreading, they were programmed to appear on a local television programme called 'Look North'. I insisted that all the family in my Nanna's house gathered to watch. After their performance, which I thought was first class, my granddad caustically remarked "Is that it then? Can't see them going very far. Nothing at all to write home about!"

In fairness I don't wish to paint 'Our Gang' as a complete bunch of degenerates and 'no hopers'. Some of them were true friends who displayed such great characteristics as trust, loyalty, compassion and the all-important unique sense of scouse humour. Who knows where my path may have led if I had gone to the Liverpool Collegiate or Institute. One thing is certain that path wouldn't have led to the happiness and fulfilment I have since found - funny old life isn't it!

Dave Watson worked in a warehouse down by the docks. It was a retail store used to supply outlets throughout the country with a wide variety of electrical goods ranging from the latest transistor radios to washing and spin drying machines. Amongst our crowd, whenever one of us managed to secure employment questions like "What are your prospects like? What pay do you receive? How many weeks holiday do you get?" were never asked. The overriding and most important question of all, which of course was always the first to be asked was "How's the fiddle?" The 'fiddle' in Dave's case was excellent but required a partner in crime. Of course he needed to look no further than his closest and ever reliable pal, yours truly!

At least one day per week I would catch a bus down to the dock area and present myself below one of the warehouse loading bays at precisely one o'clock in the afternoon. At this predetermined time the loading bay door three floors up would squeak open followed by Dave asking if it was all clear. When I confirmed that it was, Dave would call "Stand-by" and throw down a couple of brand new state of the art transistor radios, tape recorders or other such valuable items. I would then place them in a bag and disappear with the booty. We had a 'Connection' who was willing to pay, what we considered reasonable sums for our ill-gotten gains. What a routine, which was used to fund our weekend outings to the lively and exciting nightlife of Liverpool's swinging sixties.

Of course it nearly all came crashing down around our heads. One day at the established time of one o'clock I took up position at the foot of the warehouse loading bay. Dave appeared at the door three storeys up and seemed to me somewhat agitated. He quickly asked if it was all clear. After a final check I confirmed that it was. If I had known what was coming that confirmation would never have passed my lips. "Be careful Phil" mumbles Dave "this one is rather large". Thereafter he launches down nothing less than a large boxed up television set before disappearing behind closing doors. Talk about understatements!

How I managed to catch and hold on to that television I'll never know. According to the laws of physics it should have knocked me over and ended up in a thousand smashed pieces on the roadside. But miraculously I did manage to catch and hold on to this latest illegally acquired item. After gathering myself and cursing my partner in crime, I thought "How am I going to get this thing home?", a distance of approximately five miles. It certainly wouldn't fit into my bag, which I decided to reluctantly abandon. I doubted that I would be allowed on a bus with it, so left with little choice I set off walking home with my cumbersome load.

Struggling along the streets of downtown Liverpool I found myself crossing over by the entrance to the Mersey Tunnel, at the foot of St. John's Gardens. Out of the blue I felt a tap on my shoulder followed by a scary question, "What have you got there son?". Turning round, to my horror, I was being towered over by an inquisitive looking policeman. In a moment of pure inspiration I deposited myself down on a nearby bench and said "Would you believe it, a van arrived at our warehouse from T.J.Hughes (a local well known Liverpool department store) earlier to take delivery of a large order of electrical goods, including televisions. The plonker of a driver loads up his van and takes off, leaving a television behind. When my boss realised what had happened he details off yours truly to carry the damn thing up to the shop in London Road. What a job to get lumbered with. I am completely knackered". To my absolute astonishment this threatening policeman completely accepted my story and without trying to verify my spur of the moment tale, advised me to rest a while and to be careful on the remainder of my journey. With a friendly smile he bid me farewell. Thank heavens he didn't offer to escort me the remaining mile or so to T.J.Hughes!

My wasted education resulted in my old friend Ray Watson landing me the esteemed position of Junior Dispatch Officer within a cooked meats/sausage factory in Bootle. What a nightmare four or five weeks that turned out to be. As a fresh young lad with limited experience of the opposite sex I found myself walking into a den of hardy, life experienced and mischievous ladies who took great delight in reducing their new member of staff into an all shades of red, embarrassed young man. The things they got up to with those sausages are just too crude to describe in any detail.

Enduring my life of purgatory, Mr Mason, the company owner and hands-on factory supervisor, did not in any way help alleviate my ongoing misery. He always appeared to be at my side screaming out abuse for my apparent lack of effort, which didn't illicit any sort of sympathy from my work colleagues. After lunch one of my stimulating tasks was to cut up, weigh and wrap up a mountain of freshly made link sausages. Each package had to weigh precisely 16lbs. During week four, when my endurance was running low and I was having initial thoughts of running off to sea, Mr Mason stationed himself behind me as I was tackling a mountain of newly processed sausages. The abuse started flowing and I could feel this unfamiliar anger welling up inside me. 'Go away' I was muttering to myself. Of course he didn't. I then seemed to slip into a surreal world and found myself scooping up the largest amount of sausages I could hold. Swinging around I flung the link sausages at the unsuspecting Mr Mason. Thereafter I ripped off my work coat and headed out of the factory to thunderous applause and a vision of the factory owner completely draped in sausages and looking somewhat shocked and stunned.

I jumped on a bus to St.Johns Lane in the centre of Liverpool and boldly walked into the Royal Navy Careers Office. And so began my life at sea. Of course all these dramatic happenings came as a complete surprise to my unsuspecting family when I finally plucked up the courage to let them know of my plans.

My poor old Gran was devastated and my Father completely taken by surprise. Of course lots of well meaning advice came flowing my way, but my mind was made up and there was no turning back.

A couple of weeks later I didn't feel so brave when I realised I would have to return to the dreaded sausage factory to collect my P45. Arriving at the main entrance I entered the factory space. The fearsome ladies who had made my life so miserable in the past greeted me as a returning hero, making me a cup of tea and forcing a heavily sauced sausage sandwich in my hand. Before long I was summoned to Mr Masons' office. Knocking on the door before meekly entering I said a somewhat nervous "hello". Sitting behind his grand desk looking stern and imposing, he retorted "That was some performance the other week". I muttered a nervous apology, which to my surprise he graciously accepted. We went on to have a civilised and worthwhile discussion with regard to my future which ended with Mr Mason shaking my hand and genuinely wishing me all the very best for the years ahead. It just goes to show how easy it is to make hasty appraisals of people. I left that day with a renewed healthy respect for Mr Mason, the man who was so instrumental in determining the future course of my life.

One enlightening consequence of my choice of career was the fact that I finally found out that I was adopted. When asking for my birth certificate, which was required by the Naval

Recruiters, a strange sort of silence fell over the family. The more I asked the more I seemed to be ignored. Eventually, after virtually pleading for some sort of response, my dear old granddad, blinded from WW1, roared out "for god's sake tell the lad". "Tell me what?" I enquired. Compassionately he informed me that I had been adopted as a six month old baby. It all came as a bit of a shock and I recall leaving the house somewhat taken aback and totally confused. My thoughts and feeling were all over the place as I wandered aimlessly around the backstreets of Liverpool. Eventually I realised that my love for my family would never change, I just found it hard to understand why I had not been told earlier. Later on my Father had a long chat with me and explained the circumstances of my adoption. He and my Mother always intended on letting me know about my background but kept putting it off, fearing that somehow knowledge of my biological roots would affect my feelings towards them. They couldn't have been more wrong.

Time to move on. A whole new world was awaiting.

A LIFE AT SEA

TRAINING

On reflection, perhaps the most significant decision in my life was to join the Royal Navy. At the tender age of 16 years I made the brave decision to leave the encroaching 'arm of the law' behind me and take off for a life of adventure on the high seas. The decision was completely my own, helped along by the scary Mr Mason.

On a cold, wintry Monday morning in December 1962 my Father accompanied me to Lime Street station. He was there to bid farewell as I left my hometown of Liverpool for a life of travel, wonder and companionship at sea. Although sorry to see me leave, I felt he was more than a little proud to see me trying to make something of myself. After his final words of encouragement and sound advice on how to make the best of my chosen career, I boarded the steam train bound for Plymouth.

I sat down next to another young lad who was leaning out of a slide down window waving frantically to people on the platform, who I later found out were members of his family. As the train left the familiar surroundings of Merseyside we hesitatingly said hello to each other. Thereafter it didn't take long to discover we were both destined for HMS RALEIGH in Cornwall to join Her Majesty's Royal Navy. My new found companion, Mick, and I just seemed to gel, no doubt because of the apprehension we shared as we travelled off into the unknown.

Arriving in Plymouth in the early hours of the evening we were met by members of the Naval Regulating Branch (R.N. Policemen), who escorted us to a naval vehicle to transport us across the River Tamar at Torpoint and onwards to the nearby New Entry Training establishment, namely HMS RALEIGH. Lugging our suitcases we were taken to an assembly area where we were told that shortly we would be fed and then directed to our 'mess', where we would be allowed to settle in before having an early night.

The following day we were to be subjected to numerous talks and presentations before being invited to actually 'sign on'. At this stage I was actually glad to have Mick as my new mate, convinced that we were two scousers who were forever going to sail the high seas together!

The mess we were allocated was designed to accommodate approximately thirty ratings in double bunks, and after being introduced to our course Leading Hand we were advised to get some sleep as 'call the hands', our early morning call, was scheduled for 5:30am. Sleep didn't come easy that night, the excitement, unfamiliarity and feelings of foreboding all conspiring to keep most of us awake. The sound of a couple of lads sobbing into their pillows didn't help either. It seemed to be only a matter of minutes after I eventually dozed off that my world exploded into a cacophony of sound. Our beloved Leading Hand had entered the mess with a short metal pipe in his hand, which he was banging against the metal bed frames as he made his way between bunks. As if that wasn't enough he was screaming at the top of his voice "Come on let's be having you. Hands off cocks, on socks" and many more colourful naval expressions. What an awakening.

It was Tuesday, 11th December 1962, and after a hearty breakfast all the new recruits, inclusive of Mick and myself, were lined up outside an office where the evil deed of 'signing on' would be concluded. I suppose it was not an event to be taken lightly, as in those distant days once your signature had been appended to that legal document there was no going back, you were the property of the Royal Navy until the far-off age of 27 years.

Initial engagements were for nine years active service plus three years 'Reserve'. The nine years did not start until the age of 18yrs was reached, with any time served before that age, as in my case, being deducted from reserve time. There were no options whatsoever to leave before your time was served.

I was lined up behind Mick, who was joining as a Cook. As we approached the signing on desk Mick became increasingly agitated, repeatedly turning to me and expressing his doubts with regard to the monumental decision he was about to make. I had no such reservations and in my own sort of way tried to reassure him. My efforts proved pointless. As Mick approached the Officer seated behind the desk, to my astonishment he blurted out "I'm not going to do it", turned around and left the building. I never saw Mick again, but have often wondered how his life panned out. After a moment of confusion and commotion I was invited to sign on as a Junior Electrical Mechanic 2nd Class. This I did without hesitation.

The following day was a whirlwind of events, starting with a visit to the camp barbers for my first service haircut. Of course disappointingly there was no enquiry as to how I might like my Elvis Presley type crowning glory restyled, it was just a case of gritting my teeth as the close cutting shaver was directed back and forward over all areas of my head. 'Short back and sides' did not even come close to describing my new look. Next it was off to Naval Stores to be issued with our new kit, inclusive of my first rough surge, red badged, bell bottomed sailor suit, straight 'off the peg'. In fairness we were also measured up for our No.1 suits which were 'made to measure' and issued at a later date during our training. As soon as we had all our kit issued we were taken off to change. All our civilian clothes were taken off us, parcelled up and posted off to our home addresses.

The main event on the Thursday was getting paid. Lining up in the drill shed, we were called to the pay desks where we were expected to salute, take off our caps and call out in a loud clear voice our name and official service number. Being new at the game resulted in some quite hilarious performances in front of the Supply Officer and Regulating Staff. We received two weeks pay at £2.50 per week and an additional two weeks ration allowance (R.A.), I had never had so much money in all my life, close to £11!

On the Friday I found myself on my way back up north to Liverpool for Christmas Leave. I could hardly believe it, I hadn't been in the Navy for a week yet here I was sat on a train in my 'red badge' sailor suit with a pocket full of money and two weeks leave ahead of me. What a great life the Royal Navy was turning out to be - yo ho ho!

The winter of 1962/63 was severe. Returning from my first two week leave period in the Royal Navy I was keen and looking forward to getting down to the serious business of basic naval training. Once more boarding an old steam train at Lime Street Station I settled down for the long journey to Plymouth. Outside my coach window the wind was howling and the snow was falling from the heavens in a constant blanket of white. We were due to arrive at around 9 o'clock on the Sunday evening. As we progressed south the downfall of snow appeared to intensify. Just south of Taunton the train came to a standstill, which turned out to be more than a temporary signal stop.

And so begins my 'Life in a blue suit.'

After half an hour or so a guard entered our carriage and informed all passengers that the track ahead was blocked by a snow drift. He couldn't provide us with an accurate estimate of when we might be on the move again but hoped it might be within the hour. That estimate proved to be wildly optimistic. After three or four hours the situation deteriorated as the heating system failed. The temperature in the train plummeted as the snow began to drift and build up against the side of the train. I could sense a definite atmosphere of alarm from my fellow passengers as they searched amongst their luggage for garments to keep them warm. My immediate concerns did not directly centre on my core body temperature, but on the fact that I was not going to make it back to HMS RALEIGH before my leave expired at 0800hrs.

Although not in the Navy for a very long time I was very much aware of the seriousness of being late (adrift!) when returning from leave. Punishment could be severe, but I suppose necessary. The consequences of being late and missing your ship sailing could be both operationally damaging and on a personal front, financially crippling. After almost 12 hours stranded in a worsening blizzard the track was cleared and our train slowly got underway. With the heating restored and hot drinks served to all we finally trundled into Plymouth station just before mid-day. To my surprise a naval coach was waiting to transport myself and a number of other recruits I didn't realize were on the train over the River Tamar to RALEIGH. To my absolute relief the accompanying Naval Regulating Staff (Police) let us know that no charges were to be brought against us as it was accepted that our lateness was due to exceptional circumstances. What a reasonable and understanding organisation this Navy was.

The extreme weather conditions continued throughout January and indeed the full six weeks of basic training. The course at HMS RALEIGH was designed to be both challenging and enlightening with regard to life at sea. The daily routine commenced at 0600 in the dark, bleak, freezing conditions surrounding the camp. All recruits were designated various cleaning tasks to be undertaken before the start of the training day. One particular duty regularly seemed to fall my way, which in truth at any other time of the year may have been approaching a 'good number'. The parade ground at RALEIGH was a vast open area of ground that overlooked a large stretch of waterway. The Dias on which the Captain and his entourage positioned themselves when one of the never-ending series of parades took place was a rather grand looking affair with two large imposing brass cannons taking pride of place on either side of the platform. These two cannons had to be polished up daily to maintain their majestic, gleaming appearance. Collecting my cleaning clothes and tin of brasso (bluebell!), I would troop off in the dark to undertake this most important of missions. In January 1963 this mission was not one to be taken lightly. With the arctic wind howling across the deserted parade ground, the bluebell tended to begin to freeze as soon as it was applied to the gleaming barrels of the cannons. Trying to spread and polish it with virtually no feeling in your fingers was indeed a challenge. Failure to maintain the pristine condition of the cannons would inevitably incur the wrath of the scrutinising training staff, which was motivation enough for me to rub away for all I was worth. Good character forming stuff!

Training itself came in many forms inclusive of personal hygiene and how to maintain your kit, fitness sessions in the gymnasium, assault course runs, classroom periods covering naval history, routines and command structure. In addition there were damage control and fire-fighting exercises undertaken in a special unit designed to simulate the conditions to be found on an operational warship.
Then of course there was my personal favourite, parade ground training. It was here that we learnt how to march and how to handle military 303 rifles.

Not long into training I formed a close bond and friendship with a chap from Fareham in Hampshire who went by the name of Terry Stevenson. Terry came from a naval family, with his father having served for a full 22 years, achieving the rank of Chief Petty Officer Yeoman. Terry therefore had a slight insight into the R.N. as opposed to my almost complete ignorance. After overcoming the language barrier (broad scouse to a southerner is akin to trying to interpret Japanese!), the advice he had to offer was most welcome.

Where we both really hit it off was on the parade ground. The drill instructors (G.I.s), who had the unenviable task of transforming us from uncoordinated civilians to a smart well drilled military unit, were to my mind, and Terry's, born comedians. This view was not shared by the majority of our recruit colleagues. Getting some precise manoeuvre wrong would result in the guilty party having to endure a tirade of abuse and colourful language from the attending G.I. This could lead to tears welling up in the eyes of the offending member of the squad, coupled with a desire to be back in the arms of dear old mum. For some unfathomable reason such occasions had a completely different affect on me. When being bawled at for some minor misdemeanour I would find the G.I.'s language so outrageous and funny that I would start to giggle or at times actually chortle with laughter. This led to me ending up one of the fittest in the squad as I spent more time than most 'doubling' around the parade ground with my weighty 303 rifle bouncing off my shoulder. Terry was the same in his approach to parade ground training, which resulted in him laughing when I was getting a 'bollocking' and vice-versa. It was always nice to have company as I pounded around that large, windswept area of tarmac!

Training was going well and I was really enjoying the challenges that came my way on a daily basis. I was putting everything into my new way of life as I was now convinced more than ever that the Royal Navy was the way ahead. Unfortunately, this feeling of well-being was about to be shattered. One dark day

I was ordered to report to my Divisional Officer, an authoritative figure for whom I had the greatest respect. Why would he want to speak to me? It must be something serious, and indeed it was. Marched in to his office I was ordered to stand to attention in front of his desk. With an extremely serious look on his face, this figure of authority sat in front of me and solemnly informed me that I had been summoned to appear at Liverpool Magistrates Court in a week's time.

Bewilderment followed as I realised that once again one of my foolish criminal actions had, as to be expected, caught up with me. The incident related to a period before applying to join the Navy, when I was on a camping holiday in Prestatyn, North Wales with my old mates Dave Watson and Dickie Davies. Walking along a deserted section of the promenade late one evening we came across a relatively small gift shop that sold a variety of local souvenirs. Stupidly we broke into the place and helped ourselves to handfuls of inexpensive gifts on display. It wasn't exactly the heist of the century and on reflection an absolutely stupid thing to do. As we strolled off laughing a local policeman seemed to appear from nowhere. Oh dear, Liverpool Magistrates Court here we come.

The three of us were lined up in front of the Magistrate's Bench, me in my recently issued No.3 Naval Uniform. It was a clear cut case to which we all pleaded 'Guilty'. The stern looking Magistrate ordered Dave and Dickie to

be subject to background reports with a view to facing a possible custodial sentence in Borstal. Turning to me, he asked if there was anyone in the court who had anything to say on behalf of Armstrong? Fortunately for me there was, in the form of a Royal Navy Officer who had travelled up from HMS RALEIGH in Cornwall. He addressed The Bench in a clear, well spoken voice saying
"Armstrong is halfway through his basic training and to-date is performing extremely well. It is felt that he has the potential to have a successful career in the Royal Navy".

The court went quiet as the Presiding Magistrate considered the favourable remarks made on my behalf. He then looked me squarely in the eyes and proceeded to give a no holds barred dressing down. Finishing off he said "Armstrong the only reason, the **only** reason you are not being considered for the same fate as your fellow accused is because you are standing there in that uniform. Now go away and make something of your life - fined £10". What a crossroads in my life, I had been given yet another opportunity to make something of myself, and this time I was determined to do so. Good thinking Phil. Let's hope you don't push your good fortune any further!

Thank heavens my initial draft to HMS COLLINGWOOD was coming to an end. I had successfully completed my final exam and now after just on a year as a member of the Royal Navy I was eagerly awaiting the news that

I was to join one of Her Majesty's ships deploying out to the Far East or Caribbean. Disappointingly my adventures on the high seas were to be put on hold. Still things could have been worse. I was drafted to HMS ROOKE in Gibraltar where I was scheduled to work in the various radio stations and communications centres around and within 'The Rock'. Not what I was really hoping for but at least I was finally about to travel abroad to sample life in the exotic Mediterranean.

It was to be about two months before I actually departed for Gibraltar. In the meantime myself, along with my classmates awaiting to go on draft, were to work 'part of ship'. All sounds very nautical, but in fact it involved carrying out various mundane and sometimes downright offensive tasks, especially for such highly trained technicians! Jobs could range from working in the galley (washing pots and pans!) to dustbin party. I actually considered myself quite lucky to land the job of 'Training Office Messenger'. This involved being based in the camp Training Office, from where I would be dispatched to various offices and classrooms throughout that vast expanse of land known as HMS COLLINGWOOD. To assist in the delivery of this highly important documentation I was allocated nothing less than a red painted bicycle, affectionately known in naval circles as a 'Pusser's Red Devil'. Life couldn't be better. No more classrooms. No more worrying about exams. Just lazy, happy days riding my bike around the intricate road system of COLLINGWOOD.

All was going well until the day that I still consider to be the most embarrassing of my life. I was just a tender 17 year old with relatively little experience of the opposite sex. I was yet to establish any sound confidence when it came to impressing young ladies. Reporting to the Training Office shortly after breakfast I was assigned the task of delivering a letter to one of the offices in the main admin block. It had been 'pay day' the day before and as a result I had money a plenty. As I embarked on my highly important mission I decided to treat myself and dropped into the NAAFI, where I bought not a tube but a box of 'smarties'. The top of the box was opened and placed in one of the breast pockets of my working shirt. Off I set to the main admin office with not a care in the world. Riding along on my 'red devil' munching chocolate smarties, life just couldn't be better.

I arrived at my destination, parked my bike and made my way to the main admin office door. As I entered I found myself in a large open plan like office with an array of desks, around which were numerous WRNS studiously typing away at their machines. Immediately I felt uncomfortable as all eyes turned towards me. Directly in front of me a glamorous, efficient looking young lady asked if she could help. I awkwardly walked towards her, stammeringly explaining that I had a letter to deliver.

"Just put it on my desk" she instructed. I attempted to do so but unbelievably didn't quite get this most simple of tasks right. As I reached out to deposit the letter on her desk it dropped short and landed on the floor. This whole incident was turning into a nightmare as I felt the eyes of a dozen or so WRNS fall on me. The worst was yet to come. As I reached down to retrieve the letter, apologising profusely, all the smarties in my open shirt pocket spilled onto the floor. As I scrambled around picking up my little sweeties from all corners of the office I honestly wanted the ground to open and swallow me up. Red face didn't come in to it. I was beaming like the proverbial beacon as I exited that office to the giggles and I think sympathy of my female naval colleagues.

HMS ROOKE

The long awaited for day arrived and I had quite a spring in my step as I departed COLLINGWOOD to be transported to the airport and my flight to adventure in the sun drenched Mediterranean. Initially I was billeted in the main naval base accommodation facility within HMS ROOKE.

The military set-up in Gibraltar was quite fascinating with the majority of the complex communications centres being located deep inside 'The Rock'. After a month or so I was detailed to work in North Front, the site of the Transmitter Station and associated aerial field. This was a welcome development for me as it involved me moving to what might be considered first class accommodation in the form of a single story villa type building within the aerial field. Built to accommodate twelve to fifteen ratings it was more like a luxury holiday villa than a military barracks. As a bonus we had a very experienced and charismatic local chef who came in daily to prepare our meals - heaven.

Weekends, especially Sundays (our chef's day off), were wonderful. Making our own breakfasts could be entertaining, however, the evening meal was at times a complete fiasco. The Sunday routine involved us all, except duty personnel, traipsing off down to the local idyllic golden sanded beaches within Catalan Bay. The local refreshment establishment, The Village Inn, was most welcoming, stocked with a wide range of cool beers, Spanish wines and exotic spirits available to create a relaxing and joyful atmosphere. The one slight hiccup with Sundays was the main evening meal. With our beloved Chef on his day off, in turn two of us would be selected to prepare and serve the main evening meal. After a session down in The Village Inn the food presented for consumption could be far from what might be considered cuisine. What was meant to be a mouth watering traditional Sunday roast often turned out to be no more than a burnt offering.

Of course life wasn't all play and no work and over the coming months I found myself, after the Transmitter Station, working in the

Main Control Room, situated deep inside The Rock, followed by a longer period of watch-keeping in The Receiver Site at the southern end of the colony. All this technical experience resulted in me being called forward to be subject to a not too searching aural examination into my radio knowledge, carried out by my Divisional Officer. I managed not to make a complete fool of myself and shortly afterwards found myself promoted to the exalted rank of Radio Electrical Mechanic 1st class. Who would have believed it!

I had now been in Gib. for the best part of a year and with the festive season fast approaching I was hoping to maybe get home on leave for a week or so. Surprisingly, out of the blue matters turned in my favour. I was sent for by the Station Chief who, with a smile on his face said "Ah, Armstrong I hear you are hoping to get home on Christmas leave. Is that right?"
"Absolutely Chief" was my quizzical reply.
"Well there is an RAF flight scheduled to leave for Brize Norton tomorrow and they have a spare seat which they have offered to us. You are welcome to take up the offer if you so wish." My face must have looked like it was going to split in two such was the width of the smile forming from ear to ear. Of course I took up the wonderful offer and after thanking my Chief profusely, I took off to pack a bag. Scouseland here I come.

Back home in Liverpool for Christmas leave, what an unexpected and welcome turn of events.

It was not long before I had teamed up with my old friend Dave Watson who updated me on the major happenings around Anfield, which it must be said didn't come over as all that exciting. Dave was much more impressed with my somewhat exaggerated tales of life in the exotic Mediterranean.

One evening we decided to hit the bright lights of downtown Liverpool. The city at the time was the epitome of the 'swinging sixties', a teenager's paradise. Despite being in the land of opportunity as far as meeting young attractive ladies was concerned, neither Dave nor I managed to charm any of the available lovelies. Perhaps it was something to do with the excess of wine, beer and spirits we managed to consume, which for some unfathomable reason seemed to affect our power of speech. Anyway, at around one o'clock in the morning on our journey home we were walking along Edge Lane when we heard an almighty bang followed by the sound of breaking glass. A couple of minutes or so later we arrived on a scene of devastation. Someone had heaved a brick through the main front display window of a butchers shop. It appeared they were after a turkey or two for Christmas.

As good upstanding citizens we waited around for the Police to turn up so that we could avail ourselves as witnesses. Quick as a flash nobody arrived. So there we were stood in front of this smashed butcher's window with the display area still harbouring numerous turkeys and chickens. Dave and I obviously had similar thoughts as moments later we were weaving our way down various alleys and 'back entries' with our arms full of Christmas fare. Our getaway went off without a hitch as we made our way over the final couple of yards to my Gran's house in Boaler Street. Everyone was in bed as we deposited our ill-gotten gains onto the parlour floor. Planning our next move, we decided that we should transfer our array of poultry to Dave's house as his brother Ray was in the butcher trade and would no doubt give us a reasonable price for our goods.

I produced my navy 'grip' (travel bag) into which we placed our chickens and turkeys. Dave's house was only five minutes away a short distance down the road. Off we set around two o'clock in the morning on the final leg of our journey. No sooner had we started off along Boaler Street when a Police Patrol Car pulled up alongside us. A tall burly looking Police Officer approached us saying "What do have in the bag lads?". Quick as a flash I replied "Oh it's only some washing I brought home on leave. I'm in the Navy you know". This didn't appear to impress him as a feeling of dread began to engulf me. This turned to absolute horror as I glanced down and spied a chicken wing poking out from the not fully closed zip section of the bag. Inevitably I found myself in familiar surroundings, banged up in the cells of a Liverpool Police Station. Would I ever learn?

Once again there I was standing alongside Dave in Liverpool Magistrates Court, the day before I was due to fly back to Gibraltar. I was in turmoil, convinced that the Royal Navy would not want to retain my services after this latest foolish escapade. The charges were 'criminal damage' in relation to the breaking of the butcher's window and 'theft' of the aforementioned turkeys and chickens. We both pleaded not-guilty to the breaking of the window, which to our great surprise and delight was accepted, but guilty to theft.

After attentively listening to the details of the case the Attending Magistrate announced "stood over to reappear in two weeks time". My heart sank as I visualised my naval career disappearing forever. With tears forming in my eyes, I pleadingly looked over to the solicitor who had been appointed to act on my behalf. Thankfully he rose to his feet requesting to be heard. His request was granted and he went on to explain my sorrowful predicament, stating that I was a member of the Royal Navy who was due to fly back to Gibraltar the following day. The Magistrate glared at me before disappearing into deep thought. After what to me seemed an eternity he announced that he would hear the case that day. We both received a hefty fine with me once again having to endure the wrath but wise words of the man on the bench. How much longer could the Royal Navy go on saving my skin?

I resumed my duties back in HMS ROOKE, Gibraltar with no one the wiser with regard to my latest, and definitely my last, encounter with the law. A couple of weeks later my relief turned to despair when I received a very official looking letter from a branch of Liverpool solicitors acting on behalf of the damaged butchers shop. They were demanding compensation for repair of the broken window. The cost involved amounted to roughly two to three months of my pay. I was really taken aback as I pondered the situation for a number of days. Finally I responded to this unwelcomed correspondence, pointing out that I was found not guilty in a court of law to the charge of breaking their clients window, and as such felt no obligation to pay any compensation. I was on tenterhooks for another couple of weeks as I awaited a response. When it came it was even more devastating than the first letter. The solicitors involved basically stated that if I refused to pay then they would have no alternative but to inform the Naval Authorities of my criminal deeds. I was tempted to pay up, after all my whole future was at stake. However, from somewhere I found the strength to stand up to them. What they were doing was wrong. I called their bluff by writing back that they could go ahead and inform who they liked. At the same time I expressed my surprise and disgust that a reputable firm of solicitors could resort to nothing short of blackmail. The next month or so was agonising as every day I expected to be summoned by my divisional officer. It never happened. As ever, my guardian angel appeared to be looking out for me.

Just about every RN ship deploying to the Mediterranean, South Africa/America, The

Caribbean or the Far East called in at Gibraltar. Luckily I was welcomed on board quite a few of them by old friends from training. I was so envious when hearing of their exotic destinations - Cape Town, Barbados, Singapore, Hong Kong, Australia, New Zealand and many more tropical countries. Maybe understandably, although enjoying the experience of life in Gibraltar, I still longed to be at sea.

'The Rock' itself was indeed a fascinating place which on reflection gave me a sound foundation on which to build my professional career. I made many friends and with the Spanish border being open enjoyed the freedom to stroll over to a variety of towns and villages which were so authentically 'oldie world' and as yet unspoilt by mass tourism. The same can be said of Morocco, which I managed to cross over to on more than one occasion. In all it was a wonderful place to be as a teenager, but now I was looking forward to ventures new.

And so I left Gibraltar and headed home for five weeks leave. I had departed not knowing where my next adventure in the Royal Navy would be but had been assured that I would receive written notification of my next draft within the next two or three weeks.

HMS PENELOPE

I was anxious and full of anticipation as I awaited news of my future. Surely I would be joining a ship? After coming on three years in the Royal Navy I was desperate to serve at sea. Waiting for the 'postie' to arrive every day was getting frustrating. What was the hold up? Finally the longed for documentation arrived. I was to join HMS PENELOPE, a relatively new Leander Class Frigate. What excitement, a frigate was just the type of ship I was hoping for.

Leave completed, I headed off down south to Portland in picturesque Dorset. Portland was the renowned base where all ships had to undergo the dreaded 'work-up'. This involved weeks of intense training where all types and class of ships and their crews were subjected to weeks of exercise and simulated war scenarios.

I was eager to know the ship's programme. Where might I be going in the weeks ahead - The Caribbean, Far East, Australia and The Pacific? Not at all, the week after I stepped over the gangway the PENELOPE was to sail for The Mediterranean, first port of call Gibraltar!

It was strange entering Gib. Harbour, proudly fell in on the upper deck for Procedure Alpha (a routine involving the ship's company lining the sides of the ship in their No.1 uniforms). It was like coming home, however, although I was very much looking forward to meeting up again with my old mates, I was now more than ready to enjoy my new home and a life at sea.

On this initial deployment the majority of our time was spent at sea with, in addition to Gib., only a brief 'run ashore' in Malta. Still I was in no position to complain as all I had wanted for the past three years was to be sailing the ocean blue!

After a short maintenance period back in the UK we sailed for the port of Flushing in The Netherlands for a five day visit. From what the majority of the ship's company could gather our port of call was not one of the most exciting and fun places in the world. More of an area to look around numerous old museums, art galleries and the like. Pastimes certainly not the top of the priority list for young energetic sailors after time at sea. This was certainly true with regard to myself and fellow mess member Jim Willaby. We therefore hatched a plan. Approaching two of our esteemed Leading Hands we suggested that when we docked we should all take off of on 'exped' (expedition training) with a view to exploring the surrounding countryside. The idea was readily accepted.

Not long after coming alongside in Flushing we collected our kit and supplies (a couple of tents, rations of food, local maps etc) and strode over the gangway to embark on our little adventure. The nearest town of any size was a place called Bergen-op-Zoom and it was collectively agreed that that was where we should initially head for. A couple of hours later approaching mid afternoon we arrived at our destination, having hitched a couple of lifts from obliging van and lorry drivers.

The place was buzzing. What on earth was going on? It turned out that the town was celebrating an annual festival, the origins of which I can't recall, which involved days of outdoor activities and night times of dancing, drinking and general party type indulgences. Things were certainly looking up.

The next three days passed in a haze. It didn't take much to persuade our Leading Hands that we should maybe stay in this historic town as opposed to wandering off around, what we convinced them would be, flat and boring countryside. Tents pitched in the corner of a central park we set off to integrate with the local community. What a time we had. The whole place compared to Edinburgh on Hogmanay.

Of course like most things in life 'all good things must come to an end', or do they? Jim and I had met a couple of local girls which just enhanced the already great time we were having. This contributed to the foolhardy plan we stupidly agreed to follow. Even though we were very much aware that our ship was due to sail back to the U.K. in the next couple of days, we gleefully decided to stay where we where. What plonkers!

Approaching our two unsuspecting Leading Hands, who had no reason to believe we were planning to stay, we suggested that it might be best if we split into two groups of two for the journey back to the ship, and seeing that they were Leading Hands we volunteered to carry the bulk of the kit, tents, stoves etc. The logic being that it would be easier to get lifts in pairs as opposed to a group of four. The Leading Hands thought we were great and readily agreed.

They set off first to our reassurances that we would see them back on board. As soon as they were out of sight we set off to resume our life of fun and laughter. A couple of days later the serious reality of our situation began to sink in. Our ship had sailed and even if we now gave ourselves up to the local authorities we were in deep trouble. Over a beer we hatched another unbelievable plan. Prior to joining the Royal Navy Jim had spent some time in the Merchant Navy. As such he managed to convince me that if we could make our way to Italy we could quite easily sign on with a merchant vessel that could transport us off to Australia where a new adventurous and challenging life awaited us. It all seemed so straightforward to me, almost as if it was meant to be. How naive.

Bidding farewell to our new but temporary friends we departed Bergen-op-Zoom. Over the next week or so we crossed over the border into Belgium before finding our way to Luxembourg. We camped out overnight in a variety of fields and wooded areas but were rapidly running out of supplies and money. Of course we were now officially 'On the Trot', a naval term for desertion. At this rate there was no way we were going to make Italy. We needed money which dictated we needed to find work. I thought this was going to be easier said than done. However, I was truly surprised when the opportunity to boost our funds presented itself. We just rolled up to a large building site and asked, despite the language difficulties, if we could undertake any casual labouring work. To my utter amazement we were told we could start at 8 o'clock the following morning. No requests for documentation, work permits etc., it really was hard to believe.

That night as we settled down in our two man tent I engaged in some serious thinking. Surely by now my family back home in Liverpool would have been informed that I had gone missing on a visit to the continent. What on earth would they be imagining? My father would be worrying but I feared my sweet adorable Nanna would be distraught. She was fully involved in my upbringing and I know, having been told by various aunts and uncles, that she had a special place in her heart for me. And just what was I throwing away? It wasn't as if I hated being in the Navy, in fact it was quite the opposite, I loved the travel, lifestyle and varied opportunities it gave me. Would I honestly want to be virtually alone at the other end of the earth from all I had known?

Reality had firmly taken hold and it was now time to let Jim know of my intention to return home. It maybe shouldn't have come as too much of a surprise to hear that Jim was very much on my wavelength and readily agreed that we should take steps to make our way back to HMS PENELOPE. Before dropping off into a restless sleep we agreed that we would seek out the British Embassy first thing in the morning.

Early next day two rather bedraggled young souls entered the British Embassy in central Luxembourg. Crossing the grand entrance hall we presented ourselves at the main reception desk. The staff member we initially spoke to appeared, understandably, somewhat bewildered as we cheerily informed him that we were a couple of Royal Navy sailors who had missed their ship sailing. We were in the middle of Europe hundreds of miles from the sea, no wonder the poor chap was confused. A couple of phone calls later and we found ourselves ushered up to an even more opulent office where we related our story to a senior member of the embassy staff. He was also quite amazed and obviously amused as he listened to and noted down the details of the antics of the two misguided sailors seated in front of him.

As we settled down to some welcome coffee and sandwiches, telephone calls and signals were relayed to the Naval Authorities back in the U.K. This resulted in a plan to get us back to our ship. We were to be booked into a local hotel that night before being taken to the main rail station to board a train to Brussels in Belgium. There we would be met by British

Army personnel who would escort us to their barracks for another overnight stay prior to an ongoing rail journey to Rotterdam. A channel ferry would then take us to Dover where we would be met by the all important Coxswain of HMS PENELOPE.

Bidding farewell to the embassy staff, who had been so very helpful and obliging, we were assigned a charming, well presented middle-aged lady who escorted us to our overnight hotel. We were booked in and told not to worry about the bill. That would be settled later. With a cheery smile she bade us goodnight with the promise that a car would arrive in the morning to drive us to the rail station. We would be given our rail tickets prior to departure. It was hard to believe. The hotel was quite upmarket and our room bordering on luxurious. After a bath/shower we changed into the most presentable clothing we could find and made our way to the bar for pre-dinner drinks. After dinner, helped down with some fine wine, we didn't last long before needing to flop down in the most appealing and comfortable of beds.

After a truly deep and welcoming sleep and the most hearty of breakfasts we awaited the arrival of our car. I must say I was beginning to feel like a high ranking V.I.P. as opposed to what I really was - a Royal Navy deserter. This feeling of well being was short lived and changed dramatically when we were met by two Army Redcaps (Military Police) at Brussels station. The good life had ended.

The Red Caps were quite chatty and pleasant as they escorted us to their army jeep. In the back Jim and I were contemplating which mess we may be allocated to later on. Perhaps the corporal's mess, after all we were Radio Electrical Mechanics First Class. We entered the main gates of the barracks and pulled up outside the guardroom. Reality hit home as we were consigned to a cell each. Cold, bare and quite depressing. Even at that we did manage a few laughs later on. The cell doors were opened and we were ordered to 'fall in' in the roadside adjacent to the guardroom. We were to be marched down to the main canteen for dinner. Orders were barked at us from a loud and aggressive sergeant whose temper did not improve as we struggled to keep pace with the army's fast style of marching. As we stumbled and bumped into each other the sergeant's mood was alternating between anger and despair, not helped by Jim and I as we burst into fits of laughter. It's a wonder we were ever released from those cells. But released we were and after breakfast the next day we were put back on a train bound for Rotterdam.

Finally we were at sea heading for the port of Dover, onboard a vessel that was just about at the other end of the spectrum in comparison to a naval frigate. We docked and as we made our way across the gangway there was our Coxswain waiting to welcome us back. Actually he was quite pleasant and seemed genuinely concerned with regard to our welfare. HMS PENELOPE was alongside in

Portsmouth and we made the journey along the coast in a hired car. We were both looking forward to getting back on board even though we knew we would have to face the consequences of our stupid actions. Sadly there was one last unexpected hurdle we had to endure. Instead of taking us directly to the ship our esteemed Coxswain deposited us in the Naval Detention Quarters within the dockyard to spend another night behind bars. It's our belief that the Coxswain was in no rush to get back on board as he planned to visit an old flame of his who lived close by. 'A girl in every port' and all that.

Relaying our adventures to our mess mates, it wasn't long before the majority of the ship's company were taking bets on the punishment we would receive. By far the most predicted outcome was that we would be sentenced to spend anything from 28 to 90 days incarcerated in Detention Quarters (D.Q.s), a harsh regime involving prisoner's hair being shaved off on arrival.

We had no option but to plead guilty to the charges levelled at us. After all the evidence had been heard and our Divisional Officer had expressed some words of support in relation to our general conduct and performance in the navy ("completely out of character" etc.), we were 'stood over'. This meant we were dismissed proceedings to allow time for the Captain to contemplate our future. The consensus around the ship was that he was deciding on how long to send us to D.Q.s.

After a number of anxious hours we were summoned back to the 'Captain's Table'. After the more than expected dressing down we were dumbfounded and delighted to hear that we were not being sent to the fearful D.Q.s. Mind you we did receive some fairly harsh punishment, which of course we deserved. Thirty days stoppage of leave plus fourteen days No. 9s (extra work and drill commencing at 6 o'clock in the morning and not finishing until 9 o'clock in the evening). Also we were fined twenty eight days pay and ordered to meet all the expenses involved in getting us home. Hotel bill (if we had known we wouldn't have gone so wild in that bar/restaurant!), rail, ferry and car hire costs. A really costly adventure that reduced us to relative paupers for many months to come. Still we had absolutely no reason to complain as once again senior officers appeared to think that we were just immature, silly sailors who despite their foolish behaviour still had a possible positive future ahead in the Royal Navy. Once again my guardian angel had come to my rescue. However, I would have to take care, perhaps I was overworking him!

On a more serious note, when I finally arrived back home in Liverpool my family were of course delighted to see I was safe and well. Despairingly I was shocked to find out what I had actually put them through. My father produced a letter he had received from the Ministry of Defence approximately one week after we had jumped ship. The gist of the formal correspondence said "Dear Mr Armstrong we regret to inform you that on a recent visit to a port in The Netherlands your son failed to return to the ship prior to sailing. Detailed enquiries and investigations are ongoing but at this moment in time we have no reason to believe he has fallen into communist hands. We will keep you informed of developments". All rather dramatic, but it was a true reflection of the uncertain and worrying times in which we lived. The threats posed by the 'Cold War' were all too real.

I was enjoying life at sea. The travel, the friendships developed, the humour of naval life and the feeling of awe that encompassed me as I stood on the upper deck in the evenings and gazed out over the vast expanse of a seemingly never-ending ocean. That being said I was developing an inclination to serve in submarines. I had a notion that the atmosphere on a sub would be more relaxed whilst at the same time being aware of the fact that every member of the crew had an individual responsibility to ensure the safety and operational capability of the vessel. The extra pay wouldn't go amiss either!

After due consideration I completed the necessary naval request form and handed it to my section chief who in turn passed it on to my Divisional Officer (D.O.) for approval. A couple of days later I was sent for by my D.O. and therefore in eager anticipation dutifully presented myself at his cabin. I had a lot of time for this young naval officer who I always felt had the 'lads' welfare at heart. After being invited in I sat down, after which a discussion commenced on the merits and possible downsides of my request. All my D.O. was trying to establish was whether I was acting on a whim or was genuinely keen, after serious thought, to join the 'silent service'. I assured him it was the latter which prompted him to come up with a rather marvellous proposition.

We were in the middle of a three week exercise with the submarine element of the 'war games' being undertaken by HMS TOKEN, a 'T' class diesel electric sub. My D.O. asked me how I would feel if he arranged for me to spend a week serving on TOKEN. I couldn't get my enthusiastic, positive response out my mouth quick enough. "OK leave it with me" he said with a smile on his face.

The following morning I was informed that I was to be transferred to the sub later on that afternoon. I was advised not to take too much kit, just a change of underwear and socks plus toiletries. Apparently with space on TOKEN being at a premium I was to be exchanged with a suitable member of their crew who would spend his week on board PENELOPE. What a great plan.

At around 1500 (three o'clock in the afternoon) I stood in eager anticipation on our flight deck, clutching a small bag containing my essential items of kit. Making an absolutely grand appearance I was transfixed as on our starboard quarter HMS TOKEN's bow broke the surface at a sharp angle before settling approximately 200yds away in a diminishing spray of foaming Mediterranean sea. Our sea boat was lowered and to a chorus of "good luck, you'll need it" I readied myself for what I was convinced would be an interesting and enthralling week. Well it certainly turned out to be interesting, but on reflection I'm not sure if enthralling was the appropriate adjective to describe my memorable experience.

I scrambled up the side of the casing and steadied myself on the narrow ledge at the foot of the conning tower. Briefly meeting the chap who I thought was my replacement R.E.M., I shook his hand and wished him all the best as he lowered himself into the sea boat and set off for PENELOPE. A smiling member of TOKEN's crew welcomed me aboard and escorted me down into the control room. There I was met by the Coxswain who greeted me heartily, saying how good it was to have a replacement Marine Engineering Mechanic (M.E.M.) on board. Looking somewhat confused I quietly replied "I'm not an M.E.M., I'm an R.E.M.". "Oh" says the Coxswain "Well never mind you'll do. You have the first dog (1600 - 1800hrs watch) in the engine room. If you just make your way down aft you'll come across the duty L.M.E.M. who will brief you on your duties. You can't miss him, he's wearing a green rugby shirt and a top hat".

And so began an extraordinary, fascinating, eye opening, never to be forgotten week below the waves. I managed to survive the first dog watch duty in the engine room without causing any major damage to the vessel. Mind you I was more than grateful for the assistance forthcoming from experienced members of TOKEN's crew as I screamed for help when numerous orders were being relayed and various alarms sounding.

Conditions were extremely cramped with the majority of the ship's company 'hot bunking', a submariner's tradition of having to share a bunk with other members of the crew. The practise being that when you were due to finish your 'watch' you would go along to the chap who was to relieve you and if asleep give him a 'shake'. When he arrived to take over whatever duty, you would toddle off and get your 'head down' in the bunk he had just vacated. How cosy.

The week progressed as we exercised with PENELOPE. I found the experience magical and gradually built up a real admiration for the crew. They were so professional, relaxed and confident. Their sense of humour was a joy. I recall noticing a matchbox on which was printed 'THE COXSWAIN'S BRAIN'. Inside the box was a dried up walnut that indeed did look like a miniature brain. Priceless.

The all-important sense of humour was demonstrated, at my expense, a couple of days after I had been on board. We were submerged at around 100ft and I found myself needing the toilet, the type involving the requirement to sit down on the pan. Over the previous day or so I had managed to find the urinals but as yet had not sighted an actual toilet pan. Standing in the walkway between the two main engines I collared one of the stokers and asked him where the 'heads' were. At this stage I paid little attention to the slight smile he developed and the glint that formed in his eye.

"There's one just below you Scouse. Lift that deck plate you are standing on and you will see it". This I did and indeed there it was, a mini-throne set amongst a conglomeration of pipes, levers and valves. Lowering myself down I squeezed through the array of piping and, after lowering my trousers, managed to sit myself, hunched over, onto the pan. The necessary deed complete I looked around for a chain to pull. There was nothing in sight. At this stage I looked up to find my helpful stoker still in attendance by the opening I had descended from. I should have smelt a rat but in my innocence I merely asked how I could discharge the contents of the pan. He instructed me to turn around and lean over the 'throne'. Once in position he commenced relaying instructions. "See that valve to your right?".

"Yes," I responded.

"Well open it fully."

This I did. Next I was told to sharply pull down a large lever to my right. After giving said lever an almighty tug, I watched as the contents of the pan disappeared. This disappearance was accompanied by a loud rushing sound followed by an echoing thud. With me still leaning over the pan the backlash of waste returned back along the discharge piping, exiting the toilet bowl with the force of an erupting volcano. I took the full force of this disgusting motion (excuse the pun!) in the face, leaving me dripping in my own urine, faeces and toilet paper.

Still in a state of shock, I became aware of applause and laughter. Looking up to the exit back into the engine room I found myself grimacing at an array of amused faces, who were obviously delighted at initiating one of their surface colleagues into the world of submarines.

Apparently the small detail missing from my instructions was to pull down the large lever in a slow steady manner. This would have allowed pressure in the discharge pipe to gradually build up and match that of the outside sea pressure. Although the exit valve on the hull was open, quickly pulling down on the handle just meant that the accelerating discharge waste hit the pressurised sea like hitting a brick wall and hence my unwelcomed blow back. A slow steady pull would have avoided the amusing but demeaning catastrophe.

To make matters worse there were no shower facilities on board so I had to make do with a vigorous wash down at one of the bathroom sinks. Still there was a positive aspect to all this somewhat unpleasant episode in that I won the respect of the TOKEN's ship's company for the sporting manner in which I accepted their prank. I always could see the funny side of any situation, even if I was on the receiving end of it.

The time on that submarine really was a never to be forgotten experience which, as I relayed to my D.O. on the PENELOPE, only served to strengthen my desire to qualify as a submariner. Consequently my request was forwarded to the relevant departments within the Admiralty and my service documents annotated with 'Volunteer for Submarines'. Strangely enough, because of a number of developments, not least me being promoted, I never did find myself serving below the waves.

My time on the PENELOPE will always hold meaningful memories for me. As my first ship it served to consolidate my belief that a life in the Royal Navy was going to live up to all my expectations. Of course what I had to ensure was that I didn't involve myself in any similar past foolish and immature ventures involving the law. I just couldn't push my past good fortune any further - be sensible and grow up Philip!

After just nine months on my first sea-going ship I received a new draft order. PENELOPE was going into refit and I was to join the Battle Class Destroyer HMS CORUNNA in the Scottish port of Rosyth.

HMS CORUNNA

On the 1st March 1966 my train from Plymouth pulled into Inverkeithing Station, Fife, which filled me with uncertainty. Surely this couldn't be the stop for Rosyth Naval base, it was far too rural and not at all like the bustling stations at Portsmouth and Plymouth. But indeed it was and after a 10 to 15minute taxi ride I found myself entering the main gate of the dockyard naval base. HMS CORUNNA, a battle class destroyer, was undergoing a refit and looking somewhat forlorn and rust streaked when I pulled up on the jetty beside her. Reporting to the regulating office nearby, I was informed that HMS CORUNNA's ships company were accommodated in the British Sailors Society (B.S.S.) hostel just outside the dockyard gate. This turned out to be a wonderful alternative to being victualled on one of the three ships, HMS DUNCANSBY HEAD, HMS GIRDLENESS (GIRDLEPLONK!), and HMS CHEVERON which combined to make up HMS COCHRANE. I had my own cabin, enjoyed splendid meals in the hostel's restaurant and had access to a well stocked bar. Life in the R.N. was just getting better and better!

Of course true to form I had to cock it all up. Over the coming months my, what I thought amusing, antics were not welcomed by the B.S.S. manager, an Irish gentleman named Mr. Murphy. One morning an incident initiated by my mischievous ship mates found me boarded up in my cabin by strips of planking that had been screwed across my door. Escaping via my room window I still found myself adrift for the morning muster on the ship. Even more disastrously I incurred the full wrath of Mr Murphy even though I considered myself to be the innocent victim of this sorry affair.

The final straw came when myself and a good friend returned from a long and inebriating 'run ashore' in Edinburgh and thought it a great idea to transfer a large stone wheeled garden roller from the grounds outside into the hostel's snooker hall. It seemed hilarious at the time but not so amusing in the morning. All hell broke loose with Mr Murphy insisting that all members of HMS CORUNNA's crew muster in the snooker room. He was absolutely fuming and demanded the culprits responsible for this dastardly deed step forward. No response, which had him threatening to evict the whole ship's company. I and my run ashore oppo couldn't call his bluff and sheepishly stepped forward. That very day we found ourselves billeted in a rather depressing mess on board HMS COCHRANE.

Weekends on board HMS GIRDLEPLONK were somewhat hazy affairs, mainly revolving around 'tot-times' and 'run ashores'. As an enthusiastic participant in both activities I had some great laughs but not much came my way in respect of the local ladies. I think they had difficulty in interpreting my Northern England dialect, especially after over indulgence in a variety of local alcoholic beverages. This sad state of affairs came to a merciful end one Friday night when I met the love of my life at a local dance hall.

My recollections are hazy as once again I had been 'on the pop' for most of the day.

Eventually me and my good friends ended up in the Kinema Ballroom, Dunfermline. My pals were dancing away with an array of young girls as a sense of weariness overcame me. I searched out a place to rest and settled in an empty seat along the wall at the edge of the dance floor. I plonked myself down next to a rather beautiful looking young lady and before long attempted to strike up a conversation, despite the gibberish that wouldn't stop pouring out of my mouth. To my absolute amazement this vision of loveliness accepted my invitation to dance. From there on in everything was much of a blur.

The next day the first mission was to make it to the 'tot queue'. It was there that we all gathered to recount the previous day's run ashore. To a man (three of them!) all remarked on the absolutely gorgeous young female I had managed to persuade to take to the dance floor. In truth I could hardly recall events, not even the name of the lady involved. As we began to plan our next sojourn to the hot spots of Fife, I found in my back pocket a slip of paper on which was written, in lipstick, 'Annette. Tel: 01383-412830'. The boys didn't hold back, "give her a call, she's an absolute beauty".

I didn't have enough courage within me at the time, but later on after a couple of pints of heavy I steeled myself to make that fateful call. My luck was holding, Annette agreed to meet me at 7 o'clock that evening. I decided to put my sensible hat on and excused myself from the 'dinner time sesh'. Back on board I began preparations. A hot shower, iron shirt, press trousers and polish shoes.

The lady who changed my life.
The wonderful Annette.

As the fateful hour approached nerves began to get the better of me, but I was determined not to indulge in any more alcohol, well not just yet. The time came to leave and as I tied up my shoelaces one snapped, leaving not enough cord to tie the lace in a bow. A frantic request for a spare lace from my mess mates fell on deaf ears. Ingeniously I came up with a solution. Cutting a suitable length of white string from a ball in my locker I threaded it through the lace holes of my black winkle picker shoes and tied it up securely in a tight bow. The white string did not look too classy against the black leather so I quickly grabbed some boot polish and spread it over the exposed areas of string.

We had arranged to meet at the cross roads in Rosyth. As I nervously took up position on one side of the roundabout I spotted a rather classy young lady, dressed immaculately in an expensive looking light grey suit, on the other side. She looked so sophisticated and was obviously well out of my league. My heart was beginning to sink as I thought I had been stood up when the vision in the grey suit approached me and with a smile asked if I was ever coming over to say hello. I was mesmerised, surely this couldn't be. But indeed it was and as we boarded a bus to Dunfermline I was determined not to make a hash of this golden opportunity.

Sitting next to Annette on the bus I had an unnerving feeling that I was being given the 'once over'. However, I was fairly happy with my preparations and confident that that extra splash of Brut aftershave would do the trick. This confidence quickly collapsed when I glanced down at my feet. The carefully prepared shoelace had slipped round to reveal the fraud that it was, leaving me with the latest design in shoes sporting one black shoelace and one piece of white string.

Despite this setback the evening progressed well as I endeavoured to produce the best of my charm and wit. No expense was spared as I tried to impress this adorable and charming lady who had entered my life. Mind you at the final hurdle I nearly blew it. In my eagerness to create a memorable evening I had not been keeping account of the money I was spending and as we approached the bus station to return to Rosyth, to my horror, I realised I only had pennies left in my pocket. After suffering the ignominy of having to borrow money from Annette we finally boarded the last bus home. You know it's a measure of the lady that despite all my bumblings and string shoe laces she agreed to see me again. My life was about to take on a whole new meaning.

Never having been overly enthusiastic with regard to my main role as a Radio Mechanic, I was always looking for the chance to qualify as a Ship's Diver. Fortunately my chance came along and having successfully passed the aptitude test, I commenced Ship's Diver's course in early July 1966. As I've said, diving was always something I had wanted to do and, whilst under no illusions of the gruelling challenges that lay ahead, I was determined to make the very best of the opportunity that had come my way.

The four week course was held in HMS SAFEGUARD, a mine warfare establishment within the boundary of Rosyth Dockyard on the shores of the River Forth. Physically demanding, the daily challenges pushed all course members to their limits. Our diving suits were laughingly known as 'dry suits', designed to be worn with woollen under suits whilst not allowing the ingress of any seawater. Of course the suits available to us trainees were not the best maintained and that first plunge into the dark, cold, murky water of the 'Forth' was something of a shock to say the least. Why was my so called 'dry suit' allowing icy cold sea water to steadily seep into my cosy warm under suit? Still over the coming weeks it did instil into me the benefits of maintaining all your personal diving equipment.

Daily routines always involved attempting to fully dress ready for the water in under two minutes, failure to do so inevitably resulting in some form of physical torture by way of 'push ups' or long runs. Another daily inescapable joy was the 'coal heap runs'. Coal burning mine layers still operated out of Rosyth in the 'sixties' and as such there was a designated area on the quayside where all the coal and coke was stored. Towering like black sand dunes on the jetty they were the perfect set up for the sadistic instructors to put us through our paces. Trying to run up and down those black, torturous mounds was nothing short of agonising. It just seemed impossible to make progress as the blocks of coal gave way below your feet. Still the goal was certainly achieved as my stamina was built up and my physical fitness raised to new heights.

One day we were diving down a 'shot line' secured over the jetty wall and going down about 40/50ft to the muddy, slimy seabed. The instructors detailed that we were to descend to the base of the shot line and to prove that we had indeed done so, were to reappear on the surface with a hand full of mud. Down I went. At around 20ft my ears started to hurt. I tried to clear them by blowing down my nose onto my nose clip. This didn't help much and as I descended further the pain increased. At around 35ft the pain was excruciating, but all I could think about was being thrown off the course if I resurfaced without that handful of mud. Fighting the pain and gathering all the determination I could muster I struck out for the bottom. I grabbed a handful of mud just before I thought my head was going to explode. Making my way back to the surface all sorts of strange popping sounds were going off in my ears. Surfacing near some stone steps I triumphantly deposited my harshly earned handful of mud next to an instructor's foot. As I looked up at him I was surprised to see a look of worried concern on his face as he rapidly assisted me out of the water. What I didn't realise at that precise time was that my facemask was splattered, internally, in blood. It would appear that my sinuses and ear tubes were blocked and my heroic, some might say foolhardy, attempt to reach the seabed had blown them clear as a result of the increasing pressure as I descended. After the initial quayside panic all was well. I had sustained no permanent damage and in fact since that day I never again experienced difficulty in clearing my ears whilst diving. The most effective ear syringe I have had to date!

On the 12th August 1966, being awarded my diving log and badges to proudly wear on my uniform was a great day for me. I really enjoyed my diving even although initially it wasn't all a clear, tropical water, James Bond type experience. More freezing cold, nil visibility, mud surrounded operations. What I wasn't to know at the time was how much of an impact diving was to have on my naval career.

Sea trials approaching and time for the Ship's Company to move on board. For me it couldn't come quick enough, saying farewell to my hammock on the 'GIRDLEPLONK' did not fill me with any sense of sadness or misplaced nostalgia. Of course the preparatory workload increased significantly and I found myself 'turned to' for long hours setting to work on an array of radar and communications equipment. My efforts and enthusiasm must have impressed the Head of the Radio Department as out of the blue, and certainly as a surprise to me, he suggested that I take the examination for promotion to Leading Hand. Remarkably I managed a 'Good' pass which meant I was destined for another training period at my far from favourite shore establishment, HMS COLLINGWOOD.

Of course the down side of this unexpected turn in my life was that I would be leaving the CORUNNA sooner than I originally thought. It had a great ship's company and I was convinced we could have completed an outstanding commission. However, as it turned out a full commission was never to be as an announcement was made that on completion of sea trials the grand old Battle Class Destroyer was to be placed in 'Reserve' down in Chatham Dockyard - what might have been !.

Another, even more painful, offshoot of my professional advancement was the fact that I would be leaving the Scottish lass I had fallen head over heels in love with much sooner than I had envisaged.

In November 1966, on the day I was due to leave Rosyth and head off for COLLINGWOOD, I was scheduled to catch a lunchtime train from Inverkeithing. Annette worked as a hairdresser not too far from the station and the thought of leaving without seeing her was agonising. Arriving at the station in my depressed state of mind, a plan came into my head. Looking up later train times I noted there was a train due to leave in the early evening that, with a connection in London, would get me into COLLINGWOOD around 6 o'clock in the morning as opposed to mid-evening that day if I stuck to my scheduled train. Decision made, the later train it was to be.

I telephoned Annette and asked if I could come along and meet her when she finished work at 5 o'clock. She of course agreed and after an unmissable afternoon traipsing around the delights of historic Inverkeithing I found myself outside Annette's salon. Standing there in my sailors uniform accompanied by my rather large naval kitbag and suitcase raised a few well meaning smiles from her work colleagues as they left the building. Annette invited me in and we spent a wondrous hour or so together, when we expressed our love for each other and I informed the vision in front of me that I had no doubt whatsoever that one day we would be man and wife.

That day, which changed my life forever, arrived the following July. My Best Man, Steve from our early training days, and I arrived up in Scotland on the Friday evening and met up with my Father and a number of close relatives from Liverpool. The whole weekend, and particularly the wedding in Rosyth Parish Church, was magical. The only drawback was that I had to be back on board by the following Tuesday. Therefore, after our wedding night in a first class hotel in South Queensferry I had to bid my new beautiful bride goodbye. Thankfully our separation wasn't for a prolonged period as two weeks later I would be back on a fortnight's leave to enjoy our delayed honeymoon.

Where was that to be? I hear you ask. One of the Mediterranean or Caribbean islands? Hawaii perhaps? No, we were to spend a blissful time in the exotic fishing port of Lossiemouth in Morayshire. Our accommodation was also to be envied, a modest but well appointed caravan called 'Eccles'.

Of course it goes without saying that our time 'Up North' was my best leave period to date, and remains so. Annette's Grannie, Grandad and two Aunties lived close by in a magical, glorious cottage overlooking The Moray Firth. Strolls down to their little haven for a welcoming drink and first class home cooked meals served to enrich the first few weeks of our marriage. Sadly as with everything in life, all good things must come to an end, which resulted in me being back in the classrooms of HMS COLLINGWOOD.

Once again, the best part of a year in the Royal Navy's largest training establishment and for me it almost bordered on purgatory. The leadership aspect I enjoyed plus the times I had to leave COLLINGWOOD and find my way to 'Whale Island', part of HMS EXCELLENT, to make sure I stayed 'in-date' for my diving qualification. It meant missing various electronic lessons, but to me it was a small price to pay for maintaining the underwater 'minutes' required to stay in-date.

'Killicks Course' successfully completed I now awaited my next draft, praying that it would be one of the many married accompanied available throughout the world for my branch. Living abroad with my gorgeous new wife would be the fulfilment of all my dreams.

HMS HAMPSHIRE

The awaited notification arrived, I had been drafted to HMS JUFAIR, a naval base in Bahrain in the Middle East. Maybe not the most exotic of places in the world, but what the heck Annette and I would be spending two magical years together, or so I thought. The draft itself was for eighteen months unaccompanied, however I saw this as a minor technical hitch. I had only recently married and of course the naval drafting authorities would not be aware of this fact. All would be well when I explained.

Off I trudged to COLLINGWOOD's main Regulating Office to request an audience with the all-important camp Master-at-Arms (M.A.A.). I was granted my somewhat cheeky request and found myself standing on the hallowed ground in front of the M.A.A.'s desk. Gleefully informing him that I was now married I respectfully requested that he contact the drafting authorities to inform them of my new marital status, and that they could therefore amend my draft to two years accompanied. How naive can you get.

Give him his due the M.A.A. did make my requested telephone call, and after a seemingly endless chain of 'um ums' and 'I sees' he replaced the receiver and solemnly explained the situation. The draft was to stand in its stated form. There was no available family accommodation in Bahrain and therefore Annette could not accompany me.

I was dumbfounded and devastated at the prospect of spending the next eighteen months separated from my beautiful wife. It just couldn't happen. My next stop was my Divisional Officer, a young and rather inexperienced Educational Lieutenant. In an awkward but slightly aggressive manner I informed him that the only way they would get me to Bahrain would be in handcuffs as there was no way I would be leaving my wife behind for such a prolonged period of time, especially with our first child on the way. Surprisingly my D.O., seeing how uspset I was, adopted a sympathetic approach and he himself telephoned 'Drafty'. They must have been fed up of hearing the name Armstrong. It was again re-iterated that the draft stood and could not be changed. The only glimmer of hope I was given was that they agreed to look upon favourably a 'swap draft' request if I could find another LREM to take up my appointment to JUFAIR. Some chance.

The next few days were miserable as I dwelt upon and contemplated my bleak future. Then one afternoon as I forlornly supped away at my tot a fragile lifeline was thrown my way. My old friend and accompanying deserter from HMS PENELOPE, Jim Willaby, sidled up to me, "How are things going Phil? Have you got a draft yet?".
"I have actually, HMS JUFAIR. What about you?".
"HMS HAMPSHIRE" he replies.
"And what is she doing?" I asked.
"Six months maintenance period in Pompey, then 'work-up' followed by deployments to the Med and the Far East" was his response. I clicked on to the six months maintenance period and almost in desperation cheekily asked "Don't suppose you would like to swap drafts?". Expecting hoots of laughter in response, to my absolute amazement he said "Well maybe, I'll talk it over with my wife this weekend".

I was dumbstruck and after offering him a good 'gulper' of my tot I thought it only right to come clean. "That's good of you Jim", I cautiously replied, "but I think it's only fair to mention that it's an eighteen months unaccompanied draft with no chance whatsoever of having it changed to a married accompanied". At this stage I was convinced he was about to say "Oh well in that case forget it". To my complete astonishment, mainly because I was aware that just like me he had only recently got married, he pondered a while, took another good swig of his tot and said "That's ok, I'll see what my good lady has to say when I get home".

Come the following Monday morning I found myself walking down the road alongside the main parade ground. A voice called out "Hey Phil, hang on a moment". It was Jim and he was heading my way with a broad smile on his face. Obviously he was about to tell me that his new wife would have nothing to do with our hair brained plan to swap drafts, and if I was honest I had not been holding out much hope of a positive outcome. Imagine my complete astonishment when he informed me that his wife had no objections and therefore he was more than happy to go ahead with the exchange of drafts. I couldn't get him down to the Regulating Office quick enough, where we completed the appropriate paperwork that eventually sent me on my way to join the guided missile destroyer, HMS HAMPSHIRE, in Pompey Dockyard.

Jim later confided that he was a little short of money and hence the reason for him wanting to take the opportunity to serve out in the Middle East, where he planned to save up with the aim of building up his bank balance. After departing COLLINGWOOD I never saw Jim again, but I have often wondered how he got along in HMS JUFAIR and indeed for the rest of his naval career.

And so, as a young, fully qualified Leading Radio Electrical Mechanic (LREM) I joined one of the fleet's most powerful warships, the guided missile destroyer HMS HAMPSHIRE. The ship was a good third of its way through its commission and I was part of the third of the crew replacing long serving members of the ship's company, a process known as 'trickle drafting'. The ship had just returned from a trip to Eastern Canada, which was a little frustrating especially later on when I heard all the, I'm sure exaggerated, stories of what a great time everybody had had.

Normally when a ship is undergoing a three month dockyard maintenance period the ship's company are moved off to be billeted in the local barracks, in our case HMS NELSON. However, when the crew were given the option of moving into barracks or remaining on the ship whilst in dry dock, they opted for the latter, which as far as I and many of my new shipmates were concerned didn't come without its problems and discomfort. All the ship's amenities were shut down resulting in us having to traipse across the gangway to a rather rundown single story dockside building which housed basic toilet and bathroom facilities. Meals were provided from an even more depressing unit in the form of a cold steel barge like structure situated at the head of the dry dock. For the life of me I couldn't understand why my shipmates had opted not to take advantage of the far superior domestic accommodation ashore.

The Electricians mess was situated towards the after end of the ship in compartment 3P. It was the home and resting place of over sixty crew members. As was my preference I managed to find myself a top bunk, which was all good and well when the ship was fully operational but during this refit phase my newly allocated bunk space proved at times to be almost unbearable. After a couple of reasonable sleeps I was awoken one night thinking the world was coming to an end. The deck head space a few inches above me was the underside of the flight deck. Apparently a job order had to be put in to have the specialised semi-rough cast area of the flight deck removed and renewed. Hence my sharp awakening as the dockyard mateys set about their task with high powered jack hammers. All in all I have never been so happy and relieved as when that dry dock finally flooded up and we sailed out into the harbour with full domestic facilities all operational.

There was a period of absolute bliss during these challenging times in Portsmouth Dockyard and that was when I was joined by my new and beautiful bride Annette. She was joining me for an all too short four week stay, the first time we would be living on our own together as man and wife. The accommodation I secured certainly didn't fall into the luxury category, but it did leave us both with treasured memories. Our haven was the upper floor of a terraced house in the Copnor district of Portsmouth, small but cosy and functional. Unfortunately I had to leave Annette alone during the day. She coped extremely well despite some of the local shopkeepers being somewhat bemused by this wee Scotch lassie asking for unfamiliar Scottish fare such as: filleted haddock, a half loaf of bread and a bottle of Irn Bru. When the time came I managed to get the weekend off to travel back up to Scotland with Annette. Leaving her with her Mum, Dad and sister Rhona was not easy, but of course she was back home in a loving environment, which took the edge off the depressing feeling that I was deserting her.

Rum was first introduced into the Royal Navy in 1664 and, to the dismay and heartbreak of many, abolished on 1st August 1970. As the minimal age to draw rum was 20 years this afforded me the privilege of drawing my 'tot' for over four years. On the good ship HAMPSHIRE I somehow managed to get myself elected as 'Rum Bosun' for 3P mess, a much sought after and highly regarded position.

At approximately 1145hrs daily a 'pipe' would be made over the ship's main broadcast followed by those morale boosting words "Up Spirits". This was the cue for me to drop whatever I was doing (I always did have a highly developed sense of priority!) and head off down the mess to collect the 'Rum Fanny', a large pot/bucket type utensil, which was never cleaned internally. The brown stained lining build up over many years ensuring that the unique taste and character of the daily rum was not tarnished in any way.

Rum was issued to Junior Rates as 'two-in-one', which translates to two parts water and one part rum. This resulted in a full measure of close on half a pint. Senior rates (Chief & Petty Officers) were allowed to draw their rum ration 'neat', which could lead to the temptation of saving or 'bottling' up the highly toxic liquid (over 54% proof) whilst at sea. Although highly illegal, this practise did allow these highly responsible members of the ship's company to have a fine old time whilst in harbour. The fact that Junior Rate's rations had two parts water meant that it couldn't be saved and had to be drank on the day of issue. Such hardship!

3P Mess accommodated around thirty ratings who were entitled to their tot. As the Rum Bosun, this fact certainly brightened up my lunchtimes. Tradition had it that the bosun measured the designated quantity of rum into a suitable tot glass before handing it to the eagerly awaiting mess mate. Before actually departing with his precious glass of dark, longed for liquid it was beholding of him to say in a loud clear voice "have a wet bosun". This was the invitation for me to have a small drink from his ration, a longstanding naval tradition which of course explained why I was always so talkative in the afternoons.

The short refit complete, and now sea trials and a work-up period at Portland to look forward to. Thereafter back up to Scotland for a much welcomed leave period.

And so my first Hogmanay in Scotland arrived, with my dear wife one week overdue with our first child. I had heard so much about these notorious celebrations north of the border and was very much looking forward to enjoying them with my new found family. At the same time I was extremely anxious with regard to Annette's condition. We should have had our new arrival before Christmas.

Just before 9 o'clock in the evening my new friend and father-in-law George rose from his chair at the fireside and announced in his grand northern dialect "Well I'm off for a pint. Will you join me Phil?". Who was I to argue, so off we strolled the couple of hundred yards or so up the road to the 'local', The Cottars. The place was bustling but we managed to squeeze our way to the bar where George ordered two pints of heavy. Three pints and a couple of nips of whisky later we were merrily making our way back down the road to number 114. Public Houses closed the bar at 10pm at that time so we were back home just before 10:30pm. The Hogmanay Show, starring such famous Scots as Ricky Fulton, Stanley Baxter and Andy Stewart, was showing on the television and as I sat down next to my radiant wife on the settee I was overcome with a warming sense of Scottish homeliness. Mother-in-law Isobel had prepared a mouth watering array of food and as 'The Bells' approached George supplied us all with a drink to toast in the New Year. What a lovely large glass of whisky I had in my hand. 'The Bells' came, the New Year toast was made and we all kissed and shook hands, myself, Isobel, George, Annette and her young sister Rhona. Also in the company was the family dog. Small, cuddly and affectionate Sandy.

After midnight, and me being parked outside the house to re-enter as the 'first foot', things settled down a little. As 1am approached I was thinking to myself, 'Well this is very nice but not the lively raucous occasion I was expecting'. Shortly after that neighbours and friends began to arrive and the phrase 'Hogmanay Party' took on a whole new meaning. The whisky flowed, the guests sang, the skirling pipes could be heard and I was introduced to the uplifting and lively skills of Highland dancing.

At around 3a.m., with the party in full swing, I looked around for Annette. Ascending the stairs and calling her name I heard her call out from behind the bathroom door. It was obvious she was in some sort of pain and distress as I hastily sought help from her mum Isobel. It had to happen eventually, but what timing, Annette had gone into labour. As the news broke all the well meaning assembled company offered their sincere, priceless advice, albeit a little tainted by the consumption of outrageous quantities of alcohol. On reflection, most alarming was the many offers from the male contingent of a lift to the hospital. There wasn't a 'breathalyser' at that time, but the ability to be able to walk before entering the driving seat of a car seemed a sensible precaution to me. The gentleman considered most capable, George, was selected and off we set for Dunfermline Maternity Hospital. As we arrived George kissed Annette and remarked "Well there's one of you going into the hospital but there will be two coming out".

The next 24 hours proved to be both gruelling and concerning, certainly for Annette and to a far lesser extent me. Placed into a somewhat cold, bare and unwelcoming section of a maternity ward Annette was left to endure her increasingly frequent and regular painful contractions. The maternity nurses conscientiously monitored Annette but did not appear overly concerned as the painful hours passed by, in sharp contrast to both the pending mother and father. Although my first experience of childbirth, I could see that Annette was in considerable distress. After being in labour for well over 22 hours all contractions ceased. Annette was exhausted but maybe a little relieved that the never ending pain seemed to be over. Summoning a nurse, matters took a dramatic turn as it was determined that the baby had given up its struggle to enter the world. Rushed off to the delivery room as the resident maternity surgeon was called to deal with the emergency, I was left bewildered, scared and tearful as my beloved wife and unborn child were taken from me.

What seemed like an eternity later I was told that we had a baby boy weighing 6lbs 8ozs, born at 3:02a.m. on the 2nd January 1968. The joy that engulfed me was boundless. I was a father with a beautiful wife and precious son.

When taken to Annette it was apparent what an ordeal she had been through. Although obviously happy to have her beloved baby she appeared thoroughly exhausted. It appears that her contractions had indeed stopped and as a result our young son Paul was delivered by forceps which left both mother and baby bleeding and bruised. Looking at Paul for the first time through the nursery window he looked liked he had really battled to enter the world, with his face still showing traces of blood and bruising. Apart from that he was lively and healthy and as I left that hospital I was totally overwhelmed with feelings of awe and wonder. Two days later I was back at sea.

Returning from Christmas leave in January 1969 I found myself the victim of mixed emotions. I was facing months of painful separation from my precious wife and magical son. Only to be expected I suppose having opted for a life in the Royal Navy. However, being totally honest the adventurous and

I suppose selfish side of me was excited at the prospect of our imminent departure on a deployment to the Far East, inclusive of visits to various ports in both Australia and New Zealand. We were alongside in Portsmouth and as soon as I stepped onboard I could sense an air of excitement. What was about to unfold was somewhat bewildering.

The ship's Commander came on the main broadcast to announce that our expected departure to exotic lands 'East of Suez' had been cancelled. My heart sank, but this was short lived when we were informed that we were to undertake a priority trip to the Caribbean and South America. Apparently our sister ship HMS Kent had suffered a major engine failure and as a result could not take to sea.

'KENT's' planned trip was of the highest priority, both as a sales mission and an undertaking to improve diplomatic relations with developing South American countries. Britain had recently developed large scale hovercraft which could be effective in many scenarios, both civilian and military. The latest highly technically developed model was coming with us, transported on a large Royal Fleet Auxiliary (RFA)vessel. The idea was to off-load this impressive new form of sea travel and put it through its paces in all the countries to be visited. Thereafter it was hoped all the viewing dignitaries and government officials would be suitably impressed, which in turn could lead to a substantial uplift in Britain's oversees trade.

We were to sail within the week. First port of call being Barbados, followed by a transit of the Panama Canal before docking in Lima, Peru. Next came Valparaiso in Chile from where we would depart to round Cape Horn before calling into Buenos Aires in Argentina. Our last visit before departing for home was to be Rio de Janeiro in Brazil. The disappointment of missing out on our Far East deployment was of course eradicated by the prospect of our new programme - the trip of a lifetime, even in naval circles!

Berthing alongside in Bridgetown, Barbados I was so much looking forward to the five days ahead. Besides the first experience of exploring a tropical island, a diving exped had been planned. I just couldn't wait to plunge into that clear, crystal blue water. A few days later my long awaited for dream was about to come true. A team of us loaded up one of the ship's gemini fast patrol boats with all our diving equipment and set off for the waters of the aptly named Paradise beach. The dive really lived up to my expectations. The visibility within that warm, tropical sea was greater than I had ever experienced, revealing an abundance of colourful tropical fish swimming through a kaleidoscope of the most unspoilt and magnificent coral.

Sadly my moments of sheer pleasure came to an abrupt end as an incident occurred that indeed could have been more catastrophic than it actually turned out. I quote from an entry in my diving log dated 8/2/69:

> "Exped dive off Paradise beach, Barbados. Nasty experience when corlene life-line caught in props of passing speed boat. Line tightn'd round neck and dragged to surface, luckily line broke before neck! Dived in coral, numerous tropical fish to be seen".

The offending speed boat was almost certainly aware that his reckless manoeuvring had resulted in what could have been serious injury to a diver, namely my good self. Nevertheless he didn't hang about to lend any assistance, but instead powered up his no doubt expensive vessel and disappeared over the horizon in a haze of frothing sea water. As for me, I came through it all relatively unscathed, albeit I did look as if I'd had a lucky escape from the gallows, with a rather large noose like circle of bruising adorning my neck.

As if that wasn't enough, more damage to my fragile body was about to be bestowed upon me. Aware that the heat rays from the tropical sun could cause serious damage to my delicate skin I had put my 'sensible hat' on and ensured all my body and head were covered to prevent any such occurrence. However, I overlooked one vulnerable area of my predominately pallid body - namely my feet. Omitting to wear socks, I did in fact wear a pair of sandles. Unfortunately they left the upper part of my feet exposed to the sun.

The result of this oversight did not become apparent until the early hours of the following morning when I woke up in my bunk with a sensation that my feet were on fire. Gingerly getting out of my bed I made my way to the mess lounge area and with the aid of a torch proceeded to inspect the source of my agony. The size of the blisters on the upper regions of my feet left me stunned.

My visit to the ship's sick-bay resulted in me being placed on 'light duties' for a week. Very compassionate and understanding you may think - not so. The RN views such matters from a totally different angle. My consultation at the sick-bay was followed by a session in the Regulation Office, where I was charged with 'self inflicted injury'. Limping up to the 'Commander's Table', sympathy was in short supply, even as I tried to display my other uncalled for injury by way of my bruised neck. "One week's No.14s punishment" (stoppage of leave) rang out in my ears. Oh well it could have been worse - we were due to sail in a couple of days!

I always considered the medical staff in the Royal Navy to be different and quite unique, in a positive way of course. They all certainly seemed to possess a keen sense of humour, as was illustrated on one occasion when I arrived at the ship's sick-bay to undertake my scheduled annual diving medical.

The Leading Medical Assistant (LMA) subjected me to all the normal checks, weight, blood pressure etc. before turning to my ears. Examining both ears with his illuminated, telescopic probe, he exclaimed "My god you have some wax in here. How on earth do you manage to hear anything said to you?"
"What was that?" came, what I thought to be, my witty reply. The unimpressed look on his face told me he didn't consider me to be the top comedian on board. Equipping himself with a syringe, suitably topped up with warm water, and a purposely designed metal bowl in which to capture the offending wax, he was ready to commence the relatively uncomplicated procedure. Handing me the metal tray he told me to place it tight in just below my left ear. Having completed his instructions he then commenced to syringe into my right ear. Before long I could feel water and wax oozing down the right hand side of my face and onto the collar of my shirt. Very funny - he obviously thought I had very little between my ears!

On another occasion I was walking along the Burma Way (main central passageway of the ship) nursing a nagging headache, when I noticed the ship's MA approaching me. I seized the opportunity and caught his attention. "Hey Doc, I wonder if you could help, I have developed this really nauseating headache?" Looking appropriately concerned he said "Really, tell me does it increase the pain if you shake your head from side to side?"

I tried it and reported "Actually it does Doc". To which he cheekily replied "Well don't walk around the ship shaking your head from side to side". With a smile forming on his face he said "Cheerio" and continued on his way. Like I say a unique sense of humour that seemed forever present in the medical branch!

Farewell South America. We had sailed from Rio after a colourful and momentous five days. Now homeward bound after what can only be described as a top class deployment we were due alongside in our home port of Portsmouth in ten days' time.

As soon as the ship docked the lucky majority of the crew were scheduled to immediately proceed on two weeks' leave. Despite the exotic places we had visited and the fact that we had transited the Panama Canal and rounded Cape Horn in a storm, the excitement of returning home on leave was for me by far the highlight of any trip away.

We had come up through the Caribbean and were now north eastward bound across the Atlantic. There was a great atmosphere throughout the ship as we closed in on Portsmouth. With two days to go the Commander came on the main broadcast to generally congratulate the ship's company on their achievements and performance on what was primarily a diplomatic and flag displaying tour. Then came the sting in the tail, as he wished us all a good leave, painfully adding that anyone requiring a haircut would <u>not</u> on arrival be allowed to proceed on leave. What a bummer. I had a train to catch and the last thing I needed was to be traipsing around Portsmouth looking for a barbers shop before returning to the ship to be inspected by regulating staff and collecting my invaluable leave pass.

The panic started as the ship's barber (a stoker) set up shop, with his professional set of haircutting equipment, in the starboard passageway. The queue was endless and never seemed to diminish. Never mind, me and my mess oppo came up with an inspiring and foolproof plan. We'd cut each other's hair. After all there didn't seem to be a lot to it, all you needed was a comb and a pair of scissors. We tossed a coin and my oppo, Steve, lost, meaning he was first to sit himself down, worryingly, in our hastily modified 'barber's chair'. Off I went trying to emulate Annette's seemingly effortless and professional style when cutting my hair. As always it wasn't that straight forward and matters went from bad to worse as I hacked at Steve's hair and watched the uneven and irregular clumps fall onto the deck. Trying to control my giggles I soldiered on. Not expecting a tip, I announced that 'sir's' haircut was complete. Apprehensively, both for him and me, he strolled over and looked into the mess mirror. To say he wasn't overjoyed was indeed and understatement, but the job was done and his leave pass now in sight.

Now it was my turn. As I sat down I felt somewhat uncomfortable as I noticed a sly, mischievous grin form on Steve's face. Revenge is perhaps too strong a word but he certainly appeared to revel in a certain degree of satisfaction as hair was hacked from my head. The end result was far from perfection, looking like my hair had been cut with a knife and fork. Still it allowed me to walk over the gangway and off to Portsmouth and Southsea train station. I was home with my beloved wife and son right on schedule, providing a certain degree of amusement to all the family at 114 Primrose Avenue.

Back on board I found myself on the move! From the challenges associated with being a baby faced Leading hand in a mess of sixty odd sailors to the relative luxury of 3R mess. 3P mess had been quite an experience, and having to deal with quite a few 'three badge men' (over 12 years service), some of whom served in the Korean War, really did help develop my fledgling leadership skills.

My new mess was considerably less spacious, being home to only fifteen Weapons Electrical Leading Hands, how civilised. I quickly settled in, being allocated my favoured place to sleep, namely a top bunk. Then to top it all I was invited to take on the role of 'Rum Bosun', and believe me I didn't have to be asked twice. Regrettably my appointment to, what I considered to be a privileged position, was to be all too short lived.

Reflecting the gravity of the impending dramatic change to the naval way of life, an announcement was made over the ship's broadcast for all available ratings to return to their mess and await a visit from the First Lieutenant. Speculation was rife, however it turned out that nobody could have forecast the devastating news we were about to be told. A somewhat solemn First Lieutenant entered the mess and invited us all to sit down. Taking a seat himself he was obviously aiming to create an informal and relaxed atmosphere. Then disregarding any meaningful pre-amble he launched in and announced that a signal had been received from The Admiralty stating that the over three hundred year old tradition of issuing of a daily ration of rum to ratings would cease after 31st July 1970.

The stunned silence and sense of disbelief was palpable. He went on to explain the reasoning behind this momentous decision, which apparently wasn't taken lightly after months of confidential discussions at the highest levels. The prominent reason given was that the Royal Navy was now a highly technical force with nuclear weapons capability and therefore it wasn't appropriate to have 'Jolly Jack' staggering around ships when at any time he could be called upon to maintain or operate highly complex weapons systems. Whilst appreciating and understanding this reasoning, I myself thought it quite ironic that at the same time as abolishing the 'Tot' it was announced that junior ratings would receive an increased daily ration of beer and senior ratings would be allowed to have a large variety of spirits available in their messes ie. whisky, gin, vodka, brandy etc. Surely this weakened the argument as sailors, particularly senior rates, could now carry out their duties, not tipsy on naval rum, but maybe a little merry on beer, whisky, gin or whatever other spirits took their fancy.

Our varied and eventful commission was coming to an end as we made our way home to Portsmouth from our deployment in the Mediterranean. It had been a good ship on which I had made many friends and created a wealth of lifetime memories. A month or so earlier my good friend Dave had applied for promotion, was successful and was now, quite deservedly roaming the passageways of the ship as a Naval Petty Officer.

With the best of intentions Dave began to apply pressure, constantly going on as to why I hadn't applied for promotion. The truth of the matter was that although I welcomed the thought of being a Senior Rate, the world of radar, sonar and radio communications never really turned me on. How I'd ever made it to the dizzy heights of Leading Radio Electrical Mechanic (LREM) was always a constant source of wonder to me. Eventually, with the responsibility I had to my new family in mind, and with the support of the head of the Radio Department, I took the plunge and submitted a formal request to be considered for promotion to Petty Officer Radio Electrician (POREL). The selection process involved sitting a comprehensive theoretical exam followed by an interview board (if successful in the written exam) made up of the ship's Commander Weapons Electrical Officer, his deputy, a Lieutenant Commander and the Chief Radio Artificer.

Putting many hours into studying, I eventually sat the theoretical exam a week or so later. Strangely enough I managed quite a good pass. This left me the mountain to climb in the form of the 'Interview Board'. I had a reasonable idea of what sort of questions I would be asked, the most fearful being to explain the details of a complex circuit diagram relating to a unit within one of the ship's radio or radar systems. A distinctly weak area with regard to my limited technical abilities. How on earth was I going to get through this mysterious aspect of my assessment?

The day before my oral board I was presented with a lifeline. A well meaning Senior Rate from the radar department who must have thought I had some potential, approached me with a gift from heaven. He reported that a technical reference manual (BR) had been borrowed by the Commander WEO which, as it turned out, he correctly assumed was to be used to test my knowledge of interpreting a circuit diagram. He knew the contents of this BR extremely well and thought there was a fair chance I would be asked about a circuit called a 'square wave generator'. Being grateful doesn't begin to cover it especially as he used his expertise to explain to me the intricacies of this mysterious document. Of course there was always the chance that the 'square wave generator' was a red-herring and another completely different circuit diagram would be placed in front of me. In which case I would be doomed.

The big day arrived and boy was I nervous. Entering the compartment where the three board members were seated behind an elongated table I myself sat down in the isolated chair in front of them. Let battle commence! Things were initially progressing well but I knew the make or break period of the interview was fast approaching. Finally the Commander reached over and opened up the BR he had in front of him, exposing the dreaded circuit diagram that could well have precipitated my downfall. My spirits soared. There in front of my eyes was the anticipated 'square wave generator'. I had to do everything in my power to stop myself pumping my fist in the air and shouting out 'Yeah!'. Controlling myself, I went through the pretence of carefully considering what should have been an unfamiliar diagram before me. My explanation of the circuit and the answers I gave to their specific, probing questions appeared to impress them. "This boy really knows his stuff" seemed to be their impression.

Eventually the ordeal was over and I was asked to step outside as the board considered my performance. Fairly soon after I was called back and took heart at the smiling faces that greeted me. Congratulations were offered as I was informed that I had managed a 'good' pass. In a haze I thanked the board and stepped out into the ship's main passageway. Dave was waiting for me and was genuinely delighted to hear of my success. Dragging me off to the Petty Officer's mess he had a pint of Courage Sparkling Bitter in my hand before I knew it. This was supplemented by some 'neat' naval rum that Dave had been bottling up (against the rules!) in anticipation of this very occasion. The rest of the day passed in a blissful but somewhat hazy atmosphere.

My time on HAMPSHIRE had been quite an experience, but in line with life in the navy it was time to move on.

Does this never end? Back to HMS COLLINGWOOD once again, this time to complete Petty Officer Radio Electricians (POREL's) course. The one overriding positive factor of this unavoidable training period was that Annette and our new young son Paul would be accompanying me. I was scheduled to be back in the Fareham/Gosport area for approximately six months.

We were allocated a relatively new, three bedroomed terraced married quarter, with a small back garden, in the Navy's Rowner Estate, Gosport. It certainly took the edge off being back at COLLINGWOOD, with me being free to come home to my new family every night, enhanced with the free weekends we had to share.

Our time together down south left us with many treasured memories, inclusive of Paul being fascinated and intrigued when we crossed Portsmouth Harbour on the well known Gosport Ferry. He was a contented wee boy who spent many happy hours playing on his toy tractor outside our back gate, next to a small monument of a black anchor, which he never gave up trying to climb.

FLEET MAINTENANCE GROUP (FMG) ROSYTH

What next? I was due some 'shore time', which I was praying would be back up in Scotland. My prayers were answered when I received my next draft order to join the Fleet Maintenance Group (FMG) based in Rosyth Dockyard. The main workload of FMG was to assist in the maintenance of Rosyth based ships when they were alongside in their home port. However, there was another aspect of the technical support given to frontline ships, which came under the title of 'The Mobile Unit'. This involved various teams of engineers visiting ships alongside in locations outwith their home port of Rosyth. Predominatly these ports were within UK waters. Places such as Aberdeen, the Shetland and Orkney Islands, Newcastle, Liverpool etc. However, foreign visits were also programmed in Gibraltar, Malta, France, Italy and other such welcoming places. On one memorable occasion I was selected, along with another radio technician and various marine engineers, to visit the island paradise of Bermuda. Whoopee Do!!

The routine at the time involved the ship, in this case the Type 12 Frigate HMS ROTHESAY, forwarding to FMG a list of maintenance tasks requiring assistance. This was in the form of a document called the 'Mainreque'. Unfortunately in ROTHESAY's case this quite straight forward procedure never quite happened, mainly due to the fact that Britain was having to deal with a rather acrimonious postal strike. Not to worry, the quick thinking, senior Chief Artificer in charge of our department brought his vast experience into play, estimating that two radio senior rate technicians would be able to deal with whatever workload had been planned.

An area to the west of this tropical haven called Ireland Island was where the majority of visiting British Warships docked, particularly for maintenance periods. Our team, a total of eight enthusiastic technical 'whiz kids' arrived and were transported to really outstanding accommodation in the form of, what can only be described as a luxurious villa in an elevated garden area overlooking the sea. It was to be our home for the next couple of weeks, the bonus being that it was only a five minute stroll away from a famed NAAFI type establishment, namely 'The Trap', which always opened its doors when Royal Naval personnel were in the area. The prices for a vast range of alcohol and food were absolutely 'give away'.

So there we were, keen, ready and raring to go. Then we received news that ROTHESAY would be a few days late in arriving due to 'Operational Requirements'. Oh well we would just have to get on with life and enjoy the delights of our new temporary abode. Eventually ROTHESAY sailed into view and berthed alongside. Presenting ourselves to the Radio Department on board, myself and my fellow radio technician explained that due to a postal strike in the U.K. we had not received their Mainreque, but were happy to take on any outstanding maintenance they might have for us. We were both dumbfounded and lost for words when ROTHESAY's Chief Radio Electrical Artificer (CREA) informed us that they were in fact well ahead of the game in relation to maintenance and as such had no work whatsoever for us to undertake. Oh dear another ten days vacation to endure.

Over the coming days we did visit the ship during the forenoons, and whilst trying not to make a nuisance of ourselves volunteered to take on the most menial of tasks. Very little was forthcoming, but the numerous cups of coffee and tea we enjoyed down the senior rates mess was much appreciated and helped ease the occasional bouts of guilt we felt as our marine engineering team colleagues tackled their quite substantial workload. So after an arduous two weeks in a magical corner of the world we returned home grateful for the experience that came our way - you know life in the R.N. can have its moments!

Talking about 'moments', what could be more meaningful in our lives than the birth of our beautiful daughter Julie. On the morning of 7th December 1970 Annette started her contractions. Trying to remain calm we left our married quarters in Hilton Road, Rosyth, dropping off Paul at his Nanna and grandad's house, before heading off to the maternity hospital in Dunfermline. Poor old Annette, she had endured a rather traumatic experience bringing Paul into the world and was understandably more than a little apprehensive of what lay ahead this time. Matters progressed in relatively reasonable fashion throughout the day and on the advice of the experienced maternity staff I left the unit around 5pm to get back to Paul and have something to eat prior to returning for visiting time at 8 o'clock in the evening.

Father-in-law George drove me up at the scheduled time and as I entered the labour ward I was taken aside and rushed off to the delivery room. Apparently Annette was now in the final stages of giving birth. A seat was provided for me in an unexpected position at the foot of her bed, not alongside her as I imagined. Totally mesmerized as I watched Julie being delivered, I was really taken aback as one of the attending mid-wives, after weighing her, placed our new blessing in my arms. Thereafter, in a trance I seemed to float up to Annette's bedside before handing over our bundle of joy to her.

Leaving Annette and Julie to recover I made my way to the main waiting room with a broad smile on my face. The concerned look of George immediately changed as I gave him the news he had a granddaughter. Half an hour later we were sat in the lounge of the Senior Rates mess in HMS COCHRANE. The 'baby's head' was wet many times before we made it back to Primrose Avenue, where Isobel (Mother-in Law) was quite understanding in relation to our unsteady state. George was fast developing into more of a friend than an in-law!

Although enjoying life in FMG, I was well aware that it was fast approaching the time when a draft back to sea would be coming my way. Before that inevitable event I found myself undergoing the character building experience of the six week leadership course for Petty Officers held at HMS ROYAL ARTHUR in Wiltshire. It certainly was a challenging period but a time that strangely enough I really enjoyed. As such I came away with a really good report which went a long way to building up my self esteem and confidence.

Not long after ROYAL ARTHUR my expected draft order arrived. I was to join the Tribal Class Frigate, HMS NUBIAN in July 1972, it couldn't have been better. Firstly and most importantly it was a Rosyth based ship, with the added bonus being that it was currently undergoing a lengthy refit and it would be six months before sea trials were due to commence, allowing me more precious family time to enjoy.

HMS NUBIAN

With NUBIAN in dry dock, when I joined most of the days were spent in associated

'Portacabins' located on the dockside. This provided the opportunity to get to know the crew members I would be spending the following three years of my life with. They were all good blokes and I had a strong feeling that a memorable and eventful commission lay ahead. Of course there had to be a slight downside which came in the form of me having to head back down to the dreaded HMS COLLINGWOOD. I had to undertake a series of Pre-Commissioning Training (PCT) courses to familiarise myself with the radio equipment I would be responsible for maintaining when Nubian became fully operational.

The quiet time alongside was relatively short lived and before we knew it the ship was being subject to Harbour Acceptance trials (HATS) and the ship's company had moved on board. Long hours were the order of the day as we worked alongside the dockyard personnel who were responsible for handing the ship back over to the men of the Royal Navy. It was a period when I considered it essential to form a close working relationship with the highly skilled, technical experts known fondly as 'Dockyard Mateys' (many pints of Courage sparkling bitter were involved in creating this close bond!). Undoubtedly this exercise proved to be invaluable as in the months and years ahead I had many reliable technical experts to call upon in my times of operational stress!

I was rapidly approaching the critical age of 27 years and as of yet hadn't made one of the most crucial and important decisions of my married life. Should I leave the Royal Navy or re-engage until the age of 40 years?

Only a year or so earlier that decision had been quite straightforward and easy to make. I was definitely leaving. As a committed ROMFT (Roll On My Fucking Time) rating, I had had enough of separation and felt ready to settle into a nice 'nine to five' job at home. Well that was my feelings then but as decision time approached reality started to kick in as it dawned upon me that the way ahead was not as straightforward as I originally thought.

Separation was at the top of my reasons for leaving. I was finding it increasingly difficult to say goodbye to my adorable wife as I departed for yet another six or seven months at sea. This was compounded by the fact that I was now blessed with my wonderful children, Paul and Julie. I so much wanted to be a part of their lives as they were growing up. The reality aspect took the form of worrying about such important issues as 'would I get a reasonably paid job' and 'where would we live'? In short how was I going to support my family? The breakthrough came when the Royal Navy introduced an extremely attractive incentive to encourage people like my good self to re-engage.

What was on offer for people willing to re-engage until the age of 40 years was an advance of pay to be repaid over the last ten years in the Royal Navy. As such it wasn't a 'loan' and consequently there were no interest payments to be made on the money advanced. This offer was solely aligned to the purchasing of a house, which provided for a deposit, survey and solicitor's fees etc. In short a house could be purchased with no immediate personal cash payments required. The offer was just too good to miss, providing the golden opportunity to get on the housing ladder. Of course this had a profound effect on Annette and myself when trying to come to a decision regarding my future career. Gradually though we were very much leaning towards me staying in the Navy.

At the time I was taking driving lessons and one Sunday afternoon my good old father-in-law George kindly offered to take me out for a lesson in his much loved and well cared for Vauxhall Viva. We ventured into a local Dunfermline private housing estate called Pitreavie. Annette and I had always admired the houses within the estate and dreamed of one day owning a three bedroomed Wimpey semi. Driving up to the top end of the estate we came across a new development which had a number of show houses open for viewing. Back in Rosyth after my nerve jangling driving lesson I persuaded Annette to come along and view these new show houses. Off we went to see exactly what was on offer. The three differently designed houses were all detached. Were we getting carried away and looking for a home well above our station? We had set ourselves an absolute maximum budget of £4,500, and here we were considering a place at £5,250. Had we completely lost the plot?

Viewing the show houses was q experience. To say we were mighty impre was an understatement. We were edging towards making that bold, fateful decision and finally committed. To secure number 41 Mulberry Drive all that was needed was a £200 deposit, £150 of which was refundable if we changed our minds within a month. Out came my cheque book but just as I was about to start writing Annette says "Phil I don't suppose we could go for an 'N' type? ", which was a higher spec detached house incorporating an additional downstairs toilet. What opulence. I retorted "Have you gone completely mad woman, what are you trying to do, put us in the poor house?". The fact of the matter was that the 'N' type came in at £5,400, a staggering £150 dearer than the more modest abode we opted for.

A few months later we moved into number 41 having not laid out a penny, even our £200 deposit had been refunded by the Navy.

Sea trials were going well when PO Seaman Dave Allison, our Mess President, called an emergency mess meeting. Dave was an old hand, a 'three badge man' no less and well respected in the mess and throughout the ship. As we all gathered, approximately thirty Petty Officers, he announced that he intended to resign as the Mess President, explaining that as sea trials were continuing and the dreaded 'work-up' was approaching, he was going to be far too busy (weren't we all!) to carry the additional burden of Mess President responsibilities. Members were quite taken aback and I for one considered his reasoning quite pathetic. Anyway it was done and consequently a new Mess President had to be elected. Proposals were called for and you could have knocked me over with a feather when my name was put forward and promptly seconded. I was a relatively young and inexperienced 'one badge' P.O. and the NUBIAN was my first full commission in this exalted rank. A further two of my mess mates had their names put forward. Both were much more experienced than me. However, we all humbly accepted the proposals. Walking out to the passageway outside the mess, I was taken aback but somewhat proud to be part of the vote, safe in the knowledge that there was no way I could win this contest.

After no longer than ten to fifteen minutes the three of us were called back in. The announcement that I had been selected left me completely stunned. What were my colleagues thinking about? Did they think I would be a soft touch? Of course in a state of amazement I respectfully agreed to undertake this new challenge. After my short acceptance speech I pondered what lay ahead. Being 'Killick of the Mess' on HMS HAMPSHIRE had really stretched and tested my leadership skills. How was I going to fare with this, as I conceived it, even greater challenge? I knew I would have to gain all the mess's respect and thankfully that's how things panned out. I can honestly say that over the coming years I found being the Mess President of the Petty

Officer's Mess on HMS NUBIAN one of the most rewarding periods of my Naval career.

Sea trials and 'work-up' complete and operational deployments to look forward to. Where were we to sail off to in order to patrol and protect British interests? Nowhere less than the West Indies for seven months.

Alongside in Lisbon, Portugal and I found myself Duty Petty Officer. The Officer of the Day (OOD) was a young sub-lieutenant serving on his first ship after training. This should be fun. The day was passing reasonably quietly until late in the evening, when matters took a dramatic turn for the worse. Reports were coming in from ashore of a serious disturbance involving our Royal Marines Detachment. Apparently a fight had developed in a downtown bar resulting in many of the locals being the worse for wear and the majority of Royal Marines being detained in cells at the local police station. Not the most diplomatic start to our visit.

The next report we received was that the Captain, Commander Howitt Royal Navy, on hearing of the incident had stepped in to try and resolve this unwelcome turn of events. He himself was ashore attending a dinner laid on for him and a number of his fellow officers by the city's dignitaries. Word reached him of the jailing of the majority of the elite fighting force of his crew. Thereafter he involved himself in some delicate negotiations and managed to secure their release.

Apparently they were now making their way back on board.

The OOD went into an unashamed panic. "PO what are we going to do?".
"Well let's not make matters worse," I cautiously replied. "What we should aim to do is just get them down into their mess and to bed with the minimum of fuss". They started to arrive in dribs and drabs, staggering over the gangway with torn shirts and bloodied faces. It was plainly obvious that they were not in the best of moods. Greeting them at the top of the gangway we were treated to a series of grunts and menacing stares. However, they were making their way down to their mess which was a bonus in the circumstances. Matters nearly took a sinister turn as I saw one of their corporals approaching. A normally mild mannered guy who I personally got along with, as he came over the brow I said "Good evening Taff", to which he moodily replied "Fuck off". The OOD was understandably outraged as he turned to me and remarked "PO we can't have this. Arrest that man". I managed to convince the OOD that perhaps it would be better not to inflame the situation and just this once overlook this breach of naval discipline. Reluctantly he agreed.

It was well after midnight and I thought we had handled the situation quite well. The marines were all down in their mess below the junior rates dining hall and although the worse for wear should soon be asleep. How wrong could I have been. Within minutes of them congregating in the mess yet another brawl developed. Standing at the top of the hatch leading to their mess the OOD insisted that we call out the duty watch to go down and restore order. "I don't think that is such a good idea sir," I responded. "For heaven's sake why not?" he shrieked. Calmly I pointed out to him that the duty watch was predominantly made up of young sailors, who were certainly no match for the trained killers of the elite Royal Marines Corps. "Well we have to do something," he insisted "What do you suggest?". Turning to the large heavy hatch cover I released its holding pin, closed it on the combing and securely battened it down by all its clips. With a look of astonishment on his face, the OOD shouted "You can't do that". "Sir believe me it's our best option. They will be fine in the morning," I replied. "No I'm not happy," he said "Send for the Master-at-Arms". "Are you sure you want to do that sir? I don't think the Master will be too pleased at getting dragged out of his bunk at this hour of the morning," I advised. He was having none of it and 10 minutes or so later the Master-at-Arms appeared on the scene in his dressing gown and flip-flops. To say he wasn't too happy was an understatement. Turning to me he said "What's going on Phil?". I briefly explained the unfortunate sequence of events of the evening to a background of riotous fighting from below. I respectfully outlined the OOD's plan to send in the duty watch along with my solution of battening down the hatch. My briefing finished, the Master turned to the OOD and said "Don't be an idiot. Leave them to sort themselves out". He went on to say "Goodnight Phil, I'll see you in the morning. And well done".

Of course there would be repercussions in the morning when some rather battered and bruised Royal Marines would have to face the consequences of their actions by appearing at the 'Captain's Table'. Taff, as expected, personally apologised to me and all his colleagues once again adopted a respectful and disciplined manner when addressing their superiors and fellow crew members.

On station in the sun drenched Caribbean. We were scheduled to undergo a three week, mid-deployment maintenance period in Bermuda. However, at short notice we were directed to proceed to Trinidad as reports were being received regarding civil unrest developing on the relatively nearby island of Grenada. It was thought necessary that we be close at hand in order to deal with any escalation of violence.

Our unscheduled stay in the wonderful, colourful island of Trinidad was turning into a truly unforgettable experience, typified when the when the P.O.'s Mess was challenged to a cricket match by one of the local clubs. We were honour bound to accept this audacious challenge and as such set about our training programme in the mess lounge/bar. As Mess President I of course was selected for the team, although my cricketing skills were somewhat limited and indeed my knowledge of the rules involved were undoubtedly a little sketchy.

The big day arrived. The opposing team had kindly offered to lay on transport for us, which we were reliably informed would be on the jetty at precisely 1300hrs. That gave us a good hour in the mess to discuss strategy and settle our nerves over a few beers. The Quartermaster phoned down to say our transport had arrived, exactly on time. Off we went up to the gangway, the team and enthusiastic supporters raring to go. Appearing on the upper deck I scanned around looking for the coaches I expected as our form of transport. Nothing resembling a bus could be seen. Instead there were three open backed lorries with grinning drivers leaning out of their cab windows and equally happy looking assistants waving from the platform areas of the vehicles. We all heaved ourselves onto the back of the lorries and settled down on the benches that flanked the sides. Seated down we couldn't help but notice the two large oil drums in front of us. What on earth were they for? Before long, and to our absolute delight we were enlightened as to their strategic purpose. Both contained an adequate proportion of ice to keep cool welcoming supplies of local beer, rum and coca-cola. Surely the opposition weren't trying to get us a little tipsy? If they were their plan was certain to succeed.

After half an hour or so driving in the sun, down the tropical plant hedged roads of the island, we arrived at the ground. Feeling in great tune we somewhat unsteadily disembarked from our unique form of transport and with a smile on our faces and rum and cokes in our hands were escorted to our dressing room.

The game got underway in a stadium I equated to 'Lord's', not at all like the uneven, bumpy fields I had played my limited games of cricket on. The opposition went into bat and it wasn't too long before they were edging up to a 100 runs without loss of wicket. They were smashing our pathetic attempts at bowling all over the place. Some form of hero was required. So why did they call on me to deliver an over? Amid great expectation, which I felt I couldn't live up to, I made my approach and hurled the ball down towards their super talented batsman. Groans from my team mates and supporters, I had bowled a 'wide'. For my second delivery I slightly over compensated and produced another 'wide' to the opposite side of the wicket. Things were getting amusing for the Trinidadians and desperate for us. My third approach and nothing to lose, I'd already made a bit of a fool of myself. Running up, I released the ball with a passion. Moments later I was stunned in absolute amazement as I watched their opening batsman's middle stump disappear from the wicket as my speeding ball hit it square on. The whole place erupted in cheers, applause and hoots of laughter. The batsmen were marvellous and amongst the first to congratulate me, with broad delightful grins on their faces. Of course it wasn't enough for us to win the match, but I'd had my moment of glory and a great time was had by all.

On display in the Naval Museum within Portsmouth Dockyard is a treasured exhibit known as the 'Tribal Lantern'. It is an old red painted road lantern adorned with yellow paint giving the names of ships and the dates it was in their custody. In the past it was used to warn motorists of local road works, accident sites and general driving hazards. It's far more important role in the Royal Navy was to promote social gatherings between Petty Officers' messes of Tribal Class frigates.

In early January 1974 HMS NUBIAN was alongside in Rosyth Dockyard making final preparations for a seven month deployment to the West Indies. On a cold wintry morning HMS ESKIMO entered harbour and tied up alongside us. Later on that day, being President of the NUBIAN's P.O.'s mess, I had a visit from my opposite number on ESKIMO. He had come to warn me that they had the Tribal Lantern and that, in line with tradition, it was their intention to present it to our mess that very evening. Noticing the blank expression on my face he quickly deduced that I was ignorant of the lantern's existence, which indeed I was.

Gleefully he went on to explain the history and tradition surrounding the lantern. He was not sure of where and when the whole thing started but he was familiar with the rules surrounding its purpose. The ship holding the lantern had the opportunity to pass it on to any other operational Tribal Class frigate. The lantern, with a candle burning inside, would be presented to the receiving mess, who were obliged to gracefully accept it. Having gained the lantern the mess was bound to provide all members of the mess from whence it came with free beer and spirits until such time as the affixed candle burnt itself out.

Later on that evening all members of ESKIMO's P.O.'s mess arrived with a rather large candle burning brightly in the lantern. The social gathering proved to be a great success with a good time had by all, but more importantly we were now the enviable owners of the precious lantern, which according to the rules could not be passed on for at least a week. A couple of days later the ESKIMO sailed and not long after we departed for the Caribbean.

The opportunity for us to pass on the lantern presented itself a couple of months later when we found ourselves alongside in the Naval Harbour of Ireland Island, Bermuda. A day after our arrival HMS MOHAWK entered harbour and tied up just forward of NUBIAN. I could hardly get on board MOHAWK quickly enough to meet up with their P.O.s Mess Pres., who turned out to be a very amiable chap who was only too well aware of the lantern's existence and the unique traditions surrounding it. He readily agreed to host the expected ceremonies, suggesting that we visit his mess that very evening. The hunt was on to acquire the largest candle we could find to squeeze into the lantern. At around 2000hrs an enthusiastic party of around a dozen of NUBIAN's P.O.'s mess trooped over the gangway with the lantern burning brightly.

HMS MOHAWK's P.O.'s mess hospitality was outstanding, with a variety of exotic food available and beer and spirits flowing freely. After a couple of hours of joviality and exaggerated story telling the evening took a truly memorable turn. Their President turned to me and proudly proclaimed, "Do you know that we have a fleet champion in our mess and we are honoured to have him in our company this evening?". "No" says I "and just what is he fleet champion of?" "Placing 2p coins behind his foreskin" came his astonishing reply. Having reduced his visitors to stunned silence, he went on to explain the background and announced that it was the champion's intention to make an attempt on the fleet record, which we were disbelievably informed stood at 28x2p coins behind the foreskin. The intention was to try and break the 30 barrier.

The rules were explained and the scene set. Donated 2p coins were assembled on a mess coffee table, tins of talcum powder (foo-foo!) made available and various officials appointed. As the visiting Mess President I had the honour of acting as the official 'counter' and recorder of the deposited 2ps. The champion stripped off his trousers and underwear and started limbering up. What a sheet of foreskin he had! When ready he asked for an initial total of 6x2ps to be deposited behind his outstretched foreskin. The official 'coin placer' obliged and I confirmed and recorded the number of coins in place. Off he went around the mess, pulling and stretching his bewildering and expanding foreskin. After accumulating 18 coins he called for 'foo-foo' to be sprinkled over his bulging penis end. From this stage on coins had to be deposited two at a time. The build up to the fleet record of 28 was tense and absorbing, with the champ clinging on to his private parts whilst constantly calling for more 'foo-foo'. The rules stated that the foreskin must meet and touch over the coins. The sense of anticipation as he went for an amazing total of 30 was palpable. Unbelievably he managed a grand total of 32 before depositing his load into an empty pint pot. The coins had to be recounted before officially claiming the new '2p behind the foreskin' fleet record. I drew the line at this task but did oversee the final count carried out by a proud and supportive MOHAWK mess member. What an end to a rather unconventional social gathering. To my knowledge the record of 32 stands to this day!

The 18th June 1974. Still alongside in Bermuda with HMS MOHAWK. At 0500hrs I was rudely awakened from a deep sleep as the action alarm sounded throughout the ship. Not long after, the First Lieutenant announced over the main broadcast that operation awkward had been instigated by the local Flag officer.

As a priority the ship's hull had to be searched for limpet mines. In fairly quick time all the ship's divers were assembled on the jetty with their equipment. Whilst awaiting clearance to enter the water the diving officer detailed off the search team. I was to be No1 diver on the 'half necklace'. We all checked our gear and donned our breathing sets. Before putting divers in the water the diving officer must be officially informed that a series of checks/actions have been completed. These checks included such things as the propellers and rudders being locked. In addition the underwater stabilizers had to be deactivated and the sonar domes locked in either the up or down positions.

The five search divers were all ready to go when the First Lieutenant, who was himself a specialised clearance diver, appeared on the scene in a somewhat agitated state. He demanded to know why the search of the ship's hull had not commenced. The diving officer calmly informed him that the 'check clearance' had not been relayed yet. The First Lieutenant retorted in an aggressive manner "I don't give a fuck. Get those divers in the water". Consequently, contrary to all laid down procedures, we entered the water and commenced the search. Swimming forward up the starboard side we soon came to the 177 sonar dome housing. The dome itself had been raised leaving the housing to be searched. As No.1 diver I temporarily halted the progress of the team of divers strung out along the starboard side of the hull. Calling down No.2

diver we both entered the 177 dome housing in order to carry out a thorough search. The depth of the housing was approximately 4-5ft which meant that most of our bodies were inside the cavernous area as we felt around various mechanical and hydraulic parts of the sonar lowering mechanism. Nothing was found so we both resumed our positions on the search line as the team carried on swimming forward. As we reached and rounded the bows we started swimming aft down the port side. As we approached the 177 dome again, no more than 5 minutes after we had left it, I was absolutely horrified to see that the dome had been lowered and was now locked in the 'down' position. If that dome had started lowering with divers searching inside the housing, without a doubt the ship would be dealing with two fatalities.

My horror soon turned to enraged temper and as we surfaced after completing the search I ripped off my face mask whilst still in the water and bellowed out "Who the fuck lowered that 177 dome?". The First Lieutenant who had ordered us into the water was stood on the jetty next to the diving officer. They both looked understandably shocked as they realized what the fatal consequences of their failure to follow procedure could have been. The First Lieutenant slunk away as I climbed out of the water. The diving officer tried to calm me down but I was having none of it as I demanded to speak to the Captain. As the atmosphere blackened, still in my wet diving suit, I stomped over the gangway and up to the Captain's cabin only to be told that he was not on board. Apparently he was in the Flag Officer's residence debriefing the Admiral.

Finding it difficult to control my anger, I was determined to wait outside his cabin until the Captain returned. This proved to be quite a long time during which I was approached by the Weapons Electrical Officer. He invited me to his cabin to discuss the situation. He professed to fully understand my anger and concern adding that it was fully accepted that mistakes had been made and that as a result lessons had been learnt. As I gradually began to calm down I was told that in all likelihood the Captain would be spending the rest of the day with the Admiral and that I should go and get showered and changed before meeting with the WEO again in the afternoon.

After lunch I was back in the WEO's cabin, very much calmer than I had been earlier in the day. Obviously the officers had discussed the debacle and it was left with the WEO to talk me out of making a formal complaint to the Captain. To my enduring shame he managed to do just that and I never did get to tell Commander Howitt how he nearly lost two members of his ship's company. Being talked out of doing something I knew was the right thing to do haunted me for years. Why didn't I have the strength of character, at that time, to ignore the conspiracy of silence orchestrated by the wardroom and follow through on what I knew to be the correct course of action?

We sailed from Montego Bay, Jamaica, embarking on a three day passage to Veracruz in Mexico. The day after leaving port, at around 0700hrs I was in the bathroom. Alighting from the shower I was greeted by a rather solemn looking Radio Supervisor. In his hand he had a signal, the contents of which he reluctantly read to me. In stark, unemotional terms it stated ' Inform Petty Officer Armstrong son Paul admitted to West Fife General Hospital, Dunfermline. Daughter Julie admitted to Windygates Hospital, Kirkcaldy'. That was it, no further details. My blood ran cold as I tried to take in the enormity of what I was hearing. My initial thoughts focused on a car accident. Easter weekend had just passed and I knew that Annette and the children, along with her Mum and Dad had planned to travel up north to Hopeman, Morayshire to visit relatives. The route to be taken was along the notorious A9, statistically the most dangerous road in not only Scotland but the whole of the United Kingdom. My mind raced. It must be serious, why would the children be taken to separate hospitals?

Having dressed I immediately made my way up to my Divisional Officer's cabin. He had been made aware of the received signal and offered his sincere sympathies as he invited me to take a seat. At that time worldwide communications were not as sophisticated and readily accessible as they are today. I was informed that the ship had radioed off a signal to the Naval Welfare Authorities requesting further details of Paul and Julie's hospitalisation. I was in turmoil and had never felt so entrapped within a ship. I couldn't function. All I could focus on was getting home to my wife and children.

After many hours, which seemed like a lifetime, I was sent for by the Ship's Captain, Commander Michael Howitt Royal Navy. As I entered his cabin I had a feeling of foreboding, he didn't look too happy. After sitting down and being offered a drink, which I declined, Commander Howitt informed me that further details relating to my children had been received. It appeared that Paul had been admitted with severe leg pain and Julie was in an isolation ward suffering from an as yet undiagnosed viral infection. Mixed feeling engulfed me. Relief that they had not apparently been involved in a traffic accident, offset by the confusion of them suffering from apparently two unrelated complaints. The knock out punch came when the Captain quoted a reference given at the end of the signal. It referred to a section within the Naval Welfare Regulations which stated that the circumstances did not warrant me being returned home at public expense. I was dumbfounded and after gathering myself I respectfully informed Commander Howitt that as soon as the ship docked in Mexico I was heading home and that the only way I could be stopped would be to 'clap me in irons'

The Captain was magnificent. Instead of being taken aback with my attitude, he was completely understanding and promised to do all in his power to get me back to Fife. This took the form of authorising money to be made available from the Ship's Welfare Fund (an interest free loan) to pay for my air fare, to grant an initial two weeks compassionate leave and to instruct the ship's doctor, who spoke Spanish, to accompany me ashore when we arrived in Veracruz to help in arranging my passage home.

The remaining days it took to reach Mexico were agonising. I withdrew into myself which I'm sure didn't go unnoticed by my friends and colleagues throughout the ship, particularly in the mess. Eventually the ship arrived alongside around 10 o'clock in the morning. All I could think about was getting ashore to make travel arrangements to get me home as quickly as possible. The ship was buzzing with everyone keen to explore the sights and delights of this new port of call. Trying to track down the Lieutenant Doctor, who was crucial to the task in hand, proved troublesome. Without wishing to sound harsh I just got the impression he was more focused on the pending social whirl that was about to engulf the wardroom than tending to my needs.

Eventually I managed to drag him over the gangway, and in possession of an abundance of Mexican peso notes, courtesy of the ship's welfare fund, we made our way ashore to seek out the nearest travel agents. In the taxi carrying us off to the centre of town the Doc asked exactly what it was I was looking for. I replied, somewhat abruptly "I just want to get home in the shortest possible time". As we entered a rather upmarket travel agents the Doc went to work negotiating my flights and fare home. I of course didn't understand a word of Spanish and as a consequence didn't have any sense of how the conversation was going. Eventually he informed me that I could catch an internal flight that evening to Mexico City. From there I could transfer to a British Airways flight to London Heathrow, followed by a final flight from London to Edinburgh. I eagerly agreed to the offer, enquiring as to the cost, not that cost was at the top of my priorities at that particular time. That being said, I recall being a little taken aback with the expense involved. However, I was not about to launch into an argument, I just wanted that air ticket in my hand.

Mission completed we returned on board. I thanked the Doc for his assistance and made my way down to the mess to pack my travel bag. All through this worrying time I had not told my mess mates about my concerns although there was no doubt that they suspected something was not right in my life. It turned out that in my absence that morning my predicament had become general knowledge throughout the ship. As I was at my locker finalising my packing the ship's Officer's Chef, Petty Officer Davie Muir, approached me saying that the mess had heard about my troubles and were sincerely sorry to hear of the plight of my children. He then handed me an envelope saying that he had organised a 'whip round' and that I should use it to get presents on the way home for Paul and Julie. In the envelope was well over £200, not an inconsiderable sum in the 1970s.

It was a wonderful gesture which made one 'roughie toughie matelot' quite overcome with emotion, so much so that I found it quite difficult to make it into the mess lounge to say thank you. Mind you it didn't end there. The majority of the mess thought it necessary to make sure I boarded the internal flight to Mexico City, which meant a full personal escort as far as the departure lounge. Take off time was over five hours away, so with a view to temporarily diverting my thoughts away from my troubles they sat me down insisting that we have a drink or three. I was not allowed to put my hand in my pocket, both in the mess and the airport lounge, which we arrived at in a number of taxis. After once again wishing all the best for Paul and Julie they bade me farewell as I staggered through embarkation. What a great bunch of lads. It was their first night in an exotic foreign port and still they saw fit to see one of their mess mates safely on his way. Well just about!

It's lucky this flight wasn't going any further than Mexico City or I could still have been encircling the extremities of Latin America. As it was, from when I plonked myself down in my seat for the three hour flight all I remember was being awakened by a steward to be told we had arrived. With a thumping head

I collected my luggage and identified my next departure gate before taking off around the airport shops on the hunt for presents for the children. Kitted out with luggage, cuddly toys and a big hangover I eventually made my way to the British Airways International Flight Desk. As soon as I presented my documentation and passport matters took a dramatic turn. My bags were taken off me and I was allocated a personal escort who guided me to a rather luxurious lounge. Offered drinks from a bar with a vast array of top brand wines and spirits, and food which to me appeared to have been prepared by a top cordon bleu chef, I was invited to relax and told I would be informed when it was time to board the aircraft.

A couple of drinks later my hangover magically disappeared as I indulged myself in the service on offer. A British Airways member of staff eventually approached and politely asked me to follow her, as it was time to board. No queue, further boarding card checks and suchlike. No, for me, and just a few other privileged passengers, it was a short escorted walk across the tarmac to the forward boarding staircase. Up I went to be greeted at the doorway by a more than pleasant air stewardess who directed me to my seat. What a size, what leg room, what comfort. No sooner was I seated when I was offered a glass of the finest champagne. By this time the pennies were beginning to drop as I realised I was seated in first class. My well intentioned, Spanish speaking Ship's Doctor, who had acted as interpreter when arranging my passage home, obviously had other priorities on his mind such as the evening wardroom cocktail party. He had just advised me to take the first available seat the travel agent was offering, which just happened to be, in normal circumstances, well in excess of anything I could ever afford. Still I was not about to question things at this stage. I would leave that until we were up at 38,000ft and well on our way back to the U.K.

Flying high in the lap of luxury I was presented with a mouth watering exotic menu. At this stage I made my move. "Excuse me am I correct in saying that I am seated in the first class compartment of this aircraft?" "Oh most definitely sir," the stewardess cheerily replied. In a somewhat sombre and embarrassed tone I hesitatingly continued "Well I'm dreadfully sorry but I think there's been an unfortunate mistake. My booking was made through an interpreter and I suspect he did not fully take into account my circumstances." I went on to outline who I was and how my two children had been hospitalised back in Scotland. I'm sure I detected a tear in her eye as she told me not to worry. She would go away and have a word with the Captain.

Twenty minutes or so later the co-pilot arrived and sat down in the plush chair next to me. I relayed my story again emphasising the fact that I was not in such a financial position that I could afford to travel half way across the world in first class, especially with British Airways. He listened to my plight with great sympathy and understanding. Ensuring my drink was refilled, he then left to have a word with the Captain.

It was not long before he returned with a warm smile on his face. "Phil I have checked the price difference between a first and economy class ticket and it is in the region of £600." My heart sank. I would have to sell our house. Reassuringly, because no doubt he couldn't help notice my changing demeanour and the gloom descending over my face, he went on to say that he and the Captain had agreed to authorise a full refund of the amount involved. They would radio the details ahead to British Airways Headquarters and supply me with a written letter outlining the recommendations discussed, appropriately signed by the Captain.

It took me a while to register what was being said, and as the co-pilot, a splendid chap, could see I was somewhat shaken, he went on to say "Now Phil, unfortunately we are due a crew change when we stopover for refuelling in Bermuda. We don't want to cause you any embarrassment by marching you off down to economy, so just sit back and be our first class guest for the next four hours or so." He added "If we were crewing the aircraft all the way to London you would have been most welcome to stay for the full journey." Finally he declared "When we arrive in Bermuda do not disembark into the transit lounge with the remainder of the passengers. Just sit tight and a member of the crew will come and escort you to a seat in economy class." Before ordering me a large brandy (purely medicinal you understand!), he told me to sit back, relax and enjoy dinner. My faith in humanity was totally restored.

We touched down in Bermuda and as instructed I remained in my seat. Before they disembarked both the Captain and the co-pilot went out of their way to come and personally pass on their best wishes with regard to the well-being of Paul and Julie. Great guys. Not long after the lovely stewardess arrived to take me down the aisles of the empty plane to my new seat in economy. Thereafter she escorted me discretely into the transit lounge to take up my role as just another passenger joining for the final leg to London. After letting me know that the new crew would be briefed on my circumstances she wished me all the very best and bade me farewell.

Re-embarking and making my way to my somewhat smaller and hemmed in seat, I settled down, content to nod off asleep for the remainder of the flight. An exercise I knew I wouldn't find too difficult to achieve after the outstanding hospitality I had been subject to up forward.

We were airborne, the lights were dimmed and I pulled the complementary blanket over myself. In a matter of moments I began to drift into the welcoming land of sleep. Unexpectedly I received a shake. Looking up, there was a chap in the aisle who leaned over and enquired "Excuse me is your name Armstrong, Petty Officer Armstrong of the Royal Navy?" When I confirmed that I was indeed the said Petty Officer Phil Armstrong he asked if I could please accompany him. Still feeling a little drowsy, I set aside my blanket and followed him up the aisles through economy, business class and finally first class to the crew's quarters just behind the cockpit. It turned out that my unexpected escort was the Chief Steward and he could hardly contain his excitement as he pranced around and introduced me to the bevy of beauties in the form of four or so stewardesses. "Girls" he was shrieking in delight "This is Phil Armstrong and he's a Petty Officer in Her Majesty's Royal Navy". The Girls, all obviously aware that he was unashamedly gay, smiled, gave me a knowing wink and proceeded to again make me most welcome.

The remainder of the flight was spent being very well looked after in the crew's quarters with the Chief Steward, in between attending to his duties with the passengers, insisting on me relating all my naval experiences to date in the minutest detail. He came over as a really nice, if somewhat unconventional, sort of chap who at the time was residing in Portsmouth.

The aircraft had started its final approach into Heathrow and I had made my way back to my seat in economy under the quizzical gaze of my fellow passengers, who were no doubt intrigued with regard to where I had been for the past few hours. With my hand luggage in tow I made my way to the disembarking staircase. My now very good friend the Chief Steward was bidding farewell to all the passengers and as I approached his face lit up and in his most feminine of voices, raised an octave or two, he commenced his emotional goodbyes. "Oh Phil it has been lovely to meet you. Pass on my thoughts to your friends in the Royal Navy." By this time all the other passengers were smiling and perhaps feeling a little sympathetic at my discomfort. I couldn't get down those steps quick enough. Even then he was shouting over the heads of others, "Now don't forget if ever your ship is in Portsmouth please come and look me up". Nice guy as he was I just couldn't get into the terminal building quick enough!

Seeing Paul lying in a hospital bed with an array of tubes inserted into numerous parts of his body, and his plastered legs held up by supporting cables was heartbreaking. Trying to appear positive for Paul's sake was extremely difficult, as was having to leave him to travel the fifteen miles or so to visit Julie at Windygates Isolation Hospital on the far side of Kirkcaldy. Visiting Julie was just as traumatic. Isolated, as she was, in a private room just about reduced me to tears. Balancing visits to our children was not easy, we of course didn't want to leave either of them alone. The answer we came to was for each of us to separately visit one or the other throughout the day.

With this plan agreed I gave Julie a goodbye hug and left Annette by her bedside. I was on my way to drive back to Dunfermline to see Paul, returning to pick up Annette later that evening. Driving alongside the promenade through Kirkcaldy I noticed the dreaded blue flashing lights in my rear view mirror. I pulled over and wound down my window as a tall sombre looking police officer approached. He informed me that I had been clocked travelling at just over forty miles per hour in a thirty mile limit. I related to him my heartrending story of being in the Navy and having to travel half way around the world to be with my two severely ill children, who were hospitalised apart in Windygates and Dunfermline. Not a flicker of sympathy or understanding showed on his face, total indifference. A fine and three penalty points on my license followed, but never mind there was a lot more going on to be worried about.

Eventually both Paul and Julie recovered and were allowed back home. I couldn't have been more relieved or thankful to the dedicated doctors and nursing staff who provided their excellent care. Of course I now faced the prospect of returning to the good old NUBIAN. The Regulating Office in HMS COCHRANE arranged flights to the Caymen Islands, NUBIAN's next 'Port of Call', which entailed transfers at London Heathrow and Miami, Florida.

Returning on board was like a homecoming. The guys in the mess asked about Paul and Julie with genuine concern, which meant a lot to me. Of course it wasn't long before I was dragged ashore to sample the delights on offer in this tropical paradise. Once again I never had to put a hand in my pocket, with all drinks and exotic snacks being willingly supplied and paid for by my unbeatable mess mates.

The remainder of our deployment took in visits to Fort Lauderdale and Pensacola in Florida plus stopovers in a variety of Caribbean islands. We returned home in early August, unfortunately ramming into the jetty which made up the south mole of Rosyth Dockyard. I really felt for Commander Howitt as we attempted to come alongside in procedure alpha. The incident was apparently a result of the engines being shut down too early and the bows being caught by a strong crosswind which propelled the ship, with a large bang, into the entrance to the lock leading into the main basin. Of course all this was witnessed by the astonished welcoming crowd on the jetty made up of excited family members, the area Flag Officer, Royal Marine band and local press. What a way to round off an exceptional deployment.

My time on the NUBIAN will always be remembered as one of the most enjoyable and rewarding of my naval career. However, as they say, all good things must come to an end and after further periods in the Mediterranean and Scandinavia I found myself once again stepping ashore to spend more time with my precious family. Where to next? Well the welcoming news was that I was to serve my next stint ashore in good old Rosyth. Not so enthralling was the fact that I would be taking on a watch-keeping role within Maritime Headquarters, Pitreavie.

AFSOUTH

My time at Maritime Headquarters, Pitreavie was not the most fulfilling of my naval career, in fact I can honestly say I found the watch keeping (shift work) draft totally boring and not to my taste at all. The only thing going for it was that I was at home with Annette and the children.

The professional misery seemed never ending with no chance of escape in sight. After five months I was beginning to despair when a single telephone call completely changed my fortunes. It was early November 1976 and I was enduring another long afternoon shift sat at the control desk within Pitreavie. The telephone rang and to my unexpected astonishment it was the Naval Drafting Authority on the line asking to speak to Petty Officer Armstrong. After confirming that I was the very Petty Officer in question a calmly spoken Officer proceeded to offer me the opportunity to spend two years working in the NATO Headquarters, Naples, Italy, accompanied by my family. I could hardly believe what I was hearing and every fibre of my being wanted to accept there and then. Of course it wasn't that straight forward, not least because I would have to discuss the matter with Annette. The sting in the tail came when the drafting officer went on to explain why I was getting a personal call. Normally personnel are given six months notice of a married accompanied draft abroad. That was not to be in my case. Apparently another Petty Officer had been designated the post but had unexpectedly become seriously ill. In looking for a replacement my name had come up, the only drawback being that we had to be in Italy within six weeks, not six months.

The next 24 hours was an intense period, with Annette and I burning the midnight oil, discussing all the many aspects to be considered in relation to this golden opportunity that had come our way. Our main concern was the children's education. When I re-engaged to serve up until the age of 40 years it was agreed that we would not, under any circumstances, disrupt Paul and Julie's schooling. However, with Paul aged 8 years and Julie 5 years we agreed that the benefits to be gained by the experience of living abroad outweighed our concerns.

After telephoning the Naval Drafting Authorities to accept their offer we went into overdrive. So much to be arranged and organised. Packing to be taken care of, the house to be let, family and friends to be informed, just for starters. It was at this stage, and again after much soul searching and discussion, that we decided it would be a good idea to invest in a guaranteed method of contraception. This was to take the form of my good brave self undergoing surgery, a vasectomy no less.

Fiendish fellow that I am, I arranged to attend a private clinic in Edinburgh at around 6 o'clock on a Friday evening in late November. The cunning plan being to nip off (excuse the pun!) for a few pints after the evil deed was done. Over I went to be operated on by an experienced consultant. I positioned myself on the table and after a total of three anaesthetic type injections into my testicles, the butchering commenced. I felt the need for three injections to ensure the perceived pain involved did not bring a tear to my eye. It worked well as after the third needle I felt as if I couldn't feel anything from the neck down. The deed complete I eased myself off the operating table, and feeling somewhat undignified with my trousers around my ankles, wrote out a cheque for the fee involved.

In the end I decided not to hang around in Edinburgh but to get on a bus back to one of the local pubs in Rosyth. After a few pints of the amber liquid and feeling quite brave and proud of myself I put on my sensible hat and thought it might be best to make my way home.

On this particular night Annette, the children and I were staying at George and Isobel's. As I entered the house everyone immediately asked, with genuine concern, how I was. Of course I replied "Fine", which indeed was my feeling at that particular time. The triple anaesthetic injections had not quite worn off yet. Friday nights were George's time to amble down to his local pub, The Cottars, for a couple of pints and not long after arriving he invited me to join him, if of course I felt up to it. Without a moment's hesitation I replied "Would be delighted George", although I'm not sure Annette thought it was such a good idea.

Off we trundled up the couple of hundred yards or so to The Cottars. The place was well attended but we managed to find a couple of places to stand at the corner of the bar. George ordered a couple of pints of lager which were duly placed in front of us. At this stage I began to feel a little woozy, so in my infinite wisdom thought it best to take a quick gulp of the golden liquid in front of me. Of course this rash course of action didn't improve matters one iota and as George began to wax lyrical about his time spent in Singapore the room began to spin and I felt in imminent danger of collapsing on the floor. With a throbbing pain beginning to develop in my nether regions, I awkwardly turned to my Father-in law, apologies falling from my mouth amidst my mumblings that I wasn't feeling too good, telling him that perhaps it would be best if I returned to the house. Insisting that George stay to finish his pint, and mine too if he wanted it, I stumbled back into the street in a haze of pain.

The short journey involved was purgatory and as I fell through the door I had left less than ten minutes ago Annette came to greet me with a puzzled look on her face. This turned to alarmed concern as she saw the obvious distress I was in. Climbing up the stairs to the toilet was excruciating and matters were not to improve in the minutes ahead. As I dropped my trousers to inspect the region responsible for my acute agony I couldn't believe the sight my eyes revealed. My penis had completely disappeared into a large swollen, black and blue scrotum that appeared to be the size of two gigantic tennis balls. My stomach area was also all bruised which completed the depressing picture of the utter destruction of my reproductive organs. I know we didn't want any more children, but surely this was way over the top.

Annette was as fraught as I was as she shakingly picked up the telephone to talk to the doctor who, not more than three hours or so ago had performed my operation. With an emotionally racked voice she demanded "What on earth have you done to my husband, he is in an appalling state". Not long after I found myself admitted to one of the main Edinburgh hospitals. Further surgery awaited.

A week of rectifying medical procedures within the Western General Hospital Edinburgh resulted in my 'Crown Jewels' returning to an acceptable form of normality, although it took rather longer for the black and blue bruising effect to completely disappear. The sympathy and tender attention I received from the duty nursing staff was magnificent. I had never had that sensitive part of my body so gently and well cared for.

Of course my condition didn't leave me well placed to pack up our quite large and varied amount of belongings, which turned out to be quite a task as we had decided to 'let out' our property for the period we were to be abroad. Step up some good reliable old friends, particularly Pete Boath (ex NUBIAN), who made a great job of the physically demanding task of loading up quite a numerous amount of large wooden crates. All carried out in a jovial manner whilst under the close scrutiny and supervision of recuperating 'Yours Truly' - Thanks Pete.

Fit and well once more, and after emotional family farewells, we set off with our more than excited Paul and Julie for what promised to be an unforgettable period of our married life. And that it certainly turned out to be.

Arriving in Naples with my wife and children was a wonderful and exciting experience. I was really impressed with the local arrangements put in place to ensure that everything went as smoothly as possible for newly arriving families. A young REM who had been on station with his new wife for the past six months, Andy Richards, was appointed as our chaperon for the first four weeks of our tour. On arrival he was there at the airport to meet us. His cheery smile and welcoming demeanour was most settling. As we were chatting waiting for our baggage to arrive I heard a familiar voice call out above the milling passengers, "Or right der scouse. Great to see yer again". Turning around there was my old shipmate from HMS NUBIAN, none other than the ever prominent Yeoman Gauson. He had arrived three months earlier. It was good to see a familiar face, especially as Annette knew his wife, Bonnie. The signs were looking good.

Bags collected, we boarded a local taxi and followed behind Andy in his car. The hotel we were booked into for the next month, the Villa Verde, was a really pleasant, well presented lakeside establishment a few miles to the north of Naples. The staff were extremely friendly especially towards the children, who they had smiling within minutes of arrival. I was beginning to feel confident that we had made the right decision in coming to live abroad as a family, confident that the experience would benefit us all in so very many ways.

The next morning Andy picked me up at around 9 o'clock and drove me off down to AFSOUTH (Allied Forces Southern Europe). I was to undertake my initial 'joining routine' whilst Annette remained at the hotel settling in. After being issued with various passes and NATO badges I was introduced to my new Divisional Officer. Again a very engaging gentleman who took pains to explain that the priority was to get the family settled, we could worry about my duties later on. I couldn't have agreed more.

It was explained that we should look around for a flat/apartment to rent for which, to me, a quite generous allowance would be paid. Additionally I was to receive £1,200 (quite an amount in 1976) to pay for furniture. What with the overseas allowance I was now receiving I seemed to have money coming out of my ears. On the way back to the Villa Verde Andy explained that the normal routine was to view apartments that service personnel at the end of their tour were about to vacate. This usually led to a deal being struck to buy all the resident furniture at a mutually beneficial agreed rate.

Our stay at the Villa Verde was extremely comfortable with the owners and staff really making us feel like part of the family. The food was excellent but understandably predominately Italian, something Annette and I revelled in but Paul and Julie found unfamiliar and not always to their taste. What about some good old 'mince & tatties'? That shortcoming was about to be spectacularly rectified.

One bright sunny morning Annette asked the resident chef and kitchen staff if they could serve up the above mentioned, much loved Scottish dish. Shrugging their shoulders, they all looked at each other in a perplexed and defeated manner. In a moment of inspiration an answer was proposed. If Annette could source the ingredients she would be welcome to come and use the vast commercial facilities of the hotel kitchen. The head chef would be on hand along with his staff, not primarily to offer assistance but to observe how this exotic sounding Scottish meal was produced. The occasion was hilarious.

Armed with a couple of pounds or so of mince and a bag of local 'tatties', the Armstrong clan entered the kitchen. It's a pity we didn't have bagpipes playing! Annette was stopped in her tracks as she was greeted by a much larger than expected curious crowd of staff eager to expand their culinary experience. Not deterred, Annette bravely made her way to an extremely large cooker, gathered a range of pots and utensils and embarked on her mission.

To say the assembled professionals looked a little perplexed is a gross understatement. However, when offered to sample Annette's speciality none of our new Italian friends declined, and indeed were extremely complimentary with regard to the taste and quality of the dish before them. The children were of course delighted to devour their mum's cooking after a couple of weeks of digesting varying and 'yucky' types of pasta. A memorable evening which as I recall didn't lead to 'Mince & Tatties' being at the top of the Villa Verde's quite splendid and varied menu. Their loss!

Over the following weeks we viewed numerous attractive apartments and villas in which we could comfortably live in the years ahead. We finally settled for a three bedroom top floor apartment in a small town approximately fifteen miles north of Naples called Lago Patria. Our new home was first class, with an all-round outside balcony and a spiral staircase leading up to an extremely spacious roof terrace with outstanding panoramic views. We were in walking distance of the beach and service transport was laid on to run the children to school. We were in a small compound which housed other service personnel, both British and American - perfect.

With domestic family needs taken care of it was time for me to concentrate and settle into my new working life which was to be in the main NATO Headquarters Communications Centre on the small island of Nisida which was linked to the mainland by a short causeway. As always the technical aspect of my new responsibilities weren't particularly inspiring to me. However, my new multi-national technician colleagues enhanced my working environment and kept me in a happy and positive frame of mind.

Of great concern was my diving qualification and how I could keep myself 'in-date'. I needn't have worried as besides making myself available to dive with the teams of visiting Royal Navy ships, there was an established American Diving club to which I was welcomed and accepted into. Some of the dives I experienced were sensational, particularly the numerous times I swam overawed through the remains of a 'sunken city' just off shore by Lucrino in the Bay of Naples.

Life was good. Annette was happy, making lots of friends. The children loved it, quickly settling into their new school, with small class sizes and dedicated friendly British teachers. Financially we had no worries and I had taken up golf. We were certainly living the dream. But of course dreams can turn into nightmares.

Off I set for work in my pride and joy. My recently purchased, gleaming, bronze Opel Manta. I was due to finish work at lunchtime with a game of golf at Carney Park to follow - life just couldn't be better. Funny how things can dramatically take a turn for the worse, especially in Italy.

Blissfully driving down the road, I became aware of an extremely large Italian military vehicle bearing down on me. He was well over to my side of the road and as I frantically sounded my horn I tried to manoeuvre as far as I could to my right hand side. The driver of the lorry appeared to be completely oblivious of the impending catastrophe. I sat looking in total disbelief as his monster of a machine bore down on me. The wheels alone were the height of my prized Manta and as they drew alongside the extremely large protruding wheel nuts gouged into my front wing and proceeded to rip apart my front offside and rear passenger doors. It was only then that the driver realised his pathetic driving skills had caused such dramatic and totally unnecessary damage.

In a rage I didn't think was in me, I scrambled out of the damaged passenger door, no mean feat as my car was hard up against a roadside wall. The soldier driving the lorry watched as I approached, correctly assuming that I was somewhat upset and annoyed. Hastily he wound up his windows and locked his cab doors. My Italian has never been anything to shout about, but he knew exactly what I was saying as a stream of internationally known expletives poured out of my mouth. As I frantically pulled at his door in a never to be successful attempt to get it open I felt a tap on my shoulder. Turning around I was confronted by a stern looking member of the Carabinieri. Trying to explain the details of the incident in my broken Italian was futile and it wasn't too long before I found myself in the backseat of a police patrol car as we headed off to the nearest Carabinieri station. My beloved broken and tragically damaged Opel Manta was left looking forlorn at the side of the road.

The language barrier proved to be a major stumbling block and it wasn't too long before I found myself incarcerated in a squalid cell. What a nightmare, this just couldn't be happening. Maybe I would wake up soon! After spending the best part of the day locked up, a legal representative from NATO Headquarters arrived to bail me out. Of course by now I'd had time to calm down, despite the injustice involved. One of the pressing things I wanted to know was what was happening to my car? It didn't lift my spirits whatsoever when I was informed that it had been impounded and was now languishing in a damaged vehicle compound in downtown Naples, my precious golf clubs still in the boot!

Trying to retrieve my vehicle proved to be a total nightmare and a highly expensive exercise. In true Neapolitan tradition things didn't happen overnight and it consequently took the best part of two weeks and a considerable sum of lira for me to take back ownership of my car, which still needed to be repaired. The complexity of trying to claim damage expenses through my insurance, with the Italian Army refusing to accept any liability was astounding. In the end the cost of repairs all fell to me.

To say I was a little annoyed was truly an understatement. My bewilderment and sense of injustice led me to put pen to paper and formally lodge a complaint via the Senior Royal Navy Commander within the local NATO Headquarters. A week or so passed before I received a response. The British contingent appeared to be becoming contaminated with the relaxed manner of the Italians, namely 'The Domani Factor' i.e. 'No problem, relax, we'll see about it tomorrow'.

Although extremely sympathetic, the advice I received from above was not what I wanted to hear. Apparently our Admiral did approach his Italian opposite number and although all parties agreed that I had been treated appallingly, it was thought to be 'diplomatically preferable' to just let the matter drop, after all we didn't want to upset the Carabinieri and Italian Army did we! Reluctantly, although still seething, I didn't pursue the matter further and just put it down to one of life's ongoing colourful experiences.

Returning home from work late one afternoon, I walked into our apartment to find Annette laid out on the settee nursing a rather large bump on her forehead. She didn't look too well at all, which naturally led to some concern. The incident that caused this worrying episode, bumping into a not fully rolled up window shutter, really was an unfortunate accident which, although never ascertained conclusively as the root of future health problems, led to a lifetime of repercussions.

A couple of weeks later Annette confided in me that she was experiencing some strange problems with her eyes. This took the form of wavy lines appearing across her field of vision, which seemed to be originating from her left eye. I suggested that maybe her eyes were becoming a little strained and a visit to the optician could be beneficial. Up until that point Annette had enjoyed near perfect sight and had never needed to wear spectacles.

A few day later, after waving goodbye to the children as they boarded the school bus, we set off for an appointment with a well respected optician in downtown Naples. Annette was called through and I settled down in the waiting room, trying to make sense of the vast array of magazines available, all written in Italian of course! Expecting Annette to be back out after twenty minutes or so, I grew somewhat concerned when she hadn't reappeared after over an hour. Surely a straightforward eye test shouldn't take this long? My apprehension was not eased when the serious looking optician appeared and invited me to step inside his examination room.

Looking more than a little frustrated, he explained that he had carried out a thorough inspection of Annette's eyes whilst trying to improve her vision with the full range of lenses at his disposal. It was all to no avail. He went on to say that in his opinion there was something seriously wrong at the back of Annette's eyes which he was not qualified to diagnose. As such he strongly recommended that we immediately seek medical attention from a suitably qualified doctor. Thanking the optician for his thoroughness and well meaning advice, we said our farewells and headed off for the medical centre within AFSOUTH NATO Headquarters.

My thoughts, concerns and emotions were all over the place as I struggled to appear relaxed in order not to panic Annette. Explaining what had happened, the receptionist at the medical centre arranged a consultation with the resident Royal Naval Doctor, Surgeon Lieutenant Commander A. Nincompoop Royal Navy, almost immediately. Before going in

I stressed to Annette the need to emphasise the concerns of the optician she had seen not more than an hour ago.

Anxiously pacing around the waiting room, I was surprised to see Annette emerging from her medical consultation in what seemed to be less than ten minutes. She was somewhat bewildered as she told me of the outcome of her session with the esteemed Lt.Cdr. Nincompoop. Unbelievably, having explained to the Naval Doctor the background and concerns relating to her deteriorating sight, he offhandedly dismissed the concerns and findings of the professional optician, stating that in his opinion Annette was nothing more than a little stressed. Consequently she left the medical centre clutching a prescription for valium.

To say that we were a little confused is a total understatement. On the one hand we were relieved that a so called eminent Naval Doctor did not for one moment think Annette had a serious condition, but deep down we knew something was seriously amiss. These events took place in the August of 1977, and Annette bravely soldiered on taking her stress relieving pills whilst learning to live with her failing sight.

As an aside, it had been decided that Annette and the children would fly back to the UK to spend the coming Christmas and New Year with her Mother and Father in Rosyth, Scotland. I was to follow ten days or so after them due to my restricted foreign leave allowance.

Two weeks before Christmas I found myself in Naples airport, hugging the children and putting on a brave face as they left with Annette for a three week stay in Scotland. I certainly was going to miss them all. Spending just over a week without my family was not something I was particularly looking forward to. However, I had plenty of invites from friends within the Brit Community that promised to ensure I wouldn't be a sad old figure sat all alone at home with my Santa hat on.

Things kicked off a couple of days later when I was kindly invited over to Bonnie and Bill Gauson's apartment for a few drinks with a gathering of mutual friends. The evening was going really well with everyone, including myself, in fine form, not least because of the fine food and abundance of drinks on offer. Unfortunately my cheerful and increasingly happy mood was about to come to an abrupt halt. A messenger from NATO Headquarters appeared at the doorstep asking for Petty Officer Armstrong. He informed me that I was to immediately report to Command Headquarters as they had received a priority signal in relation to Annette's wellbeing.

On arriving home, Annette could not have been happier. Her mum, as always, had made 114 Primrose Avenue so welcoming, not least with the enticing aroma of 'Nanna's Soup'. Later that evening all the family settled down to an evening at the television, not a pastime that we regularly indulged in back in Italy.

As the evening progressed it really hit home to Annette how much her sight had deteriorated. The television screen was just a blur of disorientated, wavy lines.

The next morning Annette made an appointment with the family G.P. This resulted in a hastily arranged visit to a nearby opticians which culminated in an emergency admission to the highly regarded Eye Pavilion in Edinburgh. Poor Annette, she was bewildered, everything was happening so fast.

Flights back to the U.K. were arranged for the next day and as I made my way back to our apartment in Lago Patria to pack I found it difficult to grasp the enormity of what lay ahead. Our stable, idealistic, happy family life was about to be shattered.

The following day I was given a lift down to Naples airport by a good, caring and supportive neighbour. My hand luggage was negligible, however, I did have something of a challenge with me in the form of a rather large (approx 3ft x 5ft) framed oil painting. We had commissioned the painting for Annette's father, George, who had forwarded postcard type pictures of Highland cows and scenic Scottish mountains which were to be the subject of this artistic masterpiece. I already had it packaged up ready to take back to the U.K. as a Christmas present. Of course this was planned prior to the unforeseen medical emergency that was beginning to engulf our lives.

I thought that since I had it suitably packaged up I might as well take the painting with me. The airport staff in Naples were exceptionally helpful and allowed me to board the plane with my somewhat oversized piece of hand luggage, which ended up occupying three seats at the rear of the passenger compartment. Just as well the aircraft was only carrying about half of the people it could accommodate.

Touching down at Gatwick I of course had to navigate my way through customs. The painting couldn't be missed and it wasn't long before a customs official strolled over to my luggage trolley and, in a friendly manner, enquired as to what the contents of my rather large parcel might be. "It's an oil painting" I told him. "Really", was his reply "And what, can I ask, is it a painting of?" "A Highland cow" came my reply, followed by what I thought to be quite witty at the time "Well a Highland 'coo' actually". Give him his due his face did break into a restrained smile as he informed me "well I'm sorry I'm afraid I have to see it". Oh no the damn thing was turning into a liability and had taken an age to wrap. The understanding customs officer gauged my disappointment and helpfully offered to make a small tear in the brown paper covering, just enough for him to confirm that all was what I said it was. Taking a small penknife from his pocket he made a small cut in the packaging and peeled it back to reveal a majestic furry faced Highland cow staring back at him. "Look guys" he called out to his colleagues "It really is a quite magnificent looking creature". After carefully re-sealing George's picture I was allowed to continue on my way to the terminal from where the Edinburgh flight was soon to depart.

On arriving back in Primrose Avenue, my overriding priority was to get over to the Edinburgh Eye Pavilion. Hugging Paul and Julie I could almost sense their bewilderment and concern. This was not turning out to be the joyous Christmas they had been looking forward to.

Meeting up with Annette again involved an absolute explosion of emotions, very few of them positive. Annette herself appeared to be in an almost trance like state, not daring to accept what was going on in the light of the diagnosis that had recently been explained to her. In order to get a clearer understanding myself I asked to speak to her consultant surgeon, Doctor Chawla.

Doctor Chawla, a calm, compassionate and highly respected gentleman introduced himself to me, before going on to clearly explain the problems and challenges that had to be faced. The condition of Annette's eyes was extremely serious, not least because of the time that had elapsed since she first started experiencing trouble with her sight. The retina in her left eye had detached. In addition the retina in her right eye had also detached and was torn across her central vision, which came as unexpected and devastating news to us all. Time was of the essence and whereas in normal circumstances only one eye would be operated on, and allowed to heal, before attempting to repair the second, this routine could not be undertaken in Annette's case. Both eyes would have to be operated on at the same time.

What Annette was about to endure was indeed pioneering surgery. After his clear and detailed explanation of what lay ahead, Doctor Chawla politely asked if I had any questions. I had many, but the overriding concern I had, and was so reluctant to ask about, took the form of me asking "Is there a chance that my wife might end up totally blind?" He gave an honest but devastating response by answering "I'm afraid that might well be the case". I was completely stunned as the enormity of what I had just heard began to sink in.

Devastation - was that too strong a word? I suppose it depends on what concept it relates to. My thoughts and feelings were in an absolute whirl. There are so many injuries and tragic conditions that can dramatically affect someone's life, but to me blindness stands out there in a league of its own. How do you cope without having the ability to gaze at the wonders of nature? Sunsets in the tropics, the Alps viewed from the window of an overflying aircraft, the pure magnificence of the Scottish Highlands through the changing seasons. And what about the absolute tragedy of not witnessing your children grow and develop. Is that not what life is all about? To miss your son and daughter graduating, not being able to see their joy as they get married, unable to see the indescribable sense of wonder and fulfilment as their children, and our grandchildren, enter this world. No, devastation doesn't even begin to cover it.

Practicalities were also intertwined with the personal tragedy my beloved and forever thoughtful Annette may have had to deal with. Paul and Julie, what of their future? I would have to leave the R.N. What job could I get? I couldn't get a job, I would need to look after Annette. With no income we would lose our home. I felt our future life was akin to looking down into a bottomless pit of darkness. Please Lord restore Annette's sight. She is one of the most unselfish and adorable creatures you have ever placed on this earth.

Time stood still during the time Annette was in theatre, well over six hours, as I anxiously awaited to hear once again from Doctor Chawla. Finally he appeared and as he approached I found it difficult to judge his demeanour. Guiding me into a nearby consulting room he politely asked me to take a seat. He then went on to explain that the operation had gone really well although the final outcome was yet to be determined. The procedures undertaken were extremely complicated and indeed involved delicate work on Annette's retinas that had never been attempted before. It would be some time before we would know the degree of success, if any, achieved.

I was desperate to see my wife, but of course had to practise restraint as she came around from the anaesthetic. After an agonising period of time I was taken through to Annette's bedside. What greeted me was heart wrenching. She had been positioned on a sloping bed with her feet where the pillows are normally placed and her head hanging over the opposite end with a clamping arrangement fitted to restrict movement. Both her eyes were heavily bandaged. I was informed that the reason for this unusual bed positioning related to Dr.Chawla's instructions. The repair and re-attaching of Annette's retinas involved delicate laser surgery, thereafter it was imperative that her head was not subject to any movement whatsoever. 'Air-bubbles' had been inserted in both eyes in order to apply the requisite amount of pressure to keep the retinas in place. It would be days before any head movement was allowed.

My poor, poor darling wife. How must she be feeling? To come around from her life altering operation and be in total darkness with severely restricted head movement must have been terrifying. Taking her hand all I could do was to try and stop my tears from flowing whilst hoping she could sense the love that was oozing from my whole being.

Over the coming days I was reluctant to leave Annette's bedside, but of course there was Paul and Julie to consider. What must have been going through their minds is hard to imagine. With only a day or so until Christmas Annette was re-positioned in a conventional manner within her bed i.e. her head up by the headboard and her feet at the bottom of the bed. This was only a small step forward as she still had to keep her head extremely still, whilst suffering the angst of having both her eyes bandaged up.

Christmas Day arrived and George, Isobel, myself and the children all left Primrose Avenue to drive over to the Eye Pavilion in Edinburgh. George had booked us all in for Christmas Dinner at a first class restaurant in South Queensferry, overlooking both the rail and road bridges. I say 'all' but sadly that of course did not include Annette. When the time came to leave, with all my heart I wanted to stay at Annette's bedside, but unselfish and caring person that she is, she insisted that I go along with the family, all the time thinking about the children and not wanting to spoil their day. She was right of course, and as I kissed her goodbye I promised to return later that evening - what a wonderful lady.

Christmas passed and eventually Annette was discharged from hospital and allowed to return home. Her eyesight was by no means perfect but thankfully total blindness had been avoided. Consultations with Dr. Chawla were ongoing and during these sessions he modestly informed us that the success of Annette's operation was greater than he could have hoped for, especially when taking into account the procedures involved pioneering surgery never before undertaken. The breakthroughs made were, at the time and for years to come, considered to be a major step forward with regard to the use of lasers in the repair of damaged retinas. In fact in the months ahead, having been politely requested by Dr.Chawla, Annette found herself at the centre of numerous consultations where medical staff, from students to senior consultants, were invited to attend. As Dr.Chawla assessed the healing process relating to Annette's retinas, the mesmerised attending medical staff were invited to ask questions both of Annette and Dr.Chawla, which they did in a most enthusiastic manner, very much aware that they were bearing witness to a major advancement in eye surgery. Of course all this celebration within medical circles did not mean Annette had regained perfect eyesight - far from it.

Sadly despite the fact that complete blindness had been avoided, Annette's sight was severely restricted. Her left eye, which she considered her 'good eye' had an enlarged pupil which did not dilate as normal. Her right eye required laser treatment in the area of her central vision, which restricted her scope of vision considerably.

All this left us with some serious and dramatic decisions to make as a family. At the top of the agenda was the question relating to where we were going to live in the months and year ahead. I was half way through my draft to Naples, with a full year to go before being appointed back to the U.K. Did we request my draft to be cancelled on compassionate grounds or return to Italy? There was no shortage of sincere advice coming our way, all of it well intentioned. That advice, from family and close friends was predominantly to abort our life abroad and to stay at home where Annette could receive the best of ongoing care. Both Annette and I completely understood this line of reasoning but chose to take other factors into account, not least that the children really loved their life in Italy, with many friends and an excellent school which they both enjoyed so very much.

I'm sure people were amazed we were even thinking about a return to the place that brought this tragedy into our lives, however, we didn't consider it as straight forward as they obviously did. Enter Dr.Chawla. At one of Annette's appointments we sought Dr.Chawla's views on our dilemma. His advice was invaluable. Annette had to remain in Scotland for the next three months in order that her post op. condition could be carefully monitored. Thereafter, Dr.Chawla was confident her healing process would continue, and as such he saw no reason why we should not return to Italy. In fact he positively recommended it, wisely saying that he fully recognised the personal trauma Annette had endured, but now was the time to look forward and carry on with our lives. Of course returning wouldn't be straight forward, but the decision was now made, to the astonishment of friends and family and the delight of Paul and Julie.

A week or so later I found myself on my way back to our apartment in Lago Patria. It was so difficult leaving, but I was sustained and so happy in the knowledge that come April we would all be living together as a complete family once more.

It wasn't long before I was inundated with visits from our large circle of friends and local neighbours. They were all genuinely concerned for Annette, expressing their disbelief and complete shock on hearing of the seriousness of her condition. The warmth they radiated gave me a positive assurance that in the coming months when Annette and the children arrived back in Italy, we would all realise the correct decision had been made.

My first working day back at AFSOUTH promised to be somewhat interesting, and so it proved to be. I was conditioning myself to try and stay calm, whilst at the same time being determined to forcibly express the absolute turmoil and devastation my family had been subject to as a direct result of the unquestionable professional misconduct of a certain so called Surgeon Lieutenant Commander.

My first port of call was the base medical centre. Undoubtedly they had been expecting me, and as such the reception desk did not direct me to the waiting area when I politely asked if I could have a word with Lt.Cdr. Nincompoop. Instead, after he was informed via an internal telephone of my request, I was escorted directly to his office. On entering I was confronted by a rather sheepish looking Naval Officer, who rose from behind his desk, came towards me and almost stutteringly asked "How is your good wife Annette keeping?" Displaying none of my usual respect for the naval uniform in front of me, I frostily replied "Under the circumstances remarkably well, which is certainly no thanks to you?"

On completion of my hostile meeting with the architect of poor Annette's troubles I stopped off for a cup of coffee before making my way to the Base British Forces Commander for a scheduled appointment. I was still in a confrontational mood and certainly not ready to be patronised by a condescending Naval Officer, of whatever rank.

Guided to a plush armchair in the Commander's well furnished office, I once again listened to, on this occasion I think genuine, concerns and well meaning sympathies with regard to Annette's condition. Then came the crux of this get together as he stated that I must feel that my family had been let down by the Service (a massive understatement) and that he would fully understand if I wished to lodge a formal complaint. I stayed stony-faced and non-committal at this point.

He went on to say that he thought I had three options that I may like to consider:

One: To submit a formal complaint with regard to Lt.Cdr. Nincompoop's treatment of Annette, which would be investigated within the Local Command.

Two: To submit a formal complaint to the local British Flag Officer (a Commodore) which would almost certainly result in Nincompoop being court marshalled.

Three: To do nothing.

He went on to add that if I opted for course of action 'One' it would more than likely lead to option 'Two'. The commander appeared more than a little tense as he anxiously awaited my response.

Trying to stay calm and not letting my emotions get the better of me, I sternly replied "And I think you have a fair idea of which choice we plan to take, and that is option three". As I watched him trying to disguise his sense of relief, I went on to express my absolute disgust with regard to the whole sorry affair, explaining that I had no doubt that if Nincompoop was court marshalled he would, understandably, do all in his power to try and save his professional reputation. This would more than likely result in Annette having to give evidence to the court marshal, along with having to face cross-examination. Annette had suffered enough trauma and the last thing she needed now was to face further stress. As a family we just wanted to pick up the pieces and try to get on with our lives.

The Commander's response was to say "Well for what it's worth I think you have made absolutely the right decision. Furthermore, you have my personal assurance that the Surgeon Lieutenant Commander will be spoken to in the most severe terms and at the highest level (the Commodore)" My response was curt "I have no doubt you think I have made the right decision, but let me re-emphasise that my wife Annette must not suffer any more than she already has". With that I stood up, turned and left. To be fair I really do think the Commander was horrified and now had Annette's best interests at heart.

Our time in Naples will always be remembered with mixed emotions. There were so many happy times, especially for the children, but it was interlaced with the trauma of Annette's eye condition and the professional medical neglect involved. However, overall it was a period of our lives that will never be forgotten. How could we ever forget the warm, balmy evenings on the NATO Beach where a huge cinema screen would be erected twenty yards or so into the sea. Families would gather and lie down in the sand, excited at getting to watch the latest movies in such an unusual but exquisite setting, supported by a stall selling ice cream, burgers, coca-cola, wine for Mum and Peroni beer for Dad. Plus weekends spent visiting such fascinating places as Rome, Monte Cassino, the isles of Capri and Ischia, Pompeii, Mt. Vesuvius and other historic locations were magical times that will always be etched in our memories.

Our tour was due to complete in February 1978, but as always there were a number of factors to consider, the main one being Paul and Julie's schooling. Therefore, after many hours discussion we decided that Annette and the children would return to Scotland before Christmas in order that they could enrol in the local primary school with a view to starting the new term in early January. I would be travelling with them but returning to Naples in the early New Year to complete my 'Leaving Routine' before driving home in my pride and joy, my exquisite Opel Manta.

A good friend, Dave Mandall, The Base Naval Photographer, had adopted a similar plan and I was really pleased when he accepted my offer of a lift back to the U.K. It would be great to have company for the long drive home. Farewell parties complete we finally departed Naples in a fully laden car and headed north. Overnight stops in Switzerland and Germany were planned before embarking on a ferry from Bruges in Belgium to Hull in East Yorkshire.

The journey home through some of the most scenic and picturesque areas of Europe thankfully passed without any dramatic incidents, and as such was welcomed as a comforting end to quite an eventful period of my life. What next?

HMS NUBIAN (Second Time Round)

Back home from Naples and together again as a family in Mulberry Drive, Dunfermline. With quite a few weeks' leave to look forward to, life was back on track after the highs and lows of our time in Italy. The next major event hanging over us was my next 'draft chit'. Having been selected for promotion to Chief Petty Officer there was a high probability that I would find myself back at sea. In truth it was no more than both Annette and I expected, the worrying and critical aspect of 'Drafty's' intentions being, where would my next ship's base port be? I was praying I would find myself once again on a Rosyth based frigate, of which there weren't many in comparison to the numerous ones running out of Plymouth and Portsmouth.

A couple of weeks later my wildest dreams came true. Not only was I to join a Rosyth based frigate but it was to be my old welcoming and never to be forgotten ship HMS NUBIAN. What an outcome. Back on board and settling in to the Chief's Mess, who'd have believed it. I was so familiar with this ship that it felt as if I'd hardly been away. Of course I now had much more responsibilities, which didn't really faze me, especially as the communications department I found myself in charge of was more or less the same as when I left a few years previously.

May 1979 and after a short but forever necessary maintenance period we departed Rosyth for a short couple of months deployment to Scandinavia. Not one of, what I considered to be, the most exciting or desirable places to visit (the beer is far too expensive!!). After completing various exercises in the North Sea we called into Bergen in Norway for a five day visit. The first night ashore turned out to be enough. You needed to take out a second mortgage if looking for a quiet night and a few beers in one of the many, and I must say atmospheric bars. Thereafter an occasional afternoon walk around the town would be followed by evenings putting the world to right in the comfort of our very own inexpensive Chief's Mess.

Next port of call was Copenhagen, Denmark, a city I had visited on numerous occasions. Much like Bergen, it was not the most economical of ports for us poor sailors to enjoy. That being said, it is an intriguing and pleasant part of Denmark to explore and I have always enjoyed myself there. The fact that I felt I knew the place well enough resulted in me, one afternoon, finding myself left in the mess with the recently joined Chief Caterer, Brian. The remainder of our mess members had ventured ashore, but after opting to stay onboard Brian and I settled down for a couple of drinks, which turned out to be a most memorable afternoon of outrageous storytelling accompanied by the ongoing background music of just about every ABBA song recorded!

Leaving Denmark we set sail for our home port of Rosyth. During the passage the Captain came on the ship's main broadcast to inform us of, what I considered to be, devastating news. All Tribal Class Frigates, inclusive of NUBIAN, were to be 'Paid Off' into reserve. I was speechless, surely this couldn't be happening. What about our planned deployment to the West Indies. I had so many friends and acquaintances on those sundrenched tropical islands that I needed to re-contact and catch up with.

HMS SIRIUS

Paying off the NUBIAN had been a strange experience. I knew I had to serve back at sea, but finding myself back on a ship that was so familiar and from which I had such fond memories was more than I could have hoped for, and of course there was the added bonus of it being a Rosyth based ship. Now I was engulfed with that air of uncertainty. What ship would I be getting next? And more importantly what would be its base port? 'Drafty' assured me that every effort would be made to get me another Rosyth based ship. In the meantime I was to serve shore-side back up in Scotland as part of the refit crew of HMS BRIGHTON, which was tied up alongside in the main basin within good old Rosyth Dockyard.

For the next three or four months life was sweet. I was back home with my family, enjoying coming home every night and not really having to undertake any strenuous duties onboard BRIGHTON. In fact I managed to get myself enrolled on some GCE courses (Naval History and Maths) which were being run from the education centre within HMS COCHRANE. Unfortunately my idyllic naval home life was about to come to an abrupt end. I came in one morning to find I had a draft order. I was to join the Devonport based Leander Class Frigate HMS SIRIUS. Of course I was straight on the phone to 'Drafty' enquiring as to why the promise of trying to get me back on a Rosyth based ship had not been delivered.
"Sorry Chief" came the rather unsympathetic response. "We are extremely short of CRELs at the moment and we had no option but to appoint you to the SIRIUS."

I had assured Annette that I would be drafted to another Rosyth based ship. How on earth was I going to tell her of this latest development? Coward that I am I kept putting off telling her this most unwelcome news, waiting instead for that nonsensical 'right moment' which I knew within my heart would never materialise.

When that 'moment' eventually came it was truly disastrous. We were uptown in Dunfermline

with our good friends Brenda and Pete and decided to drop into a local hotel, The Bellville, for a spot of light lunch. The day had been going well and we were all in a convivial, jolly mood, although I still had this sick feeling in my stomach regarding me going back to sea. Then it happened.
Pete says "This has been a great day. Why don't we get together again sometime next week?".
To which I blurted out "Sorry can't make it. I have to join HMS SIRIUS in Gibraltar next Monday".

The silence was deafening and the disbelieving look on Annette's face remained engrained on my memory for many months to come. Needless to say our little social gathering came to an end as we all made our way home, Brenda and Pete in disbelief and me scrabbling to regain the, understandably, lost ground I had made with Annette.

After a somewhat fraught weekend I flew out to Gibraltar. Landing at around mid-day, transport in the form of an 'RN Tilly' was waiting to whisk me off to my new ship. The SIRIUS was berthed alongside the 'Clock Tower' in Gib. Harbour. Crossing the gangway I was met by the quartermaster who directed me to the Chief's Mess, situated port side aft directly beneath the flight deck. Making my way down the after hatch, at the bottom of the ladder I bumped into a jovial looking Warrant Officer who introduced himself as the Chief's Mess President.

"This way Phil" he says in a manner that gave the impression we were life-long friends. Entering the mess I was greeted by an almost party atmosphere with the majority of mess members enjoying a pint or two in what I assumed to be preparations for a good old 'dinner time sesh'. Introducing myself as the new Chief RE, I was made to feel most welcome, having a pint of Courage sparkling bitter thrust in my hand before I knew it. The chap behind the bar then pipes up "Phil I have something here for you". I was somewhat bemused as he handed me a letter taped to an expensively priced bottle of champagne. The mystery unfolded as I read the apologetic letter. It was from the Chief I was to relieve. He explained that he had been offered the opportunity of an early flight home and after securing approval from his Divisional Officer had jumped at the chance to get back home to his family after many months of separation. He apologised for not being around to give me a comprehensive handover and hoped that the champagne would in some small way make up for his absence. What could I say, popping open the 'champers' I shared it around my new mess mates, deciding to worry about the more serious aspects of running my new department later. Initial reactions were most favourable. I had a good feeling about this ship, which turned out to be quite well founded.

In 1979 my father's chain smoking past finally caught up with him and whilst on board HMS SIRIUS, alongside in Plymouth, I was called back home to say a final farewell. A telephone conversation with my stepmother Mary left me in no doubt that my father only had days left.

It was a Saturday when I travelled north, with SIRIUS due to sail to El Ferrol in Northern Spain a week on the following Monday. It is difficult to express the feelings I was experiencing at the time except to say an immense feeling of sadness overwhelmed me, not least because of the certainty of having to say a final farewell to my Dad.

Sat in a virtually empty rail carriage, staring out the window as night time encroached, words came into my head that I felt compelled to write down. This I did, literally 'on the back of a fag packet'. The following encapsulates my mood at the time:

> A journey of sorrow with no hope at the end
> One last visit to a man who is both Father and friend
> When I get to his side will the words that I say
> Be enough to bring comfort in a meaningful way
>
> In my youth he helped me when I needed a guide
> He gave me my values and sense of pride
> Without who knows where my path may have strayed
> I thank you dear Father and hope all is repaid

When you finally leave us on a day close at hand
My heart will be heavy but I'll try to understand
That you must go to end your pain
I love you Dad - Till we meet again

I eventually arrived at my childhood home of 12 Mansell Road. Dad's bed had been moved downstairs and had been placed in the front room, commonly known as the parlour. Lying there with an oxygen mask on his face, he did not look at his best. However, as I entered the room he took off his mask and managed a welcoming smile.

On speaking to the doctor, who was in regular attendance, he confirmed that my Father had only days left and indeed might go within the following 48 hours. The next two days came and went, as indeed did the next two. My Father was hanging on but visibly deteriorating as each hour passed. I kept updating my ship with regard to my Father's condition. Contrary to all expectations he was still with us on the Saturday and when I contacted SIRIUS to request an extension of compassionate leave, I was left devastated when it was refused.

Having to say goodbye early on the Sunday morning, knowing that I would never see my Father alive again, was heart wrenching. The journey back to Plymouth passed in a haze and I was not in the best frame of mind when I arrived back on board the SIRIUS.

The ship sailed for El Ferrol on the Monday morning. On the Tuesday I was sent for by the Weapons Engineering Officer, who solemnly received me in his cabin. Of course I knew exactly what he had to tell me and before he even spoke I said, somewhat aggressively "I'll save you the trouble sir, you are about to tell me that my Father has died. Well that, as we all know was very much expected. The question now is, what are you going to do about getting me home?" I was furious and the W.E.O. knew only too well that the situation had been handled badly. The ship was well into the Bay of Biscay and as such it was not practical to transfer me back to Plymouth by the ship's helicopter. The only alternative was for me to stay with the ship until we arrived in El Ferrol the following day, when arrangements would be made to get me back to Liverpool. This involved a lengthy car journey to Madrid, followed by a flight to London and a train journey to Merseyside. This was one of the occasions when the Royal Navy got it wrong. Not only did it have a disgruntled Chief Petty Officer on its hands but it also had quite unnecessary and expensive travel costs to pay.

The funeral was well attended. My only regret about the occasion was that I missed the opportunity to say a few words by way of the poem written from my heart only two weeks earlier.

When alongside, certainly in the U.K., I always made the effort, every night, to telephone my dear wife Annette. I always felt she shouldered most of the burden of our unavoidable periods of separation, certainly with regard to bringing up the children in the absence of their father.

It was a cold, wet, blustery evening in late November and once more we were berthed in our home port of Plymouth. As I trundled over the gangway, the rain got heavier - typical! My search for a telephone box was quickly rewarded not more than three or four hundred yards from the ship. Diving into the all familiar red box I picked up the phone only to find out it was frustratingly out of order. Oh well there was no doubt another public phone not too far away. Indeed there was, but unbelievably that was also defective. In total I managed to discover three completely inoperative GPO telephone boxes.

Not one to be deterred, I trudged on through the worsening weather. Eventually my endurance paid off. At, I'm sure, the furthest away point in the dockyard from HMS SIRIUS I came across a telephone that was obviously working. This fact was borne out by the line of soggy looking sailors waiting patiently outside the box. They had most probably experienced the same frustrations as me before discovering what appeared to be the only working public telephone in the vast expanse of Plymouth Dockyard.

I joined the queue of about five or six and awaited my turn. After what seemed an eternity

I entered the box, feeling somewhat cold and wet. Never mind I would soon be talking to my dearest wife. I dialled, and after a couple of rings my heart sang as I heard that lovely voice of Annette saying "Hello".
"Hello dear it's me, Phil. How is everything?". Her reply left me reeling. "Phil don't you know 'The Evening News' has just started?". Her ears must have twitched as I slammed down the phone. Boy was I angry.

My anger subsided somewhat as I made my way back to SIRIUS. As I approached the gangway I heard a 'pipe' over the ship's main broadcast, "Chief Petty Officer Armstrong, telephone call, gangway". Of course it was a very apologetic Annette who explained that she said what she did without really thinking. I apologised in return for the abrupt manner in which I terminated our short lived call. Thankfully all was forgiven as we relayed our latest news to one another.

Future calls were much more amiable, and certainly not made when eagerly awaited TV programmes were being broadcast.

Our first night ashore in Setubal, Portugal. We had been at sea for a couple of weeks so a good 'run ashore' was very much on the cards. Early evening and after a couple of pints in the mess my good friend Bill and I decided to venture ashore. Nothing outrageous was planned, just a short walk to the nearest hotel with a view to making a telephone call to our nearest and dearest back home in the U.K. Off we toddled and it wasn't too far from the ship that we came upon a somewhat upmarket hotel that we both agreed looked ideal for our mission. Entering into a grand well appointed foyer we approached the reception desk and asked if it would be possible to put a call through to the United Kingdom. The delightful young lady we spoke to couldn't have been more pleasant and obliging. She explained that she herself would try to connect to our home telephone numbers and when she got through would contact us and let us take the call in one of the three telephone booths situated just off the reception area. In the meantime perhaps we would care to take a drink in the nearby opulent lounge. What a splendid idea. Another drink or two in such grand surroundings would go down a treat.

Settling down we ordered a couple of beers in the expectation that it wouldn't be too long before we were both speaking to our families back home. It was now around 8 o'clock in the evening and we were more than confident that we would be back on board by 9 o'clock.

An hour passed and our lovely receptionist had not called us through. I wandered back to her desk and in a most polite manner asked if there was a problem in getting us a connection. She appeared almost more concerned than we were as she explained that all international lines were busy but she would of course keep on trying. With a smile I said "That's ok, just let us know when you get through". Back in the lounge Bill and I decided it might be time to try some of the local drinks, especially their world renowned, quality port.

The evening seemed to have disappeared as we were eventually called through to the telephone booths at around 11pm. The port had gone down an absolute treat as old stories and general joviality poured out of both of us. Somewhat unsteadily I made my way past reception and lifted the phone. What came out of my mouth was strange sounding, even to my ears, and in no way resembling the Queen's English. I rambled on to Annette recounting heaven knows what of my time out in the Med. I'm sure I must have asked her about the children but suspect Annette never caught on to it. The call ended and I made my way back to the lounge. A few minutes later Bill re-joined me as a cloud of common sense descended over us and as a consequence we mutually agreed to return on board. Mission finally accomplished.

A week or so later we arrived in the port of Split in the old country of Yugoslavia. Mail arrived on board and was collected by individual messes. Receiving mail was such a personal and uplifting moment. As I tore open my first letter my thoughts returned to our home in Scotland. After reading the opening paragraph I didn't know whether to laugh or cry. Annette had started, "Dearest Phil, tonight I had a call from a 'Blob-a-Lob' man.

Difficult to know what he was trying to say". What a truly unique wife I had, with a modest but outstanding sense of humour.

Eighteen years in the Royal Navy without experiencing the delights of a ship's visit to the magical and most welcoming port of my hometown, Liverpool. All that was about to change. Sailing up the River Mersey onboard HMS SIRIUS was heart warming for me and I just knew the following five days were going to be something special. My expectations were boosted as an example of scouse humour was forthcoming even before we were alongside. Procedure Alpha was the order of the day, so there we were lining the sides in our No1 uniforms. It just so happened that the guy next to me also hailed from 'Scouseland'. As the ship was manoeuvring into our docking area he says to me "Phil, you know 'our kid' (his brother) used to work in the docks here". "Really" says I "what did he do?".
"He was a diesel fitter" came his proud response, followed by "Yeah he used to unload cargo ships, many of which were importing clothing, shoes etc". In renowned docker fashion he would peruse some of the goods, announcing to his fellow scavengers "dees'le fit me Mum, dees'le fit me Dad". One of the most experienced 'dees'le fitters' in Liverpool! I exploded into laughter and immediately knew I was back home.

The visit did indeed live up to all my expectations, starting from lunchtime just after we had secured alongside. Probably well aware of the warm hospitality forthcoming from Her Majesty's Ships, a couple of local CID Officers had found their way to our mess. As a 'local' I found myself chatting away to them, reminiscing about my dubious past and generally ensuring they had a memorable 'dinner time sesh'. Feeling relaxed and wanting to be open and totally honest with my new found friends I mentioned that I had a number of bottles of fine spirits in my locker, top malt whisky, excellent brands of rum etc., which of course they were welcome to sample. Taking up my offer they went on to assure me they could help in overcoming the final hurdle of actually landing my liquid treasure. I had already explained that the risks involved in trying to get my 'booty' through any dockyard gate, especially HM Dockyards such as Plymouth, Portsmouth and Rosyth, were just not worth the penalties upstanding naval senior ratings such as myself would be subject to. "No problem at all Phil, we can lend a good friend a helping hand here" was a response that left me a little bemused. "Thanks to your outstanding hospitality, we cannot help today, but if it's alright with you we'll come back this time tomorrow and all will be well".

The following day my two friendly cops did indeed return and before partaking in a further offer of Courage sparkling beer, invited me to gather up my collection of 'spirits' which they assured me would not come under any kind of intense scrutiny whilst leaving the dockyard area of Liverpool.

My police colleagues escorting me, we made our way to the ship's gangway. The Officer of the Day looked a little suspicious as he eyed the somewhat bulky 'pusser's grip' I was trying to be indifferent about, especially as the clinking noise of its contents seemed outrageously loud to me. Not far from the ship we climbed into an unmarked police vehicle which then proceeded to the dockyard gate. A flash of my very understanding and well appreciated CID friend's warrant card to the guard manning the dockyard gate resulted in us passing through with friendly waves all round. Dropping me off at the Pier Head in order to catch a bus to Mansell Road, I invited them to drop round the mess any time, which of course they took me up on. Colourful characters - Liverpool is full of them.

Before contacting family members I decided to try and get in touch with my old friend Dave Watson, who I hadn't seen for the best part of ten years. My thinking was that a good place to start enquiring as to his whereabouts was The Raleigh pub on the corner of Boaler Street and Sutcliffe Street. I didn't have a contact telephone number but felt fairly confident he would still be causing mischief around the streets of my upbringing. My hunch turned out to be a positive move. Entering our old haunt I ordered a pint before asking the landlord if a guy named Dave Watson still used the place. "Of course he does" came his welcome reply "He now lives in Hawkins Street." Which was more or less just a continuation of my boyhood address in Mansell

Road. With his house number obtained it wasn't long before we were facing each other over his doorstep. Dave's face was an absolute picture and of course it wasn't long before we were back at the bar in the 'Raleigh'. Reminiscing was a joy and before leaving, rather unsteadily, we arranged to meet the following day for an afternoon game of golf.

Dave was always a good if not, in my eyes, outstanding sportsman, especially as a footballer. Thankfully he hadn't as yet fulfilled his potential as a golfer and as such we had a well matched game at one of the city's numerous municipal courses. After the game and the mandatory couple of pints, I invited Dave down to the ship. He readily accepted my invite and after going home to get changed we hopped into a taxi down to the docks, a familiar area to us both, mainly as a result of our slightly unlawful pastimes - enough said!

The guys in the mess gave Dave a great welcome and of course the drinks were free flowing. I could see that he was truly impressed with the life I had made for myself, possibly thinking that maybe he should have taken a similar path. However, it was not to be, but we were still great friends. Unfortunately it saddens me that over the years we have gradually lost touch. Still maybe we'll meet again in the years ahead. I certainly hope so.

Now for the family, and top of the list to make contact with was good old Uncle Bill, a loveable wartime sailor with a multitude of intriguing, colourful and never to be forgotten stories to tell. What better place to command an audience than in the Chief's Mess of a modern day Royal Navy frigate.

I could almost feel the excitement emanating from Bill as he strolled over the gangway onto the flight deck. How long had it been since he had set foot on a Royal Navy Warship? The best part of thirty four years I estimated. I had briefed my fellow mess members on the nautical background of my special guest and as I expected they all rose to the occasion, ensuring he received the best VIP treatment whilst making him feel extremely welcome.

After I'd taken him on a tour of the ship, which he found fascinating and so technically advanced in comparison to the ships he had served on during the war, it was back down to the mess to get on with the main purpose of the evening - sea stories! It was heart warming to see Bill so happy. He always was a mischievous character with a gift for telling magical stories, slightly embellished to ensure his audience's attention never wavered. Of course us modern day sailors were not to be outdone, coming up with our own somewhat exaggerated versions of outrages sea stories. The evening couldn't have gone better and as an unsteady old seaman said farewell it was not in question that a good, no great, time had been had by all.

Over the remaining couple of days I had various other members of my family on board, which they all found to be a unique experience. My only heartfelt regret was that my dear beloved Father was not with us anymore, which hurt. He would have been proud to see how far I had come since escaping from my troublesome early background in the city, which I still to this day feel so very much part of.

A prolonged period alongside in Devonport was on the horizon, as the SIRIUS was programmed to undertake a twelve month refit. I certainly did not welcome the prospect of spending a year lounging around in HMS DRAKE (Devonport shore base). Then again I felt this was unlikely as I still had eighteen months or so 'sea time' to get through. Perhaps 'Drafty' would be kind and understanding to me this time and appoint me to a Rosyth based ship - In my dreams! No sooner were we back in Plymouth when my new draft order arrived. In a month's time I was to join a sister ship of the SIRIUS, HMS ARGONAUT. Once again a Devonport based frigate.

HMS ARGONAUT - THE TRUTH

After an enjoyable leave period, during which I once again had to agonisingly inform Annette that a Rosyth based ship was not to be, I headed back down south to Devonport. As I trundled through the now all too familiar dockyard the ARGONAUT came into sight, and would you believe it she was berthed next to another Leander Class Frigate, HMS SIRIUS no less. I nearly walked up the wrong gangway. However, after having composed myself I made it on board and began yet another 'Joining Routine'.

Of course it wasn't too long (the next day) before I paid a visit to my 'old home' on the SIRIUS. In contrast to my state of mind, the majority of my old friends couldn't have been happier, which was understandable as they were looking forward to a twelve month, not too strenuous, refit period involving the added bonus of being able to go home to their wives and families at night. Of course we arranged to go out for a final farewell drink in the local pubs just outside the dockyard gates. SIRIUS was a 'happy ship' but as often in life, especially the RN, all good things must come to an end. It was time to settle into my new home, which I did with a strong feeling that I would have an unforgettable time on the ARGONAUT. Well that was a colossal understatement. The months ahead were to be both dramatic and life changing and would forever be etched in both my, and my family's, memories.

In early April 1982 HMS ARGONAUT was being subjected to the delights of 'work-up' off Portland on the Dorset coast. Whilst closed up at action stations the Captain, Captain Layman Royal Navy, came on the main broadcast to inform the ship's company that we were to be immediately detached from the exercise area and were to proceed to our home base at Plymouth at best speed. The Falkland Islands had recently been invaded by the Argentineans which had resulted in a British Naval Task

Force being dispatched to retake the islands. HMS ARGONAUT was to join the main group after collecting essential stores and additional ammunition from Plymouth Naval Base. So began the most memorable, frightening, heart-warming and proudest period of my naval career.

The activity on the jetty when we arrived alongside was extraordinary. There was an absolute mountain of stores and equipment awaiting with a vast array of technical talent in the form of 'dockyard mateys'. To say I was impressed hardly begins to describe how I was feeling. We were given two days to prepare before sailing south. At the time I was in the middle of selling my family home and was more than grateful to be granted special leave to travel home to Dunfermline in Scotland in order that I could sign over full power of attorney to my wife Annette. I spent less than 12 hours at home before having to say an emotional farewell to Annette and my precious children, Paul and Julie.

Back in Plymouth the hectic activity continued. A few hours before sailing I was called to the gangway. As the Chief Petty Officer responsible for the maintenance and operational capability of all external communications systems I was invited to sign for some advanced encryption equipment that would allow British ships to communicate with each other without tactics and vital information being intercepted by the enemy. Unfortunately the 'boffins' delivering this highly technical gear did not have time to install it. After a quick briefing on the merits and 'Star- Trek' type qualities of my new acquisition I was left to get it 'up and running' before we got in close range of the Argentineans. Thank God I had some talented radio technicians in my team!

We eventually sailed on April 19th 1982 in company with HMS ARDENT. There was not an inch of spare space on board with all passageways being used to store bags of spuds, vegetables etc. The atmosphere on the ship was electric. The excitement, exhilaration and sense of adventure felt by virtually every member of the crew was inescapable. Of course those feelings were to change dramatically in the weeks and months ahead.

On our way south the 'routines' on board began to change to accommodate the unfamiliar situation we were being subjected to. For instance there was no compulsory reason to shave, after all if we did find ourselves in a combat situation shaving would not necessarily come out on top of the priority list. Having to change into 'night clothing' for dinner was also dispensed with as we found ourselves getting ever closer to the Falklands. It just seemed to make sense to stay in our action/ working rig (No. 8s).

We were due to call into the Ascension Islands on our way south and I was hopeful that we would have the voice communications encryption equipment we had been landed with fully operational by the time we arrived there. Unfortunately it didn't quite work out that way. All the installation, wiring and local testing went off reasonably well. Problems arose when we moved to the all important practical phase of operational testing with another ship. At this particular moment ARDENT was the only other R.N. ship in range. Difficulties arose when we could not successfully establish two way encrypted voice communication between our two ships. Where was the problem - ARGONAUT or ARDENT? That particular mystery could have been easily solved if we had been in company with a third Royal Navy ship with a comparable communications fit. If one ship had problems it would have been relatively straight forward to determine which one it was by conducting a three-way communications exercise. Unfortunately with only two ships this was not an option.

Normally a frigate in the Royal Navy is commanded by an officer holding the rank of Commander Royal Navy. Frigate squadrons had a lead ship commanded by a more senior officer, namely a Captain Royal Navy. HMS ARGONAUT was such a ship and hence carried the title of 'Captain F'.

This vital communications problem was dragging on and after carrying out in-depth and wide ranging checks on ARGONAUT's equipment it was decided that a highly effective, knowledgeable and technically competent rating, in the form of Petty Officer Tony Dennis, would be transferred to the ARDENT to assist in getting to the bottom of our communications problem. Petty Officer Dennis was transferred by helicopter and, after exhaustive checks and long hours attempting to resolve our mutual problem, returned to ARGONAUT two days later.

Meeting up in the Electronic Maintenance Room (EMR) I asked Tony how he had got on. "Don't you ever send me anywhere near that bloody ship again" came his angry, forthright and unexpected reply. Although making technical progress the problem was not fully resolved. However, this was not the source of Tony's anguish. His outrage came about as a result of the general treatment he had received on the ARDENT. He had transferred in his working rig and after a long arduous day was understandably looking forward to the sustenance of a full, well presented and enjoyable naval dinner. Imagine his surprise and indignation when he was refused entry to the Senior Rate's Dining Hall because he was not in the 'rig of the day', i.e. evening clothing - we were on our way to war for God's sake!

Having had to eat his meal in an out of the way office space like some sort of leper, he chose to return to his technical tasks, not an evening of some light hospitality afforded by the Senior Rates of HMS ARDENT. The final straw came when he found himself sleeping in the settee area of the Petty Officer's mess. Far too much to expect that they may have found a bunk for him. Tony's comments were, via myself, duly passed to our Squadron Weapons Engineering Officer (S.W.E.O.).

Our S.W.E.O. passed on all concerns to the W.E.O. of ARDENT. The tone of the message I was not privy to. However, a couple of days later I had an inkling of what may have been said. The communications problem had not gone away and consequently it was decided that I myself should transfer to ARDENT to have a final go at resolving matters. The final message from ARGONAUT before I departed was along the lines of "We are sending our Chief over and we hope he receives better treatment than his P.O.".

Talk about V.I.P. treatment. As our helo landed on ARDENT's flight deck I was met personally by the W.E.O. himself who waltzed me off to his cabin for a welcoming chat. After apologising for the treatment Tony had received, he assured me that I would be given all the support I needed. If I required anything whatsoever, all I had to do was ask.

After our friendly chat I was handed over to the ship's Chief Radio Engineering Artificer (C.R.E.A.) who had instructions to stay with me at all times and to ensure I was well looked after. Numerous checks were carried out throughout the day and some minor technical faults detected and rectified, which proved to be the breakthrough - two way communications were finally established.

For the remainder of my time on board I was really given the treatment. Taken down to the

Senior Rates Mess, I was afforded the freedom of the bar and enjoyed chatting to most of the mess members as they filtered into the lounge. The majority expressed surprise at my mid-growth beard and the fact that we were maintaining regular bar hours back on the ARGONAUT. Apparently their bar hours had been severely restricted, but on this occasion the bar was opened especially to entertain me - what an honour. Eventually I found myself with the W.E.O. who was more than grateful and relieved that our encrypted communications network had been successfully established.

Before transferring back to ARGONAUT I was invited to the bridge to brief the Captain, Commander Alan Ward Royal Navy, the same Alan Ward who ended up as the head of the Royal Navy, Admiral of the Fleet and First Sea Lord no less. Without going into too many technical details I told him that we had managed to resolve all outstanding technical hitches. "So the problem was at our end was it?" he enquired in a somewhat sarcastic manner. "Well yes it was sir," I responded. To which he retorted "Well it would be wouldn't it. The problem couldn't have been on ARGONAUT because you're Captain 'F'". I was really taken aback to hear a senior officer addressing a Chief, on a fully manned bridge, in such a churlish and childish manner - astonishing.

Returning to the ARGONAUT made me appreciate what a fine well adjusted crew we had. Perhaps it was the unfamiliarity of being on another ship that made me feel more 'at home' - there was no other ship I would rather have been serving on during such perilous times. I must point out that I feel somewhat uncomfortable relating the above story as I in no way wish to tarnish the professionalism and bravery of ARDENT's ship's company, especially since a couple of weeks later on 21st May HMS ARDENT was sunk in a gallant action, resulting in 22 members of the crew being killed.

My colleagues and good friends in the Chief's mess, HMS ARGONAUT were truly a bunch of characters. It was a fine mess with the usual friendly banter between branches. The engine room artificers proved they could use their engineering skills to great effect, not least in providing all mess members with meaningful additions to our recently issued 'dog tags'. During the middle watch (1200 - 0400) they would manufacture brass tags that reflected the identity of the owner. For instance they made a small hammer for the Chief Shipwright (Chippie) and a 'golly'(common nick name) for the Chief Yeoman. The tallies were presented after breakfast in the mess lounge. I eagerly awaited my presentation, which when it came was the source of much amusement. To understand you have to see my legs to believe them. On virtually all of my ships they proved to be a great morale booster. The legs in question are extremely thin with the knobbliest of knees in the middle and the largest of feet at the ends. Whenever we changed into tropical rig (shorts) all you could hear around the ship, to the amusement of all, was 'have you seen the Chief R.E.'s legs?' Anyway my tally was in the form of a pair of shorts with two sticks protruding, bumps in the middle and large feet at the ends. 'Phil' was printed on one side and 'legs & co' on the other. I wore that tally all through the conflict and consider it to be something of a lucky charm. I still have it and occasionally wear it when travelling or climbing in the Scottish mountains.

We arrived at the Ascension Islands on the 29th April and sailed a couple of days later. In company with HMS ARDENT we were detailed to patrol the local area with orders to hunt for a possible enemy submarine, thought to be awaiting the arrival of British ships. Thankfully we never came in contact with any such underwater threat.

Slowly it was beginning to dawn on the ship's company that things were really serious. When we left Plymouth I'm sure the majority of the crew thought matters might be resolved in the period it was going to take to sail south - surely a political solution would be found? The true reality of the situation hit home on the evening of the 4th of May. The majority of off-watch Senior Rates were in the dining hall watching a movie. Half way through the film the Chief Radio Supervisor opened the door and switched on the lights. He was met with a torrent of 'boos' and abuse. This turned to stunned silence when he informed us that HMS SHEFFIELD had been hit by an Exocet missile. There were many deaths and casualties and it was expected that the ship would sink, which was its eventual tragic fate. Returning to the mess, the usual banter and good humour was missing. We were all lost in our thoughts and the realisation that there was no turning back - we were at war!

As we approached the Falklands the ship went into defence watches. Preparations intensified inclusive of exercises involving closing up for action stations at all hours of the night and day. Falling off asleep only to be rudely awakened by the ear splitting sound of the action alarm at 2 o'clock in the morning left us all feeling somewhat tired and jaded. At this stage we all remained in our action rig for 24 hours per day. It felt peculiar to have a shower in the evening and to then dress back into No. 8s instead of changing into night clothing in the form of a crisp white shirt and dress dark trousers. Sleeping in our action rig was also a necessary and practical arrangement. Throughout the evening of 20th May, the day prior to the landings, there was an atmosphere of confidence about the ship. We had all been briefed by the First Lieutenant and the plan to conduct the amphibious assault from San Carlos Water, later to be laughably known as 'Bomb Alley', seemed foolproof and a stroke of genius to us all. We were due to go to action stations at 0900 the following morning.

In the Chief's Mess a number of us settled down to a game of cards, three card brag, which of course was, and still is, a highly illegal pastime in the Royal Navy. However, not to worry, we had the Master at Arms, 'Connie' Francis as an enthusiastic member of our group, so all was well. The game went on until about 3 o'clock in the morning. The final hand, and a huge 'pot', was won by Connie with, would you believe it, the best hand in a game of brag, a prial of threes. How lucky could you get? Tragically that luck was not to hold.

Connie had asked that he be allowed to take up a first-aid role on the upper deck. His request was approved. ARGONAUT was the first ship to be attacked on the morning of the 21st May. An Argentinean Aermacchi jet swept over the headland and strafed the upper deck. The 965 long range radar aerial and some radio aerials were damaged, but more dramatically we took three casualties. Able Seaman Dalloway lost an eye and was shot in the ankle. Leading Seaman Peel was shot in the nose and arm. Sadly Connie Francis took a bullet to the chest. I vividly recall a first-aid party being called to the upper deck. The wardroom, which was adjacent to the Main Communications Office (M.C.O.), had been designated as a casualty centre and on opening the M.C.O. door I was confronted by Connie being carried on a stretcher with blood pumping from his chest. He was later transferred, along with the two sailors, to the hospital ship UGANDA. I'm glad to say he survived, but I suspected his three card brag days were well and truly over!

Throughout the remainder of the day we were subject to continuous attacks from Argentinean

Skyhawk jets. The final strike by a wave of Skyhawks proved to be the defining moment of our time down south. In all a total of ten bombs fell in the sea around ARGONAUT. Unfortunately two 1000lb bombs found their target. One penetrated the boiler room just above the waterline, struck the bulkhead separating the boiler room/engine room and settled wedged into the boiler room ladder. The bomb itself didn't detonate but it caused a boiler to explode, rupturing steam pipes and filling the machinery spaces with superheated steam. Miraculously none of the engine/boiler room staff were seriously injured. The second bomb hit up forward below the waterline on the port side. It came through a main diesel fuel tank before entering the seacat magazine and almost exiting the starboard side. A number of our own missiles were badly damaged, but once again the Argentinean bomb itself did not detonate. Tragically the two missile handlers closed up in the magazine were killed instantly. Able Seaman Stewart was 18 years old on that very day, the 21st May, and 20 year old Able Seaman Boldy who married a matter of weeks before we sailed south.

At the time the bombs hit the ship was steaming at full speed ahead. All power had been lost and we were heading towards a rocky coastline. Fortunately a quick thinking officer, Sub Lieutenant Morgan, ran forward to the focsle and let-go the anchor. This action eventually brought us to a shuddering halt but saved us from foundering on the rocks.

I was closed up in the M.C.O. and remember the horrific bangs and unnatural shaking of the ship as the lights went out. As I gathered myself 'Portland' training kicked in and I recall thinking 'switch to alternative power'. This I did and as quick as a flash nothing happened. It was then I turned to a small emergency generator which successfully restored essential communications and limited lighting. 'What next' I was thinking when it dawned on me that I should report to Damage Control Headquarters (D.C.H.Q.). This I did, but I was not long into my report before my good friend at the other end of the telephone line said "take it easy and slow down Phil". Of course I didn't realise what sort of state I was in, the words were just tumbling out of my mouth and the adrenalin must have been pumping around my body at a phenomenal rate. Add to this the fact that it can be difficult to understand a Scouser at the best of times and it's easy to appreciate the difficulties D.C.H.Q. were having to contend with!

The ship was dead in the water when Captain Layman sent the following defiant signal to HMS FEARLESS, 'We cannot steam, but we can float and we can fight'. We were of course upholding the true and honourable traditions of the Royal Navy.

Although afloat we had no power and as such were completely vulnerable to further attacks. How grateful, therefore, we were for the gallant protection provided by HMS PLYMOUTH. She quickly assessed our desperate situation and proceeded to provide protection by way of circling our position. It was not long before another wave of Skyhawks homed in on us. PLYMOUTH positioned herself between ARGONAUT and the incoming attack, which undoubtedly would have finished us off, and successfully fought off the enemy. When darkness eventually fell, PLYMOUTH took us in tow and deposited us in the relative safety of a creek off San Carlos Bay. She came alongside and tied herself up to us. Shore cables were passed between us in order that PLYMOUTH could provide us with power whilst we carried out essential repairs.

There was to be little rest for the majority of the ship's company that night. Damage control parties were trying to effect repairs. Both Junior Rates and the Petty Officer's messes up forward were destroyed and uninhabitable. The engineers were desperately trying to get some life back into the generators and engines. I myself was involved in diving operations with a view to assessing the underwater damage to our hull. The positive side to all this activity was the fact that we didn't have time to dwell on our perilous position, there was far too much to do.

The following week indeed proved to be the most dramatic, frightening and testing time of my life. Although unable to manoeuvre, when power was restored the Captain insisted on the ship being towed back into the landing area within bomb alley. We were to be subjected to constant air attacks on a daily basis whilst trying to conduct ongoing repairs, and of course there was still the small matter of two unexploded bombs to be dealt with. However, the ship's company were more than a little concerned with regard to the position the captain had placed the ship in. Most of the other ships had their bows pointing towards the entrance to San Carlos Water and the direction the majority of air attacks came from. To be different ARGONAUT was completely broadside on. Now in our minds this meant that the Argentinean pilots looking for targets to select were met with a magnificent view of our Exocet Leander. This did not make us feel comfortable at all. Of course when you think about it, it was a truly inspired manoeuvre. For one the target area, although looking attractive was in fact harder to hit because it was much narrower. Additionally, we maintained maximum arc/ tracking in relation to our weapon systems and hence a greater chance of downing the enemy, which we successfully did on numerous occasions.

One of the more colourful characters on board was our Gunnery Instructor (G.I.), namely Petty Officer Jones, affectionately known as Jonah. He was an old school G.I., straight talking, humorous and a great guy to have on board. After the initial air attack and the fact that we had taken casualties, the tension around the ship was such that you could cut the air with the proverbial knife. Petty Officer Jones had been stationed on the upper deck, the flag deck to be precise, to take charge of the port and starboard 40/60 gun crews. Another air attack came in. The members of the crew below decks were rigid with anticipation. As the enemy aircraft targeted ARGONAUT Jonah gave the following report over the action information communications network, "Four Skyhawks approaching port side. Christ they are coming in low. Bombs released". A minute or so silence, then, "Fucking shave off". At this point the Captain, who was closed up in the ops room, lifted his microphone and said "Petty Officer Jones I don't think there is any requirement for language like that over the action information intercom". Without hesitation Johah immediately replied, "You're a fucking good kid down there, that bastard just missed my head by 6ft". The ops room crew burst into laughter. The Captain just smiled and returned his mike to its holder. The reality of the situation was that the incoming aircraft had come in extremely low, below bridge height, released their bombs which hit the water approximately 20 yards or so off our port side. Two of the bombs bounced over the flag deck and splashed harmlessly into the sea about 20 yards off our starboard side.

At the end of each day, when we fell out from action stations I usually found myself involved in diving operations. The most light hearted being when two of us had to go down to try and repair the split in the starboard side of the hull where the bomb had almost exited the forward magazine. The plan was to take down soft wood wedges and to hammer them into the split. I was going to place the wedges in the split and my diving companion was to hit them with a hammer until tightly secured. The wedges would then gradually expand as they absorbed sea water and hopefully form a watertight seal. Down we went and I placed the first wedge in the split. Now it must be borne in mind that there was a 1000lb bomb and numerous pieces of damaged munitions on the other side of the hull. I gave a thumbs up which was the signal for my diving partner to strike the wedge with his large hammer. As he was about to do so, I put a finger in each of my ears. He just about spit out his mouthpiece and almost dropped the hammer. When we eventually surfaced after successful completion of the job, he jokingly said "You bastard Armstrong, that's the last place I needed a good laugh".

A more sombre dive, undertaken on 24th May, involved retrieving the body of Able Seaman Boldy from the magazine. The body of Able Seaman Stewart had floated up to the magazine hatch not long after the bomb hit and had since been removed and placed in a suitable compartment to be prepared for burial at sea. Entering the magazine, both myself and another diving buddy from the ship's team were not sure what to expect. Lighting had been lowered down which gave us a clear picture of the devastation the Argentinean bomb had caused. The body of Able Seaman Boldy was floating in a horizontal position amongst a batch of damaged seacat missiles on the starboard side. The unexploded 1000lb bomb was a matter of feet away. Lifting tackle had been assembled over the hatch of the magazine to assist in the removal of the body. Swimming over to Able Seaman Boldy we took hold of his legs with a view to floating him over to the hatch. This proved to be not as straight forward as we hoped it to be. He was firmly stuck by an outstretched arm amongst the missiles. Attempts to dislodge him were proving difficult. I indicated to my diving buddy that I would investigate. What followed proved to be one of the most difficult, grim and unwelcomed experiences of not only my time down the Falklands but indeed of my entire life.

Closing in on Able Seaman Boldy I could see that his hand was gripped on the ridge of a missile casing. To get to his hand I had to squeeze and swim along his body length. This entailed passing within inches of his head. The startled, eyes open expression on his face remained a clear and haunting image in my mind for months and years to come. Reaching his hand I found it difficult to move as a result of rigor mortis and had to put all emotion aside as I forced his fingers free. It was eerie floating his body over to the hatch. The lifting tackle was dangling in the water and we began the closing stage of the operation as we attempted to attach the body to the straps provided. One final sickening obstacle remained. Able Seaman Boldy's arm was at right angles to his body and had to be snapped down and tied to his waist in order to allow him to be hauled up through the hatch. On our signal the sailors above started the lift. It must have been a dreadful experience for them, some his mess mates, to see his dripping body emerge from that watery tomb. We still had some air remaining in our diving sets, therefore before climbing out the magazine ourselves we used the time available to remove several cases of damaged ammunition.

The 26th of May with the majority of the ship's company drained and weary. The day before we had received the shattering news that HMS COVENTRY had been sunk trying to protect the ships in San Carlos Bay from incoming enemy air attack. Could all this be real? Please let me awake from this ongoing nightmare.

Evening approached and we were stood down from action stations. Oh how I craved a good night's sleep. Looking forward to a hearty meal my plans were shattered when the diving team were ordered to 'close-up at the rush'. Banging noises had been heard on the ship's hull and the fear was that limpet mines had been attached. This was completely feasible as we were anchored not too far away from the coastline, certainly within striking distance of enemy Special Forces divers.

This was a situation for which our diving team had trained for on many occasions, the exercises appropriately named 'operation awkward'. The aim was to thoroughly search the ship's hull, usually in the form of what is known as a 'half necklace'. A long rope is deployed to attach a number of divers, in our case five, four under the water with diving sets and one surface swimmer with a mask and snorkel. The divers enter the water, say amidships on the starboard side. When all the divers are in the water and attached to the necklace, number one diver swims down and takes up position on the keel. Number two swims down until he can still sight number one from his position further up the hull. This procedure repeats itself until all divers are strung out on one side of the hull from the keel to the surface. Number one controls the speed of the search and when all divers are ready to go they take off swimming forward towards the bow of the ship, swinging round and coming back down the port side. All intakes, stabilizers, sonar dome housings, propellers and rudders have to be thoroughly searched for limpets.

I had carried out this exercise on many, many occasions over the years, but this was special, it was for real. Believe you me that hull was searched thoroughly, not a spare inch of steel was overlooked. Mercifully no offending explosives were found. Usually, under exercise conditions, a search of an R.N. frigate would take around 40 minutes. On this particular occasion none of the divers surfaced for over an hour. Given the circumstances it was a truly extraordinary feat. To understand the operation and limitations of our diving sets an explanation is required.

Our sets were known as S.A.B.A.s. They consisted of two air tanks. With the diving set strapped to your back the number one tank was opened which allowed the diver to breathe through his mouthpiece. As he continued breathing the air in the tank gradually decreased until such time as the diver found it increasingly difficult to draw air from the tank. At this point it would be necessary to 'equalise'. This involved opening a valve which allowed air from the full number two tank to run into the empty number one tank. Once the hissing noise of the air transferring had finished the equalising valve was closed and the diver once more commenced breathing from the now half full tank number one. Of course with only half a tank the time to the next equalisation was considerably shorter than the first. Naval regulations determined that after two equalisations a diver must signal and return to the surface.

All well and good, but on this particular occasion, with me on the keel acting as number one diver, the need to stretch the rules was called for, especially when the team got a little tangled up in the 'free area aft' (propellers and rudders area). Indeed I actually equalised a total of six times, leaving the equalising valve open on the sixth occasion after realising there was hardly any air left to transfer. The reasoning behind this somewhat rash decision was the fact that I felt we just couldn't afford to delay the search by coming to the surface for replacement diving sets. It was subsequently reassuring to find out that my fellow divers had the same thought process. What a great team.

Nothing was found and although a little apprehensive we were all reasonably confident that the ship was clear of mines. This confidence was justified when investigations revealed that the banging on the hull was a result of a fire hose dangling loosely over the side, swinging in the breeze and regularly making alarming contact with the ship's side. What a relief, but it didn't alter the fact that I had just completed the most nerve racking, adrenalin pumping dive of my life.

After falling out from action stations and reverting to defence watches, evenings on the ARGONAUT were somewhat unconventional for a Royal Navy ship, especially during wartime. The ship would revert to defence watches at around 2000hrs. With all the damage we had sustained up forward finding somewhere to 'get your head down' (sleep!) proved to be a bit of a challenge. However, the Chief's mess instigated a great routine. Whoever was first to the mess lounge had the honour of pouring numerous pints of Courage sparkling bitter and placing them on the bar, ready for all the members to arrive. Numerous people have since enquired as to why we were drinking during such dramatic times. Well believe me it proved to be invaluable. It gave us all the opportunity to unwind together and not merely slink off to bed, tense and unable to sleep. These were not mammoth drinking sessions, just an hour or so of de-stressing. The Petty Officers were our honoured guests on these occasions as their lounge had been destroyed when the bombs hit. At around 2100hrs the chefs had usually prepared the evening meal, which was served in the Junior Rates Dining Hall. Officers, Senior and Junior Rates all queuing up and dining together, another first in my naval career.

It had been another fraught and stressful day with the damaged ARGONAUT being subject, once again, to numerous Argentinean air attacks. As always it came as a relief when the ship was stood down from action stations and reverted to defence watches. Retiring to the mess lounge and that all important couple of pints of courage sparkling bitter I engaged myself in conversation, relating to the day's dramatic events, with my old friend Warrant Officer Graham Major. Graham was a straight talking, experienced, well respected Warrant Officer who was extremely good at assessing people's character. After an hour or so it was announced that the main evening meal was ready to be served in the Junior Rates dining hall. Graham and I decided to hang back awhile to let the inevitable queue go down. Eventually we made our way to the dining hall to be served a wonderful steak meal. R.N. Chefs really can perform miracles at times! Finding an empty table we sat down, only to be joined a few moments later by Lt. Cdr. Stevens, the W.E.O. and Cdr. Williams the S.W.E.O. Graham had served on another ship with the W.E.O. a couple of years before and on numerous occasions had told me that in his opinion Lt. Cdr. Stevens had quite a few shortcomings. One thing was for certain, Graham was not intimidated by the man or his rank and as such would not shy away from voicing his opinion, especially if he thought the policies of the W.E.O. were out of order.

This trait of Graham's was about to be demonstrated in the most startling of fashions. The W.E.O. addressed Graham and declared "Ah Mr Major I'm glad we have the opportunity for a chat. There is something I would like to discuss with you". Graham frowned, it had been a long day! "I note that a number of the men have been sat in the passageway for most of the day and I'm sure it must be very stressful for them". He continued, "Therefore, with a view to taking their minds off things and not allowing them to dwell on the imminent danger, I would like you to devise a training programme for them to engage in throughout the coming days". What a remarkable statement. The truth of the matter was that all the 'Greenies' were run off their feet connecting damage control cables, dealing with general action damage and keeping vital services running. They certainly weren't sat on their backsides all day. Mr Major slammed down his knife and fork and glaring at the W.E.O. said in a not too quiet voice, "You cunt. I always knew you were an arsehole and now you've proved it". The whole dining room fell silent. The Junior Rates present were stunned. To say the W.E.O. was taken aback is something of an understatement. He opened his mouth to protest but was frozen into silence as Graham continued, "You know I've thought of an even better plan. Why don't you take yourself off to your cabin and lock yourself in. I'll give you a knock when we are back alongside in Plymouth".

Whilst this exchange was going on I'm sure I detected the beginning of a slight smile appearing on the face of the S.W.E.O.! Finally Lt. Cdr. Stevens managed to spurt out "Mr Major I won't have you talking to me like that". To which Graham retorted, "Well somebody needs to keep you right, you prick". Then turning to me Graham stood up saying "Phil I've suddenly gone off my food, I'll see you back in the mess". As he left the dining hall I could sense that the attending members of the crew were just itching to break into applause.

It is perhaps significant that no disciplinary action was ever taken after this unusual and somewhat unique incident. A combination of common sense and the unfamiliar, dangerous and testing period we found ourselves in ensuring that it was in the best interests of all to just move on.

On the second night of these social arrangements the P.O.s had once again joined us in our lounge. Conversation was freely flowing when the P.O.s Bar Manager, none other than the ever outspoken Tony Dennis, approached me and said how grateful both he and his fellow mess members were for the hospitality afforded them. By way of contributing to proceedings he asked me to accompany him to the bomb damaged P.O.s mess lounge where he assured me there were numerous bottles of spirits (whisky, gin, rum, vodka etc.) that they would like us to accept by way of saying thanks. I of course insisted that such a wonderful gesture was not necessary, but he was insistent. So, off we ventured up forward carrying a couple of travel bags in which to load the bottles of spirits 'lost in action'! Confusion and disappointment greeted us when the said bottles of spirits were not to be found. Mind you the lounge, and particularly the bar area, was in a dreadful state with damaged articles and furniture strewn all over the place. It appeared the generous offering from the P.O.s had indeed been the victim of the bomb blast. I assured Tony that it was 'no great deal' and that their friendly gesture was very much appreciated.

After retrieving the body of Able Seaman Boldy from the forward magazine I was totally drained both physically and emotionally. After grabbing something to eat I experienced a great weariness overcoming me which left me longing for sleep. It was late in the evening, approaching midnight, as I made my way to my bunk space. In the passageway outside our mess I was approached by a rating whose face was etched with worry and concern. He said "Sorry to trouble you Chief but I think you should take a visit down to the 'Greenie's'

(Electricians) mess. A lot of guys seem to be quite upset". I needed this like a hole in the head but nevertheless made my way down the hatch into the mess recreation space. What greeted me was chilling. Virtually all the mess members were there. Why were they not trying to catch up on some sleep?

Their demeanour was dark. "What's the problem chaps?" says I in a friendly sort of way. The place erupted with searching questions and rash statements being hurled at me from all quarters. "What is the Captain doing bringing us back out to Bomb Alley? Why aren't we being dispatched home? We are all going to be killed." My attempts to reassure the lads, who without doubt had endured so much over the past few days whilst all acting in both a professional and heroic manner, were not meeting with much success. I asked for a cup of coffee and made an excuse that I had to go to the 'heads' (toilet). My concern was such that I sought out the ship's Surgeon Lieutenant. I felt pretty bad about this, being all too aware that he had been particularly run off his feet since we first entered San Carlos Water. I briefed him on the situation and without hesitation he agreed to accompany me back down to the Greenie's mess. He handled the incident magnificently, reassuring everyone that we were in the best position possible, with numerous British Warships around us to offer the best protection. Surely better than being off in mid-ocean with limited manoeuvrability and completely vulnerable to enemy attack?

The worries, concerns and need for reassurances were still coming fast and furious but he was steadily winning them over. As I was witnessing this spectacle a grim understanding began to dawn on me. Then it hit me. These guys weren't merely suffering from battle stress, they were pissed, and I knew exactly where they had managed to get hold of the amount of alcohol required to create this foreboding and reckless atmosphere.

The Surgeon Lieutenant finally left, leaving the mess members in a slightly better frame of mind than that in which he found them. Before departing myself I approached a Leading Hand who worked in my department. "Johnson, I want to speak to you in the E.M.R. (Electronics Maintenance Room) right now". I could see he was thinking of protesting but thought better of it when he saw the stern look on my face. A few minutes later he sheepishly entered the E.M.R. and I invited him to take a seat at the workbench. My opening words were along the lines of, "I am going to start talking Johnson and you will not utter one word until I have finished". Then off I went. "I know exactly what has been going on down your mess. You are all pissed after illegally taking numerous bottles of spirits from the Petty Officer's Mess". He attempted to interrupt but was silenced by a harsh glare and a command "to be quiet". "Do you have any conception of the seriousness of the offences that have been committed? We are in a combat situation for God's sake. Believe you me we are talking serious court martial offences here". I noticed his crumbling demeanour as tears began to well up in his eyes. I eased up slightly saying, "Alright you have one chance, and one chance only, to resolve this situation". At this point I handed him a travel bag with instructions to return to his mess with a view to retrieving the liquor as yet not consumed. He was to return to the E.M.R. in half an hour's time. As he was leaving he was left in no doubt that this was a one off opportunity to avoid unimaginable consequences.

In precisely half an hour Johnson returned to the E.M.R. Placing the travel bag on the workbench I heard the clinking of bottles and adopted a somewhat positive frame of mind. Why was Johnson still looking frightened and defensive? The answer came when I looked in the bag and withdrew a total of two bottles. One empty bottle of gin and one bottle of vodka with about an inch or so of spirit remaining. I exploded, "Right that's it. I am now going to contact the Regulating Staff who will undoubtedly instigate a full mess locker search and you can all stand-by to appear before a full court martial on our return to Plymouth. I know for a fact that at least eight bottles of spirits disappeared from the P.O.'s Mess, where are they?" By this time he was a pitiful sight who went on to shakily explain that all the spirits taken had been drunk. Initially I found this hard to accept, but as I calmed down I began to realise that Johnson was indeed being truthful. The temptation placed before the lads during such an exceptional time was almost impossible to resist.

Returning to the Greenie's Mess with Johnson I spoke to the members in a more understanding manner. Not condoning their actions, but emphasising the need for us all to pull together as a team if we were to see our way through this daunting period. Nothing more was ever said about this dark and unsettling affair.

Although there were dark periods during our time in Bomb Alley, in general the Ship's Company reflected the true spirit and traditions of the Royal Navy, displaying true professionalism, team work and the all important sense of humour during the most arduous of conditions. On one occasion I was closed up at action stations in the M.C.O. Once again the atmosphere was tense with hardly a word being spoken, everyone was lost in their own thoughts and fears. A young Radio Operator (R.O.) was amongst us. He was what you might call a bit of a reprobate, every 'Jimmy's' (First Lieutenant) nightmare. Always adrift from shore leave, occasionally having that extra pint too many and other such misdemeanours. In spite of his numerous shortcomings he was indeed a likeable rogue. Anyway, our young R.O. could well detect how we were all feeling. Out of the blue he stands up and asks "Who would like a cup of tea?". We were all startled. "Two sugars Chief?", "No milk for you Shiner?". After taking the full order he disappeared out of the M.C.O.

It must be borne in mind that we were at action stations, condition zulu alpha, which meant all the clips were closed on all water tight doors. This made it extremely difficult to navigate your way around the ship. About 15 minutes or so later he reappears with a full tray of tea and biscuits. How he managed it is beyond me, but it certainly brought us all back to life. He will always be my hero, despite the fact that he doesn't wear a gallantry medal on his chest.

It's difficult to express just how stressful and tiring our experience in Bomb Alley was. The need to dispose of the bomb in the forward magazine was paramount. Thankfully the bomb in the boiler room had been made safe. Not a lot could be achieved during the day as we were closed up at action stations and being subject to constant air attacks. As a result, for two consecutive nights the majority of the Ship's Company were transferred to HMS FEARLESS to allow the bomb disposal team to carry on with their vital and dangerous work. It was decided that the bomb could not be disarmed in situ and the only option available was to try and remove it through the side of the ship. This operation involved cutting holes in the two decks directly above the magazine and then cutting a further hole in the starboard side of the ship to allow the bomb to be ditched in the sea. Some of the cutting work, using acetylene torches, was carried out during the daytime, when we closed up at action stations, by shipwrights from HMS FEARLESS. Unfortunately this plan nearly had disastrous consequences.

ARGONAUT on fire whilst under air attack.

The shipwrights were cutting away at the deck when we came under air attack, again! Of course they dropped their equipment and took shelter. The deck plates where they had been working were extremely hot and within the area were traces of diesel that had been deposited all around the forward section of the ship when the bomb entered through the forward fuel tank. The diesel ignited, which resulted in a major fire. So there we were trying to fight off an air attack whilst at the same time dealing with a major fire. The forward damage control party were magnificent and eventually managed to control and extinguish the fire. Apparently it was really 'touch and go' with the Captain seriously considering giving the order to abandon ship.

During our time in Bomb Alley I can't recall ever sleeping in my bunk. On the one night I planned to HMS ANTELOPE, which was anchored next to us, blew up. Two Royal Engineer bomb disposal officers were attempting to defuse an unexploded bomb when it detonated. One of the officers was killed and the other lost an arm. Both these officers had successfully defused the bomb in our engine/boiler only a day or two before. Many of the ANTELOPE's Ships Company were picked up by us. As you can imagine they were pretty shaken up and I was more than willing to give up my bunk to someone who looked as if he really needed it. I got my head down in a passageway, although sleep was hard to find. Mind you it all caught up with me. After spending well over 48 hours without sleep, I was closed up in the E.M.R. The workbench looked really inviting and after hauling myself on top of it, I was out like a light. It was many hours later that some young sailor was giving me a shake, asking if I would like some soup. That sleep did me the world of good, especially when you consider that I apparently 'never felt a thing' during yet another air raid!

Eventually a plan was hatched to get us home. On the 30th of May we were detached from the rest of the fleet with orders to rendezvous with the repair ship STENNA SEASPREAD. Our engineers had worked wonders to allow us to get underway. Mind you we had only one boiler and a slightly bent shaft. The idea of meeting up with STENNA was to assess the underwater damage with a view to making us seaworthy enough to undertake the 9000 mile journey home. STENNA engineers would also be assisting in making good other damage inclusive of the engines and propulsion systems.

On the 5th of June we finally detached for the U.K. Prior to departure a huge amount of stores including our helicopter and ammunition were to be offloaded and transferred to other ships in the fleet. Our secure voice radio communications system was equipment designated for transfer. I made my way up to the M.C.O. to appraise the job and oversee the packaging of the sensitive units. Just before disconnecting the power, on somewhat of a whim, I put a final call in to the flagship HMS HERMES. My old buddy Warrant Officer Bill Gauson was the senior Yeoman on Admiral Woodward's staff. Bill eventually ended up on the line and could hardly disguise his surprise and delight at my call. After enquiring as to how he himself was, I asked if he had any messages I could pass on to his wife Bonnie and his two girls Jullya and Wanda. After thinking up an emotional message, understandable in the circumstances, we said our farewells with a promise to get together for a pint or three when we were both home again.

At the time of making this unauthorised call our Captain was onboard HERMES to debrief the

Admiral. Bill has since told me that he was quite taken aback by my unconventional form of personal communication. However, after gathering himself he sat down and scribbled a letter to me on a few loose pages of signal pad. Never a guy to be described as a 'shrinking violet', Bill then proceeded to the Admiral's cabin, where, via the attending stewards, he asked if he could please speak with Captain Layman. Captain Layman duly appeared whereupon Bill respectfully asked him if he could please deliver his hastily composed letter to Chief Armstrong. Our Captain undertook to take on this rather menial but highly meaningful task. Of course I was completely unaware of these unconventional events, until such time as Captain Layman returned to ARGONAUT later that evening. I was in the mess enjoying a pint with my messmates as we dared to believe that we were actually heading home. A knock was heard on the mess door and the member furthest from the entrance rose from his seat to see who it was (an old and somewhat bizarre mess tradition!). Imagine his surprise to see the Captain, no less, standing there. Our Commanding Officer politely asked if he could speak to me. I stumbled to the door to be met by the Captain eloquently posed with a silver tray in his hand. On the tray in an official envelope was Bill's letter. I was dumbfounded as the Captain handed me the only mail delivered to the ship that day. After expressing my confused words of thanks I invited Captain Layman to join us for a drink. He tactfully declined my offer remarking with a smile on his face, "I have been many things in my naval career Chief but never the ship's Postie. Have an enjoyable evening". A relatively unimportant occasion in such eventful times, but to me it reflected the leadership and true noble character of an outstanding Naval Officer.

Eventually we detached from the remainder of the fleet, retaining just eight Seacat missiles on the after launchers. As we headed north the majority of the ship's company started to relax just a little as we dared to believe that it might all be over for us. Mind you we were completely on our own, with no escort, limited ammunition and restricted speed and manoeuvrability. This feeling of security was shattered two days later when an Argentinean aircraft was picked up on radar not more than 30 miles away. The action alarm sounded as we went to air raid warning red. I've never seen people move so fast. I tell you honestly that that ship was completely closed up for action stations in less than three minutes. Mind you we were well practised at it! Fortunately no attack was forthcoming. The aircraft turned out to be a reconnaissance 707 which just circled the ship and left.

The day before, a memorial service was held for our two lost shipmates. Held in the open hangar, with the ship rolling in a heavy Atlantic swell, it really was an emotional affair. The Captain led the service, praising the courage and professionalism of Able Seamen Stewart and Boldy. Perhaps even more poignant were the words expressed by close friends of the two young lads. During the singing of the naval hymn 'Eternal Father' it was difficult to hold back the tears. After the ship's company were dismissed everyone just walked off quietly, most to stand at the guard rails lost in their own personal thoughts.

A day or so before we reached the Ascension volunteers were called for to fly off home once we reached the islands. This was mainly because over half the ship's company were sleeping in passageways, work spaces etc. As I had been in the middle of a house move when we left I put my name forward. My request was granted. The night before we arrived, the mess treated itself to a good old 'up channel night'. It was a relaxed and somewhat riotous affair that went on until the early hours of the morning after which, not wishing to miss the boat transfer, I just packed my grip (bag) and sat myself down in the mess lounge. At around 0900hrs all the lads mustered on the upper deck to see me off.

Once on Ascension we were mustered for a briefing by a fairly serious and stern looking Warrant Officer Master-at-Arms, who after congratulating us all, went on to say that we had approximately six hours before our flight departed and that we were at liberty to wander off around the local area. However, he did stress that anyone returning drunk would not be allowed on the aircraft. With this in mind I decided that I would make my way up to the headland to look down on poor old ARGONAUT.

She did indeed look battered, rust streaked and very much the worse for wear. As I was standing there a local resident, who's fine looking grand bungalow was close at hand, came over and asked if I was a member of the crew of the ship anchored in the bay. When I confirmed I was he had me 'up homers' (a guest at his house) before I could make the weakest of protests. Of course his family's hospitality was outstanding and who was I to refuse a couple of beers, fine wine and a farewell tot of rum. By the time I found myself ascending the stairs into our VC10 it took all my concentration not to fall foul of the overseeing Master-at-Arms.

Thankfully I made it and after a refuelling stop in Sierra Leone the aircraft came into land at RAF Brize Norton in the early hours of the morning. I was accompanied by a Petty Officer Steward, a Glaswegian, who was travelling up to Scotland with me. We were planning to make a quick dash off to catch a train and didn't think for a moment that there would be a reception crowd awaiting us. We were wrong, there was indeed quite a large gathering inclusive of my wife Annette and our children Paul and Julie. In truth I found it quite scary negotiating the hordes of well-wishers who had gathered. It was only when I spotted a waving Scottish flag that I realized my family were there. It really was a heart warming homecoming that was made all the more special when we boarded the coach to whisk us off to a local hotel. I could not believe my eyes when there waiting on the bus was Connie Francis, the three card brag Master-at-Arms himself. He had been resident in the Royal Naval Hospital Haslar when he heard some of the ARGONAUT's crew were coming into Brize Norton. Against doctor's advice he discharged himself to welcome us all back. It was the most uplifting of moments and a gesture I will never forget.

A few days after returning to my family and friends in Dunfermline I heard that HMS PLYMOUTH was due to arrive back into her home port of Rosyth. Keeping in mind her gallant actions in protecting ARGONAUT during our 'hour of need' I thought it only right that I should go down to the dockyard to welcome them home. With the enthusiastic help of my children we made up a large banner which read 'Welcome home and many thanks from HMS ARGONAUT'. As expected there was a huge welcoming crowd on the jetty, along with a Royal Marine Band, press and TV cameras. As the ship came alongside the Captain, Captain Pentreath who took the surrender of South Georgia, spotted our banner from the bridge wing and beckoned for us to come aboard. For all that was going on at that moment he still found time to have me, Paul and Julie up to his cabin. After being well entertained we departed for the Chief's Mess. I had some good friends in that mess and the last time I had seen them was the night PLYMOUTH had taken us in tow after being bombed. In the years ahead, when I found myself promoted and in the Naval Careers Service, Captain Pentreath was appointed to the Director of

Naval Recruiting's staff. Fortunately this gave me the opportunity to meet up with him at various functions. We developed a mutually respectful friendship and after dinner we always found ourselves tucked in the corner of the bar spinning old sea dits (sea stories). On his retirement from the R.N. Captain Pentreath CBE DSO Royal Navy found time to write to me and wish me well for the future - a true gentleman. It is a letter I treasure.

So, what did the Falklands Conflict mean to me personally? For one it made me immensely proud to be a member of the Royal Navy, but maybe more importantly it very much made me realise that war is not all glory and heroics. It is brutal, frightening, exhausting and a humbling experience.

In closing it must be said that undoubtedly there are many, many unsung heroes who have gone unrecognised by the establishment. However, they feel no resentment and carry on in life secure in the knowledge that their close comrades and family know their true worth.

HMS CAMPERDOWN

ARGONAUT was to undergo an extensive refit, understandable in the circumstances, and as a result the majority of the ship's company anxiously awaited draft orders. When mine came in I couldn't have been happier. I was to return north of the border to Scotland as an Instructor at the Royal Naval Reserve Unit, HMS CAMPERDOWN, in bonnie Dundee. With just over three years to serve until pensionable age, this was surely going to be my last appointment? No more 'sea time' for me.

Although only an hour's drive from my home in Dunfermline I was to receive 'lodging allowance' with a view to renting accommodation in or around Dundee. This was most acceptable to me as the weekly routine involved attending two 'Drill Nights' every week in order to train up enthusiastic reservists.

I was surprised at how well the unit was equipped. Besides having a resident minesweeper, HMS CUXTON, it also housed a fully equipped diving store. Most unexpected and very much welcomed. The mess facilities were also first class with lounges overlooking the River Tay, along with the impressive road bridge. I could see myself settling in here very nicely.

My arrival at CAMPERDOWN couldn't have been more welcoming. The Falklands War was not long over and as a 'veteran' I found myself the centre of attention. Especially so at the bar where full time naval personnel and reservists alike hung onto my every word as I colourfully outlined my experiences, laced with both humour and tragedy. Needless to say I was not allowed to put a hand in my pocket, my new shipmates' hospitality always leaving me with a fine glow as I rather unsteadily made my way to my digs and a welcoming bed.

"Yeah, or right then" was my casual and dismissive response. The Unit's Regulating Petty Officer had just presented me with what I immediately identified as a hoax draft order. I was too long in the tooth to fall for that one. I had just served on three ships, one after the other, and was confident that my sea-faring days were over. I was now looking forward to spending my remaining three years in the Royal Navy in good old HMS CAMPERDOWN. The lads were trying to wind me up. How could they ever think I'd fall for such an obvious scam. I'd left HMS ARGONAUT just six months ago. There was no way I'd be sent back to sea after such a short period ashore.

My self-assured confidence in my future within the R.N. was about to be severely dented. I was sent for by my boss, the Unit's Senior Regular Service Staff Officer, who enquired, "Why haven't you signed for your draft order Chief?"
Although alarm bells started to go off I still responded with a knowing smile on my face, "So you're in on it too Sir?"
"In on what? I have no idea what you are implying."
My smile turned to a grimace as the realisation that I really was to join the Fishery Protection Vessel HMS GUERNSEY hit home.
"I thought it was some sort of Permanent Staff joke," I continued.
"I assure you it isn't Chief. I'm not long off the phone from the Drafting Authorities who were enquiring as to the delay in you acknowledging your orders. I would suggest

you sign your draft order and then, if you wish, telephone 'Drafty' yourself to discuss the matter, although not for one moment do I think they will cancel your draft."
Shell shocked, I retired to the mess to contemplate my future.

Later on that day I did indeed contact the Drafting Authorities, but as suspected to no avail. Whilst sympathetic, it was explained to me that there was a shortage of Chief Radio Electricians, especially with my background and experience. The duration of my time on GUERNSEY was to be eighteen months, not the usual two and a half years normally spent on a destroyer or frigate. Trying to be positive I looked upon this shortened period as a bonus. Unfortunately I was in for a rude awakening as I later discovered that the time actually spent 'at sea' was astronomical in comparison to that of conventional front line warships.

HMS GUERNSEY

This couldn't be happening, finishing my time on a mere Fishery Protection Patrol Vessel. I was a frigate and destroyer man for heaven's sake, my talents shouldn't be wasted on a civilian looking, lightly armed patrol vessel. How wrong my misguided and ignorant thought process turned out to be.

The 9th of January 1984 and I was back down in Rosyth Dockyard to join my new ship, which was undergoing a short maintenance period. I must admit that on first looking around my 'new home' I was quite impressed. GUERNSEY was certainly not like any of the warships I had served on in the past. It had more of a civilian type leisure cruiser feel to it, with its broad passageways and easily negotiated, wide stairwells. The Senior Rate's mess, designed to accommodate up to seven CPO/POs, was really quite welcoming and well fitted out.

Over the coming weeks I endeavoured to fulfil the age old naval necessity which came under the phrase of 'know your ship'. Poking around up forward I opened a door on the port side and entered what I thought to be a storage space for the seaman's branch - ropes, fenders etc. As I took in my surroundings it began to dawn on me exactly what this compartment was designed for. Beyond a doubt it was a diving store. This was evident by the presence of an air compressor and numerous points to recharge sub-aqua bottles. All sorts of exciting thoughts began to enter my head relating to the virtually impossible dream of creating a fully equipped, operational diving team on board HMS GUERNSEY. There would be so many hurdles to overcome, not least the challenge of mustering enough trained crew members to form a viable team that could conform to the abundance of strict regulations that diving operations were subject to.

I returned to the mess to gather my thoughts. Of course I would have to approach the Commanding Officer to seek approval to orchestrate my, some might say, hair brained plans.

Members of GUERNSEY's Diving Team.
Phil A. centre (look at those knees!).

Lieutenant Commander Colin Ferbrache Royal Navy was an approachable, fair, hardworking and ambitious Naval Officer who was experiencing the heavy responsibility of his first command. I had requested a meeting with him to discuss the merits of forming a fully operational diving team, in the hope of gaining his approval and support. He listened with interest to my proposals whilst regularly asking pertinent and searching questions. I had prepared well and as such was able to reassure him that, although not wishing to underestimate the scale of the venture, I was confident that it could be achieved. My closing remarks highlighted the operational advantages of HMS GUERNSEY being the only Island Class

Patrol Vessel with a diving team on board. With an assuring smile on his face he granted me permission to go ahead with my plans. I left his cabin full of enthusiasm. Perhaps my time on board a mere Fishery Protection Patrol Vessel wasn't going to be such a waste of time after all.

The maintenance period was complete and preparations were underway to sail on my first eight day patrol. I found it strange having to personally report to the Captain on the bridge that the ship, as far as the Weapons Engineering Branch was concerned, was in all respects ready for sea. On my previous ships it was a case of me reporting my department to the Chief Artificer, who reported to the Deputy WEO, who in turn spoke to the WEO, who eventually reported to the Captain. Quite a number of safety buffers as far as my responsibilities were concerned! However, that turned out to be just one of the many challenging aspects of serving on a Royal Naval Patrol Vessel.

Sharing my cabin with the ship's Petty Officer Mechanical Engineer (POME) proved to be a bonus as the POME also undertook the duties of the ship's Supply Officer, my source of equipping out the diving store/team. It wasn't too long before he was due to leave the ship and when he did he was relieved by POME Dave Newell, who ended up being a really close friend of mine, to the extent that I had the honour of acting as the 'Best Man' at his wedding.

Dave picked up the task of equipping The Diving Team with great enthusiasm and it was only a matter of weeks after he joined that we were ready to enact the next phase of my ambitious venture - training! Over the coming months I dedicated a considerable amount of my time to forming a diving team, which had to comply with the numerous and varied laid down associated naval regulations. Eventually with two qualified ship's divers (one being my good self) and three enthusiastic volunteer members of the crew trained locally to act as 'attendants', we were ready and raring to go.

Our eight day day patrol period was coming to an end as we headed for the first of our numerous forty-eight hour 'stand-offs' in the colourful port of Aberdeen. Coming alongside at 0900 we were due to sail exactly two days later. It was at this time I was made aware of yet another peculiarity of the 'Fish Squadron'. In the 'Proper Navy' shore leave was granted subject to fairly strict rules, i.e. all members of the crew had to return to the ship by a laid down, specified time, say 0700, with somewhat harsh punishment awarded to personnel who failed to return on time, known as 'being adrift'. Patrol vessels ran a much more relaxed routine which I suppose was reflective of the trust and responsibility afforded to crew members. As mentioned, GUERNSEY was scheduled to sail two days later at 0900, and unless on 'duty', crew members could stay ashore for just about all of that time, as long as they were back on board an hour before sailing. Of course certain ratings had to be back earlier if they were required to 'ready the ship for sea'.

Numerous differences in my new found life at sea were about to unfold over the coming months, the majority being most welcomed and positive in nature. It was always recognised and accepted that on board Island Class Patrol vessels the ship's Engineering Chief Artificer (Marine Engineering Officer - MEO) would undertake the respected role of the Senior Rates Mess President. When I joined this position was held by a great guy named Ron Beck. It turned out that Ron actually lived not far away from me in Pitcorthie Estate, Dunfermline. We really got on well together and I truly admired his sense of judgement, professionalism and cheerful sense of humour. He was always there ready and willing to help anybody out if they needed it. Regrettably he was due to leave the ship only a matter of months after I joined.

The new MEO, a Scotsman who hailed from Edinburgh, named Don Gillies, joined when we were alongside in Stromness in the Orkney Islands. Two days later Ron left nursing a throbbing hangover, having succumbed to the age old naval tradition of having one final memorable 'run ashore'. Back on patrol we were having a 'stand easy' down the mess when I asked Don how he felt about taking on the role of Mess President. Unexpectedly, and to my great surprise, he came up with "Well I'm not too fussed Phil, you are welcome to take on Mess Pres as far as I'm concerned,

I'm sure you'll do a great job". And so began one of the many fulfilling and rewarding roles I found myself subjected to whilst serving in my last operational ship in the Royal Navy.

Once settled-in the opportunity to take on a couple of different but nonetheless essential responsibilities, in relation to maintaining the morale of the whole ship's company, came my way - Canteen Manager (Can Man) and Film Officer. The ship was built with a compartment specifically designed to act as a 'shop'. Quite spacious with ample refrigeration and storage space, it had a large counter area which opened onto the main passageway. Being mid-ships it was ideally suited to serve all members of the ship's company, inclusive of Officers, Senior and Junior Rates. On main line RN fighting ships, frigates, destroyers, aircraft carriers etc. the ship's shop was run by the NAAFI. It was managed by a civilian NAAFI Manager, who was usually accommodated in a Senior Rates mess. Now that role was coming my way and I couldn't wait to get started in 'setting up shop'!

The Film Officer's role was just as important in maintaining moral, mainly due to the fact that we spent so much time actually at sea. There was a Fleet Film Library located not far from the dockyard gate in Rosyth. Prior to departing on patrol it was my responsibility to visit the library to select a varied range of engrossing films to entertain and captivate an expectant audience, namely the whole ship's company. The films in the fleet library were stored and classified into three distinctive groups:- 1. Relatively newly released films which had received rave reviews from the general public and professional film critics. 2. Older films with mediocre story lines. 3. Rather obscure films starring actors who should have maybe stuck to their day jobs. Having verified with the senior film librarian exactly how many days we would be at sea whilst away on patrol, let's for argument's sake say sixty, I would then be invited to select twenty films from each category. No matter how much I switched on my scouse charm I could never persuade the distributing librarian to offset our allocation with slightly more films from category 1, which made my job of producing an enthralling ship's patrol film programme all the more challenging.

The 'Can Man' job was rewarding in many ways, both professionally and financially. I had complete free reign to stock up with items I considered appropriate - soft drinks, confectionery, crisps, biscuits, washing powder, toiletries etc. I found myself visiting a local retail store to provision a shop that had no local competition to deal with, which was going to be run by a friendly and accommodating proprietor. It was left to me to determine the price of all the items on sale which, being an honest scouser, I did with true integrity, always taking into account the needs and welfare of my valued customers. Honestly I did not scam the lads but the role did afford me a small but reasonable profit that helped towards the funding of quiet 'runs ashore' when alongside.

It was quite fascinating to slowly realise just how much the roles of Can Man and Film Officer intertwined. Producing a film programme was no easy task. Trying to balance up the sequence of films involved not showing all the classics in turn and in the same vein not showing all the less entertaining movies one night after the other. A well thought through balance had to be produced. Of course on film nights it fell to me to promote the programmed show. During the day members of the crew would approach me and ask "What movie is showing tonight Chief?". Whatever category of film it was I would always respond with something along the lines of "It's an absolute stormer. Make sure you get a good seat in the mess before the 8 o'clock start, you don't want to miss a single minute of this epic story". This was stated with such conviction that for most of the time it was actually believed. The trick was to inject one of the really good films just as my credibility was beginning to wane.

The entertainment systems on board included the installation of a large display television in every mess, on which the films could be screened. Prior to the 8 o'clock start I would open up the ship's shop at 7 o'clock, encouraging passers-by to stock up with 'nutty' (sweets and confectionery) plus cans of coke/lemonade and to make sure they got a good seat in the mess for the evening's 'must not miss' movie. This approach proved to be, in the most part, a sound sales pitch. Mind you, on the days after I might have slightly exaggerated the quality of the film shown I found it advisable to keep a low profile.

Much to his mother's disapproval our son Paul was developing a serious interest in joining the Royal Navy. Of course Annette laid all the blame on me, with accusations of brainwashing. Actually there might well have been an element of me unwittingly painting a positive picture of naval life, after all the tendency was to highlight the adventure, visits to exotic lands and forged lifetime friendships. Talk of long, boring days at sea, family separation and other negative aspects of 'life in a blue suit' rarely took precedence in my story telling. That being said Paul was certainly aware, more than most people, of the reality and horrors of war. The Falklands Conflict had had a profound effect on him.

With a view to giving him a realistic insight into life at sea, I asked Paul how he would feel if I could arrange for him to spend a couple of weeks at sea on the GUERNSEY. Unsurprisingly he jumped at the opportunity. I approached Captain Ferbrache with my proposal which he supported wholeheartedly, suggesting that Paul might wish to bring a friend along who also had an interest in service life.

New Year's Eve 1984 and we were due to sail at 1500hrs. Joining the crew as fit and excited volunteers were Paul and his good friend from school Michael McLeod. Michael was considering his options with regard to a career and, undoubtedly being influenced by Paul's enthusiastic portrayal of life in the Navy, decided to take up the offer of a couple of weeks away on fishery protection duties.

Sailing under the magnificent Road and Rail Bridges, we headed off down the Forth and out into the North Sea. The boys were allocated a cabin and given time to settle in before I took them on a tour around the ship. Paul was fascinated whereas Michael appeared a little disinterested and rather pale looking. Of course we were out on the high seas now and the ship was beginning to rise, fall and roll with the ever increasing sea swell. It turned out that Michael just could not find his sea legs and in fact he spent the majority of the following two weeks in his bunk, no doubt longing to be back shore side on terra firma.

Over the time on patrol Paul willingly engaged in numerous activities, inclusive of: Joining a boarding party to ensure fishing vessels were operating within laid down lawful regulations. Taking an active role in a 40/60 bofor guns live firing exercise. Manning the Bridge and joining a watch down in the engine room. He also joined the diving team for a rather interesting harbour dive, and of course he acted as the Film Officer's and Can Man's assistant!

The interesting dive we embarked on took place in Lerwick Harbour in the Shetland

Isles during our first forty eight hour 'stand-off'. After a detailed and appropriate briefing Paul went down with me. It turned out to be a most enjoyable and intriguing dive. In fact I managed to uncover, buried in the sea-bed mud, an old white clay pipe which had fascinating inscriptions on its bowl which to me appeared to be Viking in origin. I still have it to this day but have never got round to having it verified as an ancient artefact - one of these days!

Another eight day patrol and into Aberdeen for our second 'stand-off'. At this stage Paul and Michael, after a farewell audience with the Captain, disembarked to make their way by train back to Dunfermline. Paul had found the whole experience extremely rewarding, and in fact went on, much to his mother's dismay, to join the Royal Navy as an Engineering Officer. As for Michael, who remained bunk bound for just about all his time on board, unsurprisingly he did not opt to follow in the wake of Nelson and other famed sea-farers. However, he has been tremendously successful, taking up an academic path and ending up as a professor no less, not of nautical studies I hasten to add!

The ship's canteen (shop) provided an ideal storage area for a number of sets of golf clubs held by the ship under the category of 'sports equipment'. Coming alongside in the tranquil fishing village of Stromness in the Orkney Islands, I decided to try and break away from the trap of excessive drinking whilst alongside. The plan was to take off for a game of golf with Dave Newell and another couple of shipmates. My colleagues had rarely, if ever, handled a golf club, therefore being the most experienced I was to act as instructor. At 3 o'clock in the afternoon the ship was alongside and by 4 o'clock we were teeing off at the local club's first hole, feeling rather pleased with ourselves that we hadn't had a drink. Halfway round things started to go wrong for me. One green lay just by a road with a small stone dyke at the back of it. Unfortunately I over hit my approach shot and my ball landed on the tarmacadam road. Foolishly instead of picking it up and throwing it back over the wall I tried to be a right smarty pants and attempted to chip it back over. I lined up, chipped and then everything went black. Apparently the ball took off like a rocket, hit the dyke, rebounded back smashing my glasses and splitting my lip. This proved to be too much for my students who were hysterical with laughter and lacking any sort of sympathy or assistance. Still the game went on with more than the occasional titter as we proceeded down the remaining fairways. After a memorable game we ended up in the clubhouse around 8 o'clock in the evening.

Feeling rather pleased with ourselves for being such sober and upstanding ratings after the ship had been alongside for all of five hours, we thought we rightly deserved a few quiet pints, but unfortunately things didn't quite go to plan. It seemed we had picked the one night of the year when the Ladies Annual Prize Giving was to take place. Before long a band arrived carrying their accordions, chanters etc, followed by a bevy of the more elderly ladies of the island. A microphone was rigged up and the presentations duly commenced, with an assortment of silver cups and bowls being awarded. Shortly afterwards theses containers were topped up with a variety of numerous bottles of malt whisky and passed around the club. Being visitors we kept a low profile, taking up station in a quiet corner of the bar. However, the local ladies would have none of it insisting that we took part in the local tradition by helping down the abundant supply of excellent whisky. For my part I thought it would be purely medicinal and a help to my poor old split lip. Anyway suffice to say that hardly any of us remember leaving that club and how we managed to arrive back on board with all our golf clubs intact is still a mystery. So much for a relaxing game of golf. What with my split lip and raging hangover in the morning I felt as if I'd taken part in an England v Scotland rugby match at Murrayfield or gone fifteen rounds with Muhammad Ali.

One of the highlights of the year was our deployment to Gibraltar to undertake a ten day maintenance period, boosted by a three day visit to Bordeaux in France on the way down. The time in Gib. offered the opportunity for the ship's company family members to visit. Although predominantly operating in UK territorial waters, the family separation of serving on a Fishery Protection Vessel was quite considerable, consequently I didn't have to think twice about flying Annette out to join me in sunny Gibraltar, a place I was more than familiar with. An additional bonus was that our daughter Julie was to come out as well. Unfortunately poor old Paul, her hard working brother, was tied up with his all important and numerous school leaving exams.

The majority of the ship's company bringing out their family members, including my now close friend Don Gillies, were to be accommodated in well appointed, spacious caravans situated in a most convenient area of the Naval Dockyard. I didn't take up this offer as our old friends from Naples, Bill and Bonnie Gauson, were enjoying a two year appointment to Gib. and insisted that we stay with them for the duration of our visit.

The week in the sunshine was memorable. It provided me with the opportunity to show Annette and Julie all the places I used to work from when stationed in HMS ROOKE, the local RN shore base, as a young sailor straight out of training. This was enhanced by the many and varied social occasions that we found ourselves invited to. All in all one of the highlights of my time on GUERNSEY.

Still all good things must come to an end, and after saying an emotional farewell to the two most precious females in my life, I made my way back to the ship to try and resolve a complex technical problem I had been struggling with during the work periods of the week gone by. The eventual outcome of this challenging dilemma proved to be most welcoming for both myself and the majority of the crew.

The ship's main computerised navigational system had developed an intermittent fault which resulted in the large display table malfunctioning without warning. I had initiated numerous operational checks to the system which resulted in a number of defective components being identified and replaced, and although I now had the system working I still felt uneasy with regard to its reliability. We were due to sail on the Monday morning, however, Captain Ferbrache was well aware of my efforts to get the ship's main navigational equipment fully operational. On the Saturday he asked me for an update. I was completely honest with him, pointing out that although the system at that particular time was working, I couldn't guarantee that the niggling fault wouldn't return. As such I reluctantly but respectfully informed him that failure of the system whilst we were in the Straits of Gibraltar or the Bay of Biscay could prove to be somewhat problematic. Quite an understatement. He thanked me for my honesty before asking for my thoughts on the way ahead. The system itself was not in general use throughout the fleet and as such the manufacturers, as part of their contract, provided assistance by way of having their technical expertise readily available to assist as and when required. Considering this one such occasion, I therefore suggested to the Captain that we initiate this option with a view to gaining the reassurance he was seeking. He thanked me again for my frankness, agreeing completely with my line of thought.

As a consequence an Op Def (operational defect) signal was raised and the manufacturers' assistance requested. This of course resulted in the ship's sailing being postponed. The Captain made an announcement over the main broadcast which was greeted with at first disbelief followed by hearty cheers, making me somewhat of a local hero in the process.

The manufactures' rep, a chap named Alan who I now knew quite well from previous calls for assistance, arrived on board late the next day. Within twenty four hours the problem was resolved. Alan, forever the gentleman, reassured me that the course of action I took was indeed the correct one as the defective component board we eventually (well 'he') diagnosed, with the help of his sophisticated, high tech, diagnostic test equipment, had a history of unreliability. He did not have a spare board with him, so consequently we had another twenty four hours delay as we awaited the arrival of a replacement from the UK. Alan of course was more than pleased with his prolonged stay in Gib. as he rarely found himself travelling abroad to assist struggling so called technical experts in the Royal Navy.

The next couple of days proved to be memorable, with both Alan and myself never having to put our hands in our pockets to purchase a drink. All my grateful, fellow crew members took care of that aspect of our forays ashore. Even Captain Ferbrache ensured we were in good spirits (literally) by offering us generous measures of refreshment from his well stocked bar during our debrief in relation to the progress of the ship's main navigational aid. We eventually set sail back to the UK five days after our original scheduled departure date.

My time on GUERNSEY had been more fulfilling than I could ever have imagined. The responsibilities placed upon the WEO were considerable, but the rewards of self-belief, growth in self-confidence combined with the general camaraderie shared with the Ship's Company were truly exceptional. In September 1985 I found myself back at HMS CAMPERDOWN safe in the knowledge (surely?) that I would not be drafted back to sea prior to my scheduled retirement date in May 1986. My situation was bordering on perfection, there I was back in familiar surroundings to see out my remaining nine months of naval service - wonderful!

Returning to CAMPERDOWN I was more than pleased to find the Diving Store still fully equipped. This gave me the golden opportunity to reform a diving team, which of course ensured that I myself stayed 'In-Date'. Of the many dives I organised and took part in, one of the most interesting was a security related sea-bed and hull search of the historic ship, RSS DISCOVERY, which had returned to Dundee in March 1986 with a view to being exhibited as a major attraction to celebrate the city's ship building past. Discovery was a Polar Research Ship famously used to take Captain Robert Falcon Scott to the Antarctic in 1901. The security aspect was considered essential because of a planned visit by the Reigning Monarch, Her Majesty Queen Elizabeth 2nd.

My time in a 'Blue Suit' was fast approaching an end. Of course I was 'Dined Out' on more than one occasion, which added to the anguish beginning to build up inside me. I was starting to miss the Navy already. How would life in 'Civvy' Street measure up? What kind of future lay ahead?

SHORESIDE

Although I had complained on many occasions about the time I was spending at sea, which regularly resulted in me expressing that good old naval saying of ROMFT (role on my fucking time), the truth was I was not particularly looking forward to a life in 'Civvy street'. I had secured a job with a local electronics company which entailed calibrating electronic test equipment. It was undoubtedly a wonderful opportunity, however, the thought of me spending the rest of my working days cooped up in a laboratory made my blood run cold. After 24 years in the electronics world it was an area of employment that didn't particularly turn me on.

My lifeline came by way of the Naval Careers Service. I had applied to join and indeed had attended the two day selection course at Admiralty Buildings in London. The whole selection process was extremely competitive and I was completely overjoyed to be offered a place, not least because it guaranteed me a further 15 years in uniform with the added bonus of not having to serve at sea. The best of both worlds.

The two day board in London was a challenging and thorough affair involving various psychological tests, group discussion sessions and individual presentations, culminating in appearing before a board of senior naval officers. It was at this stage that I thought I had blown it. Sat on a chair facing the board, presided over by a Naval Captain, I had managed to provide acceptable answers to the varied and searching questions posed by the various members of the board. Finally came the main man himself. He had in front of him a questionnaire I had completed the previous day. There had been a time limit on completing the document which put candidates under a certain degree of pressure. One of the questions related to pastimes and hobbies. Various activities were listed and you were invited to highlight those you were interested in. For some obscure reason I had underlined 'reading' and 'writing'. Looking over the rim of his glasses, the very imposing Captain said "I see you are interested in both reading and writing, could you please expand". Without hesitation I wittily replied "well I hope to be able to do both by the end of the year sir". My attempt at humour did not appear to impress him. He merely grimaced and moved on to further questioning. My one ray of hope was the fact that I detected amused smiles on all the other members of the board.

My concerns for the future were banished in a moment when I was offered an appointment in the Naval Careers Service. I accepted without any misgivings and was more than overjoyed when I was informed that my first posting would be to the RN & RM Careers Office in Lothian Road, Edinburgh. I joined the office in the first week of May 1986. The Officer in Charge, Lieutenant Harry Bell Royal Navy, informed me it would be two weeks before I attended the three week 'Interview Training' course at Admiralty Buildings, London. In the meantime I was to link up with the School Presentation Team who were in the area. I was to accompany the team around numerous secondary schools in the Edinburgh area to witness them giving highly professional presentations on career opportunities in the Royal Navy and Royal Marines to third and fourth year students. My role was to just watch and learn.

The following day, off I went with my new highly experienced colleagues, feeling quite excited and looking forward to the challenges ahead. I was determined to make a success of this new direction my naval service was taking. Arriving at a well populated school in Wester Hailes I was very much impressed by the way the School Liaison Team went about setting up for the presentation. They appeared completely relaxed as they set up projector equipment and screens on the raised stage of a substantially sized assembly hall. Finally the pupils and staff began to file in resulting in a seated audience of well over 200 boys, girls and teaching staff. My brief was to stand in the wings and observe. The Warrant Officer in charge of the presentation team addressed the assembled audience, introducing himself and briefly explaining the format of the presentation. I was greatly impressed by his confidence, self assuredness and general relaxed manner as he opened proceedings. Perhaps one day I would feel as comfortable when speaking to such a large body of people. Standing in the wings feeling quite safe with no great expectations on me, a feeling of disbelief engulfed me as I heard the presenting Warrant Officer saying "And finally we are lucky today to have with us a Chief Petty Officer who has just recently left an operational warship and who is now going to give you a short brief on his naval career. Please welcome Chief Petty Officer Phil Armstrong. I felt myself being pushed from the security of the wings to centre stage. Staring at that sea of faces full of expectation I thought nothing but a squeak was going to come out of my mouth. Anyway after composing myself I launched into an unrehearsed short talk highlighting the major events of my naval career, I even managed to raise a few laughs! Returning to the side of the stage to the sound of appreciative applause I settled to watch the professionals in action, hardly believing what had just happened.

Afterwards I approached the Warrant Officer and said something along the lines of " You might have let me know that you were planning to get me up to speak". To which he replied "If I had you probably would have been a nervous wreck. As it was you were first class, well done Phil". Of course he was absolutely right and my baptism of fire certainly gave me a sound basis of self confidence on which to build.

I had been in the Lothian Road office for approaching a year when Lt. Harry Bell called all the staff together in the main office. The 'Troubles' in Northern Ireland were continuing at a ferocious level with little sign of any agreement to curtail the conflict in sight. Lt. Bell informed us all that a Careers Adviser, Ron McGuiness from the Belfast office, would be joining as a member of our team in the morning. Apparently this development had arisen as a direct result of intelligence received relating to a priority IRA threat to the life of Chief McGuiness. Undercover personnel from the RUC had come to speak to Ron not long after he had arrived at his office to start work. They told him he was to return home immediately to collect an overnight bag and say farewell to his wife and children, after which he would be taken to a remote harbour to rendezvous with a Royal Naval coastal patrol vessel. From there the ship was to sail to a port on the west coast of Scotland, from where Ron would be collected and transferred to HMS CALEDONIA in Rosyth.

Ron and I really got on well together. He was an experienced Careers Adviser and I welcomed his advice and counsel. We appeared to have a mutual respect for each other which was cemented one dreadful evening a couple of weeks after he joined our office. I arrived home just after 6 o'clock in the evening after a busy day in the office. My dear wife had my dinner prepared and we both opted to eat through in the lounge, our meals set out on a tray and balanced on our knees. Switching on the television news I was horrified and transfixed as the headlines announced the death of a Naval Officer in the centre of Belfast.

Disbelief engulfed me as the name of the murdered officer was announced as Lieutenant Alan Shields Royal Navy, The Careers Information Officer (CIO) for Northern Ireland. A bomb had been placed under his car which was triggered by a mercury switch. The bomb had been activated when he slowed down to stop at traffic lights. I'd met Alan on numerous occasions and found him to be a great guy with a warm and welcoming personality.

Of course Ron was a much more close acquaintance of Alan than I, in fact they were extremely close friends. As I watched the full story unfolding on the television my concerns turned to Ron and the devastation he must have been feeling. Standing up, I placed my half consumed meal on the lounge coffee table and solemnly told Annette that I had to go down to the Chief's Mess in CALEDONIA, just to be with Ron at this dreadful time. Of course Annette was completely understanding and no doubt as shocked as I as the realisation of the dangers we were all subject to began to sink home.

Not surprisingly I found Ron in the Chief's Mess bar with a large Irish Whiskey in his hand. It was difficult to know what to say, but the welcoming look of gratitude on Ron's face as I approached him eradicated the need for awkward words of sympathy. We stayed at the bar until it closed at 11 o'clock, talking through the 'troubles' in Northern Ireland, the reality and dangers involved in being a British Serviceman serving in The Province and the traumatic affect it could have on family life. When I finally left for home Ron expressed his sincere thanks for my visit, eloquently letting me know how much it had meant to him. For the remainder of my time in the Royal Navy Ron and I were more than close friends. We had developed a true understanding of each other and the values, sometimes taken for granted, of friends and family.

Two years working out of the office in Lothian Road quickly passed. It was a busy office and conducting two interviews a day interspersed with school visits and attendance at careers fairs ensured I was shaping up well in my new profession. The truth was I felt I had really found my 'niche', I just loved what I was doing and in fact couldn't wait to get to work each day. Fortunately my enthusiasm and dedication to my new role didn't go unnoticed. Consequently one day, to my utter astonishment and disbelief, I was called into Lt. Harry Bell's office where he told me he was very impressed with what I had achieved since joining and as such was recommending that I should attend the Admiralty Interview Board with a view to being promoted to Lieutenant Royal Navy. Wow!! When I had joined the Navy back in 1962 as a Junior Electrical Mechanic

2nd Class, never in my wildest dreams did I ever think I would reach the dizzy heights of a commissioned Royal Naval Officer.

But of course being recommended for promotion and actually achieving it were two completely different matters. I was so overwhelmed that I decided to give it my very best, if only not to make a complete fool of myself at The Board. The two day ordeal within the Admiralty Buildings, situated at the entrance to The Mall in London, was indeed extremely testing. However, having told myself to try and act naturally by just being 'myself', I found the whole experience to be quite exhilarating. After the discussion and presentation phases the main event, responding to searching questions from The Board members, was the crucial element of the whole selection process. The Captain of the Four Man Board was none other than the relatively newly appointed Director of Naval Recruiting (DNR), Captain David Hart-Dyke Royal Navy, a fellow 'Falklands Veteran'.

Trying to stay calm under the watchful glare of Board members I managed to come up with reasonable replies to their testing questions. Eventually the most crucial aspect of my assessment arrived as Capt. Hart-Dyke looked me in the eyes and opened his grilling with "Good morning Chief, I see that you were a member of HMS ARGONAUT's ship's company during the Falklands Conflict?". Well aware that he had been in Command when HMS COVENTRY had been sunk by an overwhelming Argentinean air attack,

I replied "Yes Sir, I was". His next question really floored me "And what did you think of your Commanding Officer, Captain Kit Layman?". As I began my reply he and I seemed to merge into a sort of 'bubble'. Of course he was well aware of our perilous situation after being hit by two bombs, so listened intently as I described the fear and reservations held by the majority of the Ship's Company. This was followed by me saying that as matters progressed I truly understood the tactical position Captain Layman adopted. Explaining this involved me asking to borrow the pens and pencils of other Board Members, which I used to illustrate the layout of ships under constant attack in Bomb Alley. As I said, by this stage Capt. Hart-Dyke and myself were in a little world of our own. Finally I answered his question by stating that I sincerely believed that Capt. Layman was an extremely brave and outstanding Naval Officer who, although initially thought to be somewhat 'gung-ho' by the majority of his ship's company, rightly earned their respect and loyalty. An outstanding leader. He appeared satisfied with my reply, after which he carried on asking what might be considered more 'standard' questions.

Travelling back to Scotland I reflected on my performance over the past couple of days, concluding that I had given a reasonable account of myself. Not that I thought it was enough to get me promoted but it was an invaluable experience which could stand me in good stead for another attempt next year.

A few days later Lt. Harry Bell appeared to be genuinely delighted to inform me that I had impressed The Board and as such was to be promoted to Lieutenant Royal Navy. I would be informed of my new appointment in the months ahead. My bewilderment was all consuming. It almost goes without saying that my friends and colleagues in the office determined that celebratory drinks were the order of the day. What a week it had been.

A couple of months later I was promoted and appointed as the Careers Information Officer for an area covering a large proportion of Yorkshire working out of the RN & RM Careers Information Office in Hull. Apparently I was one of the youngest Careers Advisers ever to be promoted. Just shows you where enthusiasm, dedication and a love of the job can get you.

Paul had settled into his life studying for his engineering degree at the Royal Naval Engineering College, Manadon, Plymouth. He had recently passed his driving test and of course was 'champing at the bit' with regard to buying himself a car, an absolute necessity for a young aspiring Naval Officer. Home on leave for the weekend, he asked me to join him on a mission to acquire a suitably impressive motorised vehicle commensurable with his status.

Off we set with a somewhat restricted budget (around £500 as I recall). The numerous second hand car garages of Edinburgh and its suburbs were thought to be the best hunting ground. In my opinion the second garage we visited had a car for sale that was perfect for Paul. A six or seven year old blue Ford Anglia. Relatively low mileage, full year's M.O.T. and a fine reputation for reliability. Paul unfortunately was not as enthusiastic as me although he did concede that the vehicle had numerous merits.

"Let's look around a couple of more garages Dad. If nothing else catches my eye we'll come back here and I'll go for the Anglia".

Paul was obviously looking for something more sporty, surmising that the Anglia was more of a 'family car'. A few garages later the astute salesman we were dealing with sensed what Paul was looking for.

"We have something recently acquired that may be of interest to you sir" he mischievously announced. Taking us to an isolated corner of the garage he introduced us to a yellow, convertible, two-seater M.G. sports car. To my eyes it looked like a wreck just about ready for the scrap yard, but all Paul could visualise was himself and some beautiful young lady speeding along the country lanes of Devon with the wind blowing through their hair.

The salesman could sense he was onto a winner and proceeded to make outlandish promises with regard to refurbishing the heap of scrap we were all looking at. I persuaded Paul to come for a coffee in order to consider his options. Of course I was pushing for the Anglia but was onto a 'loser' from the beginning. Paul's mind was firmly made up. He wanted the M.G. despite his Father's many reservations.

I hate having to say "I told you so" and in fact managed to refrain from actually launching into a tirade of such sentiment a week or so later when yours truly went to collect Paul's new image maker. Paul had returned to Manadon and was looking for me to deliver his new acquisition to his college. I picked up the car from the rather smug looking salesman and set off for Fife. Approaching the pay booth of the Forth Road Bridge the engine cut out. I managed to 'bump' start it again, paid the toll and perhaps foolishly headed off over the bridge. Thankfully I made it over to Fife although the spluttering, jumpy performance of the vehicle was not overly inspiring.

A day or so later the engine completely gave up. The garage who sold the car, although I suspect expecting my call, displayed no concern or sympathy whatsoever, pointing out that the vehicle was sold 'as seen' and without any sort of warranty. The 'big end' of the engine had failed and after calling in many favours from local friends I found a well recommended car mechanic who agreed to undertake repairs at what was undoubtedly a reasonable cost, although almost as much as the price paid for this dream machine.

Repaired and looking good, the next part of the operation was to affect delivery. Julie, my daughter, who was seventeen years of age at the time, agreed to accompany me on the long journey south. On collecting the car from the saviour mechanic we were strongly advised not to exceed a speed of 60mph for the first 500 miles of travel. Apparently this caution was necessary as a 'running-in' process for the virtually new engine.

With overnight baggage crammed into the small restrictive boot we said farewell to a rather anxious and understandably worried Annette and headed off for the M74/M6, hopefully to be back home within three days. The journey was to involve an overnight stay at Annette's Aunt Winnie's in St. Helens, Lancashire. Thankfully the weather was fine which allowed us to drive with the hood down. Mind you our speed limitation was excruciating. Bumbling along in the inside lane this now classy looking speed machine seemed so out of place. Being passed by pensioners in reliable old Fords and Vauxhalls was humiliating, especially when such manoeuvres were supported by a smug honk on the horn and a sympathetic wave. Totally deflating.

Manadon was approximately 500 miles away from our home in Dunfermline, so after our self-controlled crawl south down the high speed motorways of Scotland and England we finally arrived at our destination. Paul was jubilant as he met us at the gates to his college. His joy was further enhanced when we told him that the car was now fully 'run-in' and he was at liberty to put it through its paces. He couldn't take possession quick enough, those country lanes and open roads of Dartmoor were beckoning.

After a hearty lunch and genuine expressions of gratitude, Julie and I bade farewell and headed off for Plymouth Railway Station and the long rail journey home. For years to come I couldn't understand the sort of in-bred reluctance I seemed to have developed with regard to offering my son advice when purchasing motorised vehicles.

The 21st of December 1988, a date etched in the memory of people throughout the world, certainly a day that will never be forgotten within the Armstrong family.

On that fateful day Pan Am Flight 103, bound from London to New York, was subject to a terrorist attack and at 7:00pm, whilst at a height of 31,000ft, exploded over the peaceful border town of Lockerbie. A total of 270 innocent people were killed. For an agonising period of time Annette and I feared our beloved son Paul could have been amongst the casualties. Paul, studying for his degree at the Royal Naval Engineering College (RNEC) Manadon, was due home on leave that day. How very much we were looking forward to having him home to share and enjoy a happy family Christmas. Expecting him to arrive around 7-8pm, our dreams were shattered as the news came through of the terrible disaster.

A couple of days before Paul had telephoned and told us that he hoped to get away on leave at around 11:00am. Over the years I had driven from Plymouth to Dunfermline many, many times and as a result was well aware of the timings involved. If he did indeed get away on schedule I was hopeful he could have been beyond Lockerbie when the tragedy occurred. But then again how many stops may he have made and for how long?

With Annette in a state of shock and glued to the updating news being broadcast on the television, I decided to phone RNEC Manadon to determine just when Paul had left the establishment. I managed to get in touch with the college, the various members of staff who I spoke to being completely understanding and sympathising with my concerns. Via various people who knew Paul, it was established that he did indeed leave the college at 11:00am, but was planning to return to his shared accommodation in Plymouth before heading north to Scotland. This of course made matters more worrying as the prospect of him being in the vicinity of Lockerbie at the crucial time was even more likely.

Annette and I spent an agonising evening glued to the television, which only served to increase our foreboding as details of the devastation, carnage and death toll involved were reported. The pictures being screened were horrific. With the phone by our side we were both willing it to ring so we could hear Paul telling us all was well and he would soon be home. 9 o'clock, 10 o'clock, midnight, 1&2 o'clock in the morning - silence. To say we were distraught is a complete understatement. Then at approximately 2:30am our prayers were answered as we heard the front door being opened, followed by a familiar loud cheery 'Hello'. It was Paul. The sense of relief we felt cannot be put into words and my eyes welled up as I watched Annette throw her arms around and embrace the precious son we thought we had lost.

Paul's story was dramatic to say the least. It transpired that he in fact did not leave Plymouth to travel north until around 1pm. This resulted in him approaching Lockerbie on the A74 at the same time Pan Am 103 exploded. He watched in horror as a section of the plane crashed down into a residential estate close to the carriageway he was travelling on. In fact he estimated he was no more than nine or ten cars down from vehicles that actually sustained damage.

Caught up in the ensuing mayhem, he was at a loss on how to proceed. With emergency services racing to the scene, the blue flashing lights and cacophony of sirens served to add to the surreal and horrific situation Paul found himself in. He spent the next three to four hours at the roadside talking to various traumatised drivers who, like himself, were at a loss of how to deal with this dreadful situation. Was there any way they could assist the emergency services? After a while a lorry driver came along and said it was possible volunteer blood donors would be called for. Sadly it was not long after that the news filtered through that blood was not required as the death toll was expected to be extremely high.

Eventually, with absolutely no prospect whatsoever of continuing north on the A74, he managed to cross over the central reservation with a view to heading south and hopefully finding a diversion route to take him to his destination in Fife. This he managed to do, initially having to avoid rescue vehicles travelling at speed on the wrong side of the motorway, understandable manoeuvres in the circumstances.

The family had a truly joyous Christmas. We just loved gathering together with George, Isobel, Rhona and her two girls Adele and Claire. Of course, it was made all the more meaningful due to the fact that we were all together, despite the dramatic events on Paul's journey home.

Having recently been promoted, I was scheduled to join the Royal Naval College Greenwich to undertake the Special Duties Officers Course, affectionately known as the 'Knives and Forks Course' - they were going to try and turn me into a gentleman! Paul was due to return to RNEC Manadon in early January and very kindly offered to give me a lift down to Greenwich, even though it involved a considerable detour for him.

Bidding a loving farewell to Annette and Julie, we began our journey in the late afternoon of the 8th of January 1989, another day that would prove to be unbelievably tragic. Having stopped off for refreshments, at around 9pm, we were well on our way, approaching London via the M1 motorway. The musical radio station we were listening to was suddenly interrupted by an important news flash. At 8:25pm a British Midland Boeing 737, en route from London Heathrow to Belfast, had developed engine trouble and crashed onto the embankment of the M1 motorway near Kegworth, Leicestershire, while attempting to make an emergency landing at East Midland Airport. Of the 126 passengers and crew on board 47 had been killed and 74 injured.

This couldn't be happening. We had just passed that very location less than half an hour ago. What were the odds of two major air disasters (Lockerbie and Kegworth) occurring so close to each other within such a short period of time? Furthermore, on a personal front, who would have ever imagined almost being caught up in both events. That was the case with Paul. Even today it's hard to believe he managed to avoid serious injury, not once but twice.

Being witness to such tragedies certainly brings home the fact that the airline industry, despite the abundance of safety measures they have in place, can involve dangerous incidents for staff to cope with. To his credit, for all Paul witnessed over that unforgettable Christmas Leave period, he was not deterred from following his dream. As such he is now a successful, experienced commercial airline pilot - a Captain no less!

The unique experience of passing through the Royal Naval College Greenwich was now behind me and I was brimming with self confidence and ready to face the world armed with a deeper understanding of the complex political world in which we lived. Additionally my social skills had been finely tuned and as such I was ready to wine, dine and generally converse with all members of society, whatever their background.

Taking up my new appointment as the Officer-in Charge of the RN & RM Careers Information Office Hull, with responsibility for an area covering the whole of Yorkshire, it wasn't long before I found myself attending my first Regional Conference as a Naval Officer. Presentations and discussions throughout the day were followed by a formal Naval Dinner in the evening. It was an event I was really up for and very much looking forward to. The Director of Naval Recruiting, Captain David Hart-Dyke Royal Navy, was the guest of honour with the Regional Commander acting as president. Dinner went off wonderfully well with fine food, engaging conversation and entertaining after dinner speeches. After completing the traditional Royal Toast to the Queen with the finest of port, all attendees retired to the lounge to continue consuming an array of further after dinner drinks.

I was in fine fettle, ready to listen to amusing anecdotes and general words of wisdom from my colleagues, whilst eager to keep them enthralled with my own vast array of stories and opinions.

As the evening progressed there was a noticeable increase in the background noise, with general conversation competing with bouts of hearty laughter and over expressed opinions. Standing in a small group with my colleagues, putting the world to rights, the drinks were flowing freely and I was feeling all was well with the world. Matters were about to take a somewhat more serious turn.

The Regional Commander joined our group, himself in fine spirits, and easily slipped into the general jovial atmosphere of the occasion. After a short time he turned to me asking "Enjoying the evening Phil?".
"Absolutely Sir, it's quite splendid" came my enthusiastic reply.
"A bit of impending news for you. Hot off the press so to speak. It is shortly to be announced that WRNS are to be allowed to serve at sea. What do you think of that then Phil? Positive progress don't you think?"
I was stunned. Of late there had been rumours circulating that 'WRNS at Sea' was being discussed within The Admiralty, but I had personally dismissed the speculation as absolute nonsense.
"I find the idea quite a frightening prospect," came my terse reply. "Just what type of ships are they planning to send our female colleagues to serve on?" I enquired.
Seeing that I was by no means enthusiastic with regard to his revelation the Commander ventured "Well my understanding is that they will be serving on support type vessels such as survey ships and maybe inshore patrol vessels."

Feeling myself getting a little agitated I responded “All well and good but before long we will no doubt find WRNS serving on front line frigates and destroyers.”
“Well I don’t think that’s on the cards at this stage, but if it was Phil would it be such a bad idea?”
With my relatively recent Falklands experience very much in mind and trying to control my tone I sternly replied “Let me give you a scenario to consider. A ship is at action stations, condition Zulu Alpha. Two ratings, a male and a female are closed up in a small compartment below the waterline. The ship takes a direct hit. Both ratings are blown off their feet. As things settle down the male rating, who is not seriously injured, takes stock. He notes that the clips on the compartment’s water-tight door have been blown off and consequently seawater is seeping into the compartment. At the same time he is horrified to see that his female shipmate is quite seriously injured. What should he do? The answer should be obvious as a result of basic naval damage control training. Firstly get the compartment door securely closed with a view to preserving the water-tight integrity of the ship and the safety of all the crew. Thereafter see to his injured colleague. If the above circumstances involved two male sailors I am absolutely sure correct procedures would be followed. However, I would suggest that with an injured female colleague in the compartment priorities could be jeopardised, especially if the two concerned were in any sort of relationship. It’s just bloody human nature”, I concluded.

"I think you may be slightly over exaggerating Phil", came his measured reply.
"Far from it," I responded in a loud and agitated voice. The fact was I felt strongly that the historic decision about to be made was a monumental mistake.

Whilst trying to maintain my respect for the Commander's rank I found it difficult to stop myself from pressing on with my firmly held views in an ever increasing loud and forceful voice. At this point my naval career was salvaged by a good friend, Lieutenant Dave Jones B.E.M. Royal Marines, who was chatting in a nearby group. He was of course distracted by my angry tone, as I'm sure were many of the Officers in my vicinity, and weighing up the situation came to my aid. Approaching, Dave politely said "Sorry to interrupt Phil but there is someone over by the bar I would like you to meet." Thereafter he casually but firmly led me away from what could have developed into a disaster during an otherwise magnificent evening. After calming down I thanked Dave for his intervention, bought him a drink and reverted back to my calm, amusing and engaging persona. Mind you it was a really close call!

One of the main reasons for my decision to apply for promotion was the fact that my son was now a young Naval Officer and I was still a 'Rating', albeit a vastly experienced Chief Petty Officer with many years' service to my name. I was getting a little fed up of Paul calling out "How about making a cup of tea

Chief" when we were both home on leave. My plan worked and as a Lieutenant I now held a higher rank than my 'Sprog' of a son. No more demands for refreshments, I had finally risen above the status of Midshipman's Steward.

An annual event took place at RNEC Manadon which was one of the highlights of the social calendar. It was called 'Fathers' Night' (affectionately more commonly known as 'Lads' and Dads' Night') and involved a formal mess dinner with a high ranking Naval Officer invited to attend as guest of honour. Invited along by Paul we were both very much looking forward to a night of naval formality, engrossing conversation and intriguing company.

The Fathers in attendance inevitably came from very mixed, interesting and varied backgrounds, ranging from farmers, bus drivers, company chairmen, Naval Admirals and countless other positions. Let the evening commence - I was genuinely looking forward to what promised to be an unforgettable evening, and unforgettable it certainly turned out to be.

Pre-dinner drinks loosened up my tongue and put me in a fine frame of mind. I was itching for engaging conversation over what I was confident would be a splendid meal. Entering the main dining hall was breathtaking. A vast array of tables were formally set, for the literally hundreds of guests, with the finest tableware, crystal glasses, impressive candelabras and fresh bouquets of flowers. Members of the Royal Marines Band Service playing soft music in a discreet corner of the hall served to wonderfully complete the truly magnificent atmosphere that had been created. Believe me no one does it better than the Royal Navy.

Paul was sat opposite me with his friends and fellow students, plus their fathers of course, stretching out either side of us. Paul, perhaps understandably, had made all his colleagues aware of my varied and colourful naval background, which of course meant that I had a certain reputation to maintain. In fact my reputation appeared to be enhancing as the evening progressed and stories started flowing off my tongue with elegant wit and perhaps naive openness. I certainly seemed to be holding the genuine interest and respect of my fellow guests and hosts. However, my world, and that of Paul's, nearly came crashing down around our heads during the Royal Toast. After dinner all tables are completely cleared and port decanters placed at various 'stations'. All attendees have a port glass placed in front of them ready to receive the decanter as it is passed along the table. On receiving the decanter an adequate amount of port should be poured into the glass before passing it on to the next guest. The port is definitely not to be touched until the Royal Toast is announced. Naval Messes have the privilege of being allowed to remain seated during the Royal Toast, a tradition dating back to the days of wooden sailing ships with low deck heads.

The decanter arrived at my placement as I was relating one of my more colourful sea stories. I held everyone's attention. Casually lifting the decanter, I started pouring the port into my glass. More interested in getting my story out than the task at hand (i.e. pouring my port), I was not really concentrating on what I was doing. Looking across at Paul I noticed his eyes were wide open and there was a look of both horror and impending disaster on his face. To his left and right there were looks of amusement and disbelief. 'What on earth is the problem?' I thought. Looking down, still pouring, I could see that my glass was rapidly filling and about to overflow. In the event of an overflow my self-esteem and reputation would have been tarnished forever. I would have been the talk and laughing stock of Manadon. As it was, without interrupting the flow of my engaging tale, I calmly placed the decanter back down on the table and passed it on. My glass of port was defying the laws of physics as I noted the deep red liquid literally hanging over the rim of my glass. The slightest touch and it was sure to cascade down onto the polished mahogany table. Paul and surrounding Naval Officers stared in disbelief not knowing whether to laugh or applaud. I smoothly and calmly finished my story before giving thought on how to retrieve this perilous situation.

When the toast was announced perhaps I could carefully pick up the glass and with hopefully a steady hand guide it to my mouth? This option was fraught with danger, with a calamitous outcome being a distinct possibility. As I was considering my course of action the President's gavel banged and I heard the inevitable words "Gentlemen, The Queen". Without a moment's hesitation I reached over, grabbed my glass and in a swift, gliding motion directed it to my mouth. Not a drop of port found its way to the table. The relief on Paul's face was a look I'll never forget. The surrounding guests also had looks of disbelief and I'm sure felt inclined to break into applause. I'd gotten away with it. My reputation as an experienced, interesting jolly old sailor was intact, and indeed enhanced. From there on in the evening could only get better, an indeed it did.

The guest speaker turned out to be a much respected senior Naval Officer, namely Captain Hunter Royal Navy. As he started speaking I immediately recognised him as the Senior Engineering Officer I served with as a Petty Officer on HMS NUBIAN back in 1974. At the time I was Mess President and he was the mess's supervising officer. Indeed it was Lt.Cdr Hunter, as he was at the time, who oversaw the unfortunate incident when the mess fell foul of an audit, with over 25 barrels of beer going missing. His speech was electrifying, informative and totally captivating. He deservedly received a rapturous ovation on completion.

After the speeches all assembled company were invited to retire to the bar to indulge in further interesting and amusing anecdotes.

As I was making my way down the crowded passageway to the bar with Paul and his now admiring friends we passed Captain Hunter.
"Good evening sir," I ventured.
"My god it's Petty Officer Armstrong," he surprisingly replied. "How the devil are you? And many congratulations on your promotion".
Of all the many people vying for his attention, inclusive of very Senior Naval Officers (Commodores, Admirals etc.) he chose me to retire to the bar with. What a time we had reminiscing about our time in the Caribbean. Laughter and tales of days gone by could be heard by all. I couldn't have scripted a better evening. It almost certainly cemented forever my reputation as the "Old Man of The Sea".

My cousin Sue (Chrysula) was visiting from Australia and a Armstrong family reunion was organised by my other cousin Pauline, in her family home in Liverpool. It was only a three hour or so journey over from Hull so I was more than happy to accept my invitation to take a trip down memory lane.

There were so many of my aunts, uncles and cousins happily enjoying themselves, reminiscing over days gone by, both happy and sad. I was particularly pleased to meet up with Sue again, we really had been quite close during her stay with me and my Dad at 12 Mansell Road.

As the evening progressed and the drinks flowed freely I found myself chatting away in a corner with my uncle Harold. Harold was the youngest of my Father's brothers and I had always found him to be a kind and pleasant man. He worked as a conductor for the Crossville Bus Company and led what many people might consider a somewhat non-eventful, routine, married family life.

I was aware that Harold had been a prisoner-of-war of the Japanese in WW2, but had no detailed insight into his experiences. He of course was aware that I had served in the Falklands Campaign and was eager to hear of my experiences. He appeared genuinely intrigued as I relayed my stories, sometimes amusing but mostly alarming, laced with fear and the unremitting strain of warfare. Of course this opened up the opportunity for me to ask of his war experiences. What he relayed stopped me in my tracks and has had a positive effect on my outlook of life ever since.

Harold was taken prisoner by the Japanese whilst fighting in the jungles of Sumatra. After enduring stays in a number of atrocious camps throughout the Far East he eventually ended up in a hell-hole of a camp just outside the city of Nagasaki in Japan. Hearing of this I couldn't help myself asking "Surely you weren't there when the Americans dropped their second Atomic Bomb?"
"Yes I was Phil" came his somewhat nonchalant and casual reply.
I was dumbfounded as he went on to explain that he was in fact hospitalised when the bomb dropped and although being subject to

the appalling aftershock and blinding flashes of light, the explosion did not destroy the building in which the hospital was housed.

Going on to describe his eventual liberation and journey home was heart warming. After many disappointments relating to American flights out of Japan being cancelled at the last moment, he eventually found himself aboard a liner bound for Vancouver, Canada on the far side of the Pacific Ocean. Of course he and his colleagues were well treated but had to be careful and resist the temptation to gorge on the splendid and nutritious food that was made available to them, after years of surviving on minimal portions of slops. Harold was just over six stone in weight when he was liberated.

From Vancouver they boarded a train bound for the east coast of Canada. At every stop they were greeted by flag waving crowds, bands playing patriotic tunes and a genuinely thankful and admiring nation. A further voyage across the Atlantic Ocean with the homeland port of Southampton beckoning made up the final leg of their eventful journey back to the U.K.

By this time the family back home in Liverpool had been made aware of his planned arrival date. A homecoming party had been arranged and all the family gathered at Lime Street Station eagerly awaiting the arrival of the train from Southampton. Disappointment followed when an announcement was made that due to signalling and track problems the train journey would terminate at Edge Hill, the station before Lime Street. A quick plan was hatched and agreed. All the family would return home whilst my Dad would jump in a taxi and head off to collect Harold.

Harold raised a smile as he told me about stepping down from the train, glancing down the platform and recognising my Father immediately. This was in sharp contrast to his elder brother's experience, who almost walked past Harold, not recognising the virtual emancipated body before him. Even after his protective journey home Harold still only weighed in at just over 7,1/2 stone. Still with a glint in his eye, Harold told of going for a pint in a local pub before heading off to the awaiting family reception. Still I suppose he was hardly going to get a telling off from his overjoyed mother.

I was spellbound as Harold casually told me of his war experiences. He was a man who had been part of such a unique, horrific and significant part of history. And yet he was so unassuming, accepting all he had endured as part of his duty. How could you resume a normal way of life after such horrific and inhumane treatment? But, like so many of his generation, regain normality he certainly did. He was such a kind, generous individual. A devoted family man without an ounce of bitterness within him. What a hero and what a fine example to us all.

What lay behind my adoption was always lingering at the back of my mind. I had managed to extract some information from my Father but always felt I was not being told the full story. Now that I had a family of my own I felt a certain responsibility to trace the origins of my natural parents. Did they suffer from any hereditary illnesses that I needed to be aware of? Of course I also openly admit that there was a strong element of personal curiosity. Consequently I visited the 'Adoption' Department of Liverpool Council, housed in an impressive grand building just off Dale Street. On making enquiries relating to the circumstances surrounding my adoption I was somewhat disappointed and more than annoyed at the response I received.

Directed to a rather supercilious female administrator, I briefly outlined my story and asked if I could be provided with some factual information relating to my early past. The uncalled for response I received from the pompous lady in front of me was along the lines of, "Undoubtedly we have your file, in fact it could well be over there in that filing cabinet in the corner. Unfortunately, present legislation does not allow me to divulge your records". Which indeed, I found out later on, was true. However, it was her lack of compassion and totally indifferent manner that left me so angry and confused.

A year or so later matters took a turn for the better. Laws were passed entitling people such as myself to be given details of their adoption. Time to visit Liverpool once again.

Annette and I made arrangements and set off for my home town to spend the week expressly looking into my past.

The next visit to the Adoption Department in downtown Liverpool was a totally different and encouraging experience to that of my previous visit. The administrator who dealt with me on this occasion was completely at the other end of the scale in comparison to her rather dour colleague, who was thankfully conspicuous by her absence. This pleasant, charming and completely understanding young lady could not have been more helpful. This resulted in me leaving the building armed with a variety of relevant information, not least my natural mother's name and her address at the time of her giving me up at the age of six months. It was also confirmed that my adoption was arranged and actioned via the Salvation Army, who apparently operated from a premises in the Sefton Park district of Liverpool. Before leaving I promised to revisit my new found friend in the council office to let her know how we got along with our search.

The following days involved visiting various districts of Liverpool, looking through local telephone directories and talking once more to my various relations throughout the city. Finally we arrived outside an address in the Dovecot district of Liverpool. I was over 90 per cent certain that we were at the right place. So was Annette, especially when her eyes fell on a young gentleman working away in the front garden. "Phil that could be your brother. He looks so much like you." I sat in the car feeling an unbelievable range of emotions. We'd done it. All I had to do now was walk down the pathway, knock on the front door and introduce myself. So why wasn't I getting out of the car? The truth was my mind was working overtime. What if my natural Mother was inside and more importantly what if she hadn't told her family about me? I could be an absolute secret that could possibly wreak devastation and disbelief on a stabilised, happy family. I was also extremely content and fulfilled with my life. Did I really want to introduce an unknown factor and possibly destabilise my wonderful and contented life? After ten minutes or so of deep, calculating thought I slipped the car into gear and drove off.

As promised the next day we returned to the adoption centre where I relayed the past day's events to my friendly, understanding administrator. I included my reasoning behind not taking those final few steps up to the front door of my Mother's house. My new found friend empathised and responded, "For what it's worth Phil I think you made the correct decision. And who knows what you may learn in the years ahead". Her wise words were appreciated and indeed in the years to come some quite outstanding revelations would come to light.

Friday lunchtime and time to leave the office and head off north and home for the weekend. I was not driving up on this occasion as I was taking advantage of using one of my monthly 'separation warrants' and travelling by train, for free! After a quick pint in Hull railway station, I boarded the train for York, a relatively short journey of just under an hour. Arriving at York I discovered I had some time to wait before my next train to Edinburgh arrived. No prizes for guessing where I headed off to await the arrival of my express train north - absolutely correct, the bar.

After consuming a tasty sandwich washed down by a couple of extremely welcoming pints of lager, I boarded my train which was precisely on time. Finding a seat at the window, I settled down contemplating whether to stroll off to the bar for one final refreshment. Just then a well dressed gentleman sat down opposite me and offered a cheery "Hello". Before long that last drink was forgotten as we engaged in light hearted conversation. I really was in a chatty mood and before too long was just about outlining my full life story to my new found friend. In response he was just as open regarding his background. It turned out that in fact he was a Major in the Salvation Army who had recently completed a theology course at the Salvation Army's college in London.

There was no stopping me now as I went on to relay the stories surrounding my adoption and the steps I had taken to find my birth mother, not omitting the fact that I was placed for adoption via the one and only Salvation Army. He was totally intrigued as I told him of the week Annette and I had spent trying to track

down my mother in Liverpool. He was even more impressed when I gave him my reasons for not making that final move to meet the lady who actually brought me into this world. Understandingly and with great compassion, he asked if I still felt the need to meet my mother, whilst fully appreciating my reluctance to perhaps cause devastating upset.
"It will always torment me in a frustrating sort of way." I replied.

He then went on to offer what appeared to me to be the perfect solution to my dilemma. Apparently there is a department in the Salvation Army's Main Headquarters that deals solely with adoption issues. The Major went on to explain that they could contact my birth mother to let her know that I wished to meet her. If she was willing a mutually convenient meeting place could be arranged and a date set for us to get together. Absolutely no one else needed to be aware of these arrangements. After this initial meeting it was entirely up to us both to agree to meet up again or to go off on our separate ways. Of course the almost irresistible draw for me was the fact that I could at long last be told who my natural father actually was. However, there was a potential sticking point to this almost unbelievable development and that was the fact that if my mother declined the opportunity for us to meet then that was the matter closed.

We eventually arrived in Edinburgh after what I felt was an incredibly short period of time. It's amazing how engaging conversation can appear to distort the passing hours. I gave the Major my business card highlighting the address of the RN & RM Careers Information Office in Hull as we said our farewells, with him promising to forward me the documentation required to instigate the search for my mother.

True to his word the relevant application form from the Salvation Army arrived in the mail the following week. I read through the paper work in front of me many times, confident that the opportunity presented to me could undoubtedly provide the answers to all the questions that had been frustrating me over so many years. Of course all the doubts and concerns I had felt in relation to contacting my birth mother resurfaced. Consequently that Salvation Army application form is still in my old briefcase, uncompleted, approximately twenty five years after I received it.

I was sat at my desk one fateful morning catching up on unavoidable paperwork when a young sailor on loan to the office informed me that a gentleman was in the reception area requesting to speak with the Officer in Charge. He had mentioned that it was something to do with the Humber Bridge. Intrigued and needing a break from the mound of letters and folders before me I told our temporary member of staff to escort our visitor through. A whirlwind entered my office. A larger than life character approached my desk with his hand outstretched introducing himself as "Darvill, Alan Darvill, ex Royal Marine". Smartly dressed and proudly sporting a Royal Marines tie, he went on to explain the reason for his visit. "Every day I pass the Humber Road Bridge on my way to work, which has inspired me to want to abseil down from the top of one of its towers." He enthusiastically went on "However, I realise that if I approach the bridge authorities with regard to my plan they would undoubtedly but politely tell me to 'go away'. Then it dawned upon me that they may co-operate if approached by the Royal Marines, especially if it was done to raise funds for the fast approaching annual Children-in-Need appeal. Can you help?". I was somewhat taken aback by his pure energy and presence. After a more general chat over a cup of coffee it emerged that Mr Darvill was the Managing Director of a large haulage company (I.B.C.). I gave him an assurance that I would make a few enquiries and get back to him. After presenting me with his business card he left in the same whirlwind he had arrived in. What a character.

Not long after he departed I was left thinking 'Was that man for real or just a crank out for a bit of mischief?'. With a view to verifying his status I called the number on the business card in front of me. On asking to speak to the Managing Director, Mr Darvill, I was informed that he was not available as he had left for a meeting at the Royal Navy & Royal Marines Careers Office. 'Well there you go' I thought, it appeared the man was indeed who he said he was.

Subsequent calls to the Royal Marines at their base in Poole, Dorset established that they would be willing to provide a team of abseilers as long as agreement/permission could be obtained from the Bridge Authorities. A couple of days later I contacted Mr Darvill with the positive news. He was absolutely delighted, even when I added the small caveat that the event could not take place unless I was included in the team. "Have you ever abseiled before?" he enquired. "No I haven't," I replied. "But I consider that a minor detail." After a hearty laugh he accepted my terms. And so began yet another challenging, magnificent and unmissable experience in my life.

Before long Mr Darvill had arranged some training sessions at the local fire station. As an ex-Royal Marine Alan was familiar with abseiling but I suspected it was many years since he had actually participated in this adrenalin inducing activity. In truth he was quite a good instructor, which is just as well as I was not long in realising that you need to have confidence in a man who is encouraging you to lean out into open space 60ft or so high up in a fire station training tower. After overcoming initial nerves and building faith in the equipment (ropes, harnesses etc.) I found abseiling to be quite exhilarating. A week or so later Alan managed to arrange for us to carry out further advanced training from the actual Humber Bridge. It was decided to video tape the session to allow us to study our efforts later on. I found myself harnessed up and leaning out into space about 120ft above the shoreline where the bridge met the River Humber. Alan, whilst video recording, asked if I was ok and did I have any concerns before making this epic leap of faith. Looking directly into the camera I asked "does my hair look ok?" At this point I felt a large boot kick my feet off the precarious ledge I was standing on, which sent me hurtling off into space to the receding sound of hearty laughter.

During my next weekend leave at home I mentioned my involvement in abseiling from the Humber Bridge for Children in Need. Annette looked at me with a withering stare that seemed to imply "silly old fool, when are you ever going to grow up?". Still at this point there was no strong objection to my latest venture.

The following week back at my office in Hull I gave my son Paul a call. At the time he was still studying for his engineering degree at the Royal Naval Engineering College, Manadon. After enquiring as to how his studies were progressing I dropped in that I was going to be abseiling from the top of the Humber Bridge with a team of Royal Marines. "Dad", he says, "that is absolutely great, but of course your mission now is to get me on the team". What a good idea thinks I. Father and son, two Royal Navy Officers involved in such a daring activity to raise money for such a good cause. "Leave it with me and I'll see what I can do" was my response. Within a couple of days

I had called Paul back with instructions to find his way up to Humberside for training. He was chuffed to pieces.

Of course this excellent piece of organisation didn't go down too well with Mrs Armstrong. Back home again I judged Annette to be in a reasonable state of mind as I said to her "Remember dear I was telling you of my abseiling plans?" She replied in somewhat bored fashion "Yes", as I continued "Well Paul is also going to be part of the event." Annette's response took me back as she cried "What, surely you haven't got our son involved in one of your hair-brained adventures?". Such concern was quite touching. However, after calming down she of course gave us both her blessing.

The big day arrived and true to form Alan had ensured the event was adequately covered by the media. Annette had travelled down to the glamorous city of Hull with her sister Rhona. The weather was fine and I was truly looking forward to the challenges of the day.

All the participating team members, inclusive of Paul and myself, gathered in a field close to the Humber Bridge. We were fully briefed on the planned proceedings for the day, after which we were issued with our specialist items of kit (harnesses, karabiners, leather gloves etc.). On reflection 'issued' was hardly the correct term to use. What actually happened was that we were told that the equipment we needed was in the back of a close by military vehicle and that we should go over and help ourselves. Paul was a little slow off the mark when it came to collecting these essential items of kit which resulted in him claiming two well worn left hand gloves with holes forming in a number of the finger tips. With a mischievous grin on his face he then seriously suggests "How about swapping Dad?".

"Not on your life" says I "You should have been quicker getting over to the lorry". At this point he threateningly declared, in a light hearted manner, "I'll tell Mum". What was I to do, I had no choice but to hand over my almost new pair of protective leather gloves to my smiling son.

The planned format for the event was that the team of eight Royal Marines, three Royal Navy and one ex-Royal Marine (Alan) would embark in a RN Wessex Helicopter to be flown to a position approximately 50ft above the main north tower of the bridge. In turn we would all abseil out onto the main upper cross section of the tower. From there it was a 400ft drop to the road where local police vehicles would be waiting to transport us to the centre of the bridge span. Another 150ft drop to the river below then awaited, where an inflatable fast patrol craft would be stationed to take us to the shore line.

As a final training session we all embarked on the helicopter which had landed nearby in our field. Up it went and maintained a hover at approximately 50ft. Leaning back and falling into space from the helo's starboard door was exhilarating and really fired me up for what was to come. Disappointingly the weather gave cause for plans to be amended. The wind was deemed to be too high for the helo to safely remain on station above the north tower. As a compromise only one extremely experienced Royal Marine Sergeant would make the descent as a more than suitable representative of the team.

Having arrived at the top of the tower by a lift in the maintenance shaft, we took up our positions on the cross section. Four ropes had been pre-positioned and Paul and I were to descend next to each other. Attaching ourselves to a rope each we clambered over the guard rail and awaited the order to drop. What a height it seemed as I peered at the minute people making up the watching crowd below. My heart was racing and I felt so very much alive. The order came and after giving a quick thumbs up to Paul I launched myself off into the void. Far from descending at a rapid rate, a few feet down I almost came to a halt. This of course was the result of the weight of the lengthy section of dangling rope acting as a brake. The only way to overcome this effect was to lift the rope which then allowed downward movement. What a weight that rope was and as a feeble matelot I feared that I wouldn't have the strength to induce motion. My fear of humiliation came to the rescue as I endeavoured to live up to my name of 'Armstrong' and as I repeatedly heaved at the rope my rate of descent gradually began to increase until I was flying down at great speed. By this time I felt the only liquid in my body was adrenalin.

The bridge had been closed to the general public for the occasion and as we hit the road we unclipped and were escorted to waiting police patrol cars. Beaming from ear to ear Paul and I sat back in the back seat of one of the vehicles as we sped off to the centre of the bridge, blue lights flashing and alarm sounding for effect. Over the barrier once more, we clipped on before making the final drop to the waiting craft in the river below. Once on board we took off at high speed to the waiting, cheering crowd on the shoreline.

The whole exercise was a resounding success and really gave me a personal lift, perhaps I wasn't destined to be desk bound for the remainder of my naval career. Annette and Rhona appeared to be suitably proud as we posed for numerous photographs taken by friends, relatives and the local press. That evening all the team and guests enjoyed a grand meal and lively evening at a nearby upmarket hotel. The perfect end to what had been the most memorable of days. To top it all we were later informed that our gallant efforts had raised just over £25,000 for that year's Children in Need Appeal.

The success of the Humber Bridge exercise only spurred on Alan to think of and plan even greater events. Without a doubt he was totally revelling in his resurrected and new found involvement with the Royal Marines. Alan and I were becoming quite close friends and I was really developing a clear insight into this extraordinary individual. I could certainly see why he was such a successful businessman. He was so driven and motivated. Once he had set himself a goal he wouldn't allow anything to stand in the way of his aims. Magnificent to witness.

It therefore should have come as no surprise when one day he said to me "Phil, how would you feel if I organised and attempt, to be undertaken by a team of Royal Marines, to break the world record for abseiling down from one of the world's tallest buildings?"
"What building did you have in mind?" says I.
"The Empire State Building, New York," came his nonchalant reply. Quite taken aback but trying to appear composed, I commented "Well Alan I'm sure I could get The Corps to support your idea, however, as before the powers that be will undoubtedly want the exercise to be of zero cost to The Service. And of course this venture will not get off the ground unless there is a guarantee of my personal participation."
"Totally accepted Phil and it goes without saying that your involvement is assured."
Music to my ears.

Alan went into action, which unfortunately involved a number of setbacks. The Empire State Building management team, when approached, did say they would consider the merits of the proposal put to them. Within a week their negative response was received, pointing out that the building did not need the publicity involved or their perceived disruption to the inhabitants of their iconic building.

Not deterred, Alan concentrated his efforts on New York's Twin Towers, which the world knows were the tragic target of the most outrageous terrorist atrocity approximately ten years later. Initially success was to the fore as tentative approval for the venture was given. Sadly a week or so later this approval was withdrawn after an episode involving a sky diving adventurer, without authority or approval, hurling himself from the top of one of the towers in a pretty fearful, dramatic and publicity seeking gimmick. It appeared that although the Twin Towers management team fully accepted that our venture would be a well organised military operation they didn't want to build up a reputation of allowing their premises to be used for outlandish stunts.

Where to now? Alan turned north and set his sights on the vibrant city of Toronto, Canada. The CN Tower is an impressive looking structure which dominates and enhances the city's skyline. Tall enough to accommodate an attempt on an abseil world record, it was as if it had been awaiting the arrival of a Royal Marine/Navy team. Alan went to work and before long he had secured approval to organise the record attempt. One condition laid down that was absolutely not negotiable was that the venture had to include the involvement of the Canadian Rescue Services. Apparently they held a record for abseiling, or repelling as they called it, from the restaurant/observation deck of the tower. It was our intention to go one better and descend from the sky platform which was an observation area situated even higher up the tower at a height of 1430ft. On reflection I can totally appreciate their stance, why should they sanction a foreign team to come and take their record?

By this time I had been re-appointed from the RN & RM Careers Office, Hull to the North Region Headquarters in Rosyth. It was with mixed emotions that I departed Hull. I had found it a rewarding two years in which I had made many friends but of course I was now back home and close to my family. The fact that I was now north of the border didn't mean that I was any less involved with Alan, in fact it very much encouraged me to stay in contact. True to form Alan didn't leave a stone unturned as he went about meticulously planning our little adventure. Amongst his considerations was getting the backing of world renowned sponsors, not least British Airways who magically agreed to fund all our transport costs to Canada.

It was somewhat strange being back in Regional Careers Headquarters (North) after a break of two rewarding and unforgettable years in Humberside. I knew virtually all the staff and now I was preparing to take over from my old boss, Lt Harry Bell MBE RN. An interesting handover awaited.

All the offices in the Region had to be visited from Inverness in the north to Liverpool in the south. Undoubtedly the visit that deeply affected me was the one to Belfast. The memory of the loss of Alan Shields was still raw and certainly brought home the reality and brutality of a conflict within the borders of the United Kingdom. As a result of the escalating threat to the RN&RM Careers Staff stationed in Belfast the necessary decision was made to move the Careers Office from its public building in the city centre to the relative security of Palace Barracks.

Landing at Belfast airport following a Loganair flight from Edinburgh, we were picked up by one of the office staff and driven off to the barracks a thirty minutes or so journey away. Harry Bell and I were welcomed into the office and quickly supplied with coffee and biscuits. It was interesting to hear how the office operated whilst having to adapt to the unique circumstances of the troubled region.

As lunchtime approached we excused ourselves and made our way over to the Officers Mess to be allocated a cabin in which to deposit our overnight bags. After a light lunch we returned to the office. It wasn't long before Colour Sergeant John McFail Royal Marines asked if I would like a tour of the local area. It came as a bit of a surprise, but with encouragement from all I accepted his unexpected offer of what I was sure would be something of a 'Magical Mystery Tour'.

Off we went straight into the centre of Belfast where all the main buildings were pointed out. We also took in Stormont, the seat of the Northern Irish Parliament, which is a really impressive building set within magnificent grounds. Before long we were driving through renowned trouble spots harbouring the core of known and suspected IRA terrorists. The areas were symbolised with huge anti-British murals painted on the gable ends of terraced street houses and kerb stones painted in Irish tricolours - orange, white and green. To be honest I was beginning to feel a little uncomfortable by this stage.

After an hour or so we found ourselves in Carrickfergus, which is where John lived with his family. "Fancy a pint?" says John. In normal circumstances I wouldn't have hesitated in giving an enthusiastic reply of "Certainly, let's go". However, now I wasn't so sure, especially as some tricoloured kerb stones still seemed close by. My apprehension increased as just before we entered the pub John lent over and whispered in my ear "Don't speak too loudly Phil, after all you do have an English accent and we don't want to raise suspicions". Was he having me on?

The beer was good but it was the first time I had engaged in conversations utilising a series of grunts! I couldn't believe this was

John's, a Northern Irishman by birth, local. All the guys in the pub were friendly enough, but I couldn't shake off the feeling of vulnerability.

Back at Palace Barracks I thanked John for making me aware of the environment they had to operate in. It was certainly a world away from the relative safety of Hull and the majority of offices on mainland U.K.

With a vast array of sponsors in place, Alan, quite correctly, deemed that a 'recce' (reconnaissance) was needed as a matter of priority. A four man team was to visit Canada to assess and plan the mission. Alan was naturally part of the team plus Capt Rob Metcalfe RM who had been appointed commander of the venture. A Warrant Officer Mountain Leader Royal Marines was to act as the technical expert and bringing up the rear was yours truly. What an honour.

In April 1992 we departed, courtesy of British Airways, to Toronto. We were booked into a rather plush city centre hotel (one of our sponsors) for the four day visit. The first day after our arrival we made our way to the tower. It was truly impressive and after being given an initial detailed guided tour of the structure I was so grateful that fortune had resulted in me being part of this adventurous project. Looking out from our planned point of descent on the sky deck, the reality and technical difficulties involved in our record attempt really hit home. That being said I never had any doubt that we would be successful. After all I was now part of an extremely professional and elite team of Royal Marine Commandos.

An immediate problem was very apparent. A few hundred feet or so below the sky deck the restaurant observation area protruded out from the main tower. The challenge was to create some form of structure that would allow the abseilers to descend over this enormous obstacle without actually touching any part of the building. Apparently to gain world record recognition the descent had to be made without making physical contact with any part of the tower.

Hours of discussion with our Canadian colleagues finally resulted in an inspired solution. A large framework secured on the roof area of the restaurant would be constructed so as to reach out and overhang our challenging obstacle. The plan being that as abseilers approached from the sky deck they would enter the iron framed area where they would carefully unhook themselves and transfer to the rope that would take them down the remaining 1200ft or so to the ground. This fiendishly clever manoeuvre would of course have to be completed without touching any part of the tower and without any physical assistance from the support team.

A final social evening with our new Canadian friends and the recce was complete. The visit was deemed to be a resounding success and

I personally realised the value of such an important exercise. The information gained was invaluable and would form the essential basis to perfect preparations prior to the full team's departure, scheduled for the last week in June.

Preparations back in the U.K. went off really well with the full team of twelve RM & RN personnel getting together at Royal Marines POOLE in Dorset for briefings and advanced abseil training. We were all more than delighted when informed that negotiations to have us supplied with the latest Special Forces (SAS/SBS) abseiling equipment had been successful. A day or so later this top notch gear arrived and we all set about familiarising ourselves with the techniques involved in getting the best out of our new and most treasured acquisitions.

There was one small hiccup on the personal front prior to the team's departure to Canada. At the time my new boss in Regional Careers Headquarters (North) was himself a Royal Marine, Lieutenant Colonel Sandy Lade. When I requested to be released for two weeks for operational reasons my mentor did not respond in the positive manner I was expecting. I went on to enthusiastically outline the reason for the deployment, with hopefully a successful outcome resulting in the Royal Marines/Royal Navy being holders of a new world record. What excellent publicity for The Service. He did concede that it was a worthwhile venture and indeed expressed admiration for the personnel involved in the actual abseil. What he was having difficulty with was my involvement, which he perceived to be nothing more than a supportive/PR sort of role. When I explained that I was an actual member of the abseiling team he was quite taken aback, after all I was just a 'silly sailor'. To his credit he was extremely supportive and encouraging after our little discussion, agreeing that I did not have to take two weeks of my annual leave to partake in the forthcoming venture, which I had threatened to do, and that he completely agreed that my absence should come under the heading of 'operational requirements'.

Having departed London Heathrow on a British Airways jet there was a tangible air of excitement amongst the team as we crossed the Atlantic bound for Toronto. The scheduled date for the record attempt was 1st July 1992, which just happened to be Canada's Independence Day. In fact 1992 was a special year as it was the 125th anniversary of Canadian Independence. Being a national holiday a large crowd could be expected to witness our record attempt. We arrived on 27th June which after settling in gave us three days for pre-event training. It couldn't come quick enough for me.

The CN Tower dominates the skyline of downtown Toronto and arriving onsite for our first day of training the structure appeared no less impressive and challenging than it did on our 'Recce' week. The centre of the tower from the extremely high up revolving restaurant deck down to ground level is hollow. Access points lead onto relatively narrow railed off platforms that extend around the full circumference of the central support walls. They are strategically placed approximately every 100ft or so from the base to just below the restaurant floor.

Day one of training and after the full guided tour we assembled inside the Tower on the highest access platform, which provided a nerve jangling 1100ft drop down to ground level. I was truly impressed with my Royal Marines colleagues as they set about securing ropes in a central position over our drop into oblivion.

The first down were the more experienced Marines in our company. Finally my turn arrived. After checking my harness and additional equipment for the umpteenth time, I was passed a rope onto which I connected my carabineer. Climbing over the rail I steadied myself for the swing out into the centre of the Tower. Psyching myself up to let go of that rail took some doing but there was no way I was going to let myself down in the presence of my professional friends. Off I stepped, falling into the abyss. My free fall, which seemed to go on forever but in fact was only a matter of feet, was arrested as the all important attendants held me until I was manoeuvred into the central position. I found out later that I was in fact allowed to fall for a greater distance than my fellow abseilers, something to do with building up the adventurous spirit of a mere matelot! "Ok Phil, when you are ready off you go." The weight of 1100ft of rope doesn't lend itself to a swift departure, in fact building up to descending momentum was always a concern of mine as it took a lot of strength to lift the rope to allow the descent to commence. Off I went with my speed gradually increasing. I'm sure the speed was directly proportional to the amount of adrenalin coursing through my veins.

The enterprising attendants at the bottom of the ropes had brought a portable radio/tape recorder with them and were playing some stirring music, in my case I recall it was a rocking Beatles number, which echoed around the huge chamber of the Central Tower. Hurtling down at a controlled rate, the music gradually increasing in volume was such an uplifting and awesome experience and one I will certainly never forget.

My sister-in-law Rhona and her husband Iain were also by chance in Toronto visiting their good friends Myra and Tom. We'd met up during my training period but, somewhat sensibly for me, I refrained from socialising at that point as I was sure we'd more than make up for it later.

The big day arrived and the weather could not have been kinder to us. The wind was negligible, which was crucial. Anything much more than a strong breeze and uncomfortable decisions would have had to be made on whether it was safe to go ahead with the record attempt. An absolute bonus was the fact that the sky was a cloudless magnificent blue.

It being a national holiday, combined with the excellent weather, resulted in an overwhelming turnout. The gathering crowd were in full holiday mode and the local media were out in force.

Up on the sky deck at 1,400ft, my Canadian colleague and I hooked up to our respective ropes prior to our descent. Check, check and check again was my philosophy of the day. We were to be the fourth pair down. Climbing out of one of the window sections where the framed glass had been removed for the occasion, we fell out on to the support of our ropes and applied our 'brakes'. Composing ourselves, we looked up for a quick photo shoot before setting off to the transfer section at the top of the restaurant/observation platform. I was so impressed with the special forces equipment our team had been loaned and my confidence grew as we hurtled down.

The transfer over the protruding roof section of the restaurant was tricky. It had to be completed without the abseilers actually touching the structure of the tower and involved members of our team assisting in unhooking us from the downrope attached to the skydeck and connecting us to the one overhanging the revolving restaurant. Exercise complete and we were at liberty to complete our mission.

As I steadily moved down I couldn't believe my eyes. There sat at a table and waving madly were Rhona and Iain. Grinning broadly, I waved back as I noticed cameras clicking from all angles.

Mainly for diplomatic reasons it had been agreed that each pair should hit the ground together. As we set off on the final and longest section of our descent I was in a special place and on such a high (who needs drugs!). Clear blue sky above me, panoramic views of Toronto all around and a magical feeling of almost being in flight. I was picking up speed, this equipment really was superb, and getting carried away, it wasn't long before I was leaving my Canadian colleague and his somewhat antiquated kit behind. Thankfully common sense kicked in as I realised I was nearing the ground. I slowed myself down allowing my partner to catch up. We hit the ground together to rapturous applause and cheering. What a moment. It was sensational. I was now a world record holder.

It was to be a further five days before we were scheduled to fly home, and believe me that time wasn't wasted. Our new Canadian friends ensured we were never at a loose end, organising games of golf, caving expeditions and the not to be missed trip to the relatively close by Niagara Falls. All this was interspersed with nightly 'Up Homers' invites to attend well provisioned, both in terms of quality food and copious amounts of drink, Barbeques.

World record holders.
Phil A. 2nd left, back row.

The inevitable departure date arrived and we found ourselves sat around in the departure lounge of Toronto airport. It was an overnight flight and with us all being a little worse for wear I didn't envisage any of us experiencing any difficulty in falling into a sound sleep. With our luggage already checked through we were all sat around in a rather dishevelled bunch.

From out of nowhere one of the lads came up with what turned out to be an inspired question. Addressing Capt. Rob McCalf he casually remarked "Hey Boss what do you think are the chances of us all getting an 'upgrade'? Worth a try don't you think?" To my surprise

Rob arose from his chair and sauntered on over to the check-in desk. Mustering all his worldly charm I watched as he engaged the attractive looking young attendant lady in his persuasive art of conversation. After what seemed to be a longer time than needed he came walking back with a rather solemn look on his face. He was greeted with "No joy then Boss", to which he measuredly responded "Sorry lads couldn't get us an upgrade to business class", which was met with expected disappointment, "But they can fit us all into first class". What a player, this Royal Marine Officer training must be top notch!

Rejuvenated, we all found ourselves being offered glasses of top quality champagne as we took our seats in the grandeur of the British Airways first class cabin. No chance of sleep now, this experience had to be savoured and fully appreciated. As we touched down in Heathrow the overwhelming need for sleep had magically disappeared. To a man we all felt our mission had been well and truly accomplished.

We were World Record Holders, officially acknowledged as such by the Guinness Book of Records. We had achieved the ultimate in the world of abseiling - not so! Mr Darvill, never one to just sit back and savour his achievements, already had further plans forming in his overactive brain. There was a world abseiling endurance record, at that time held by the Parachute Regiment, that was just hanging there as an open invitation to be broken, especially by the ever competitive men of the Royal Marines.

Alan set about his mission with his usual energy and enthusiasm, and in a matter of weeks had all arrangements agreed and in place. The event was to take place in Plymouth and involved a 200ft descent from the roof of the Civic Centre in the central area of the city. A team of ten abseilers, which I had the honour of being a member of, was to continually make the 200ft drop over an eight hour period. Quite an undertaking.

A robust, secure steel structure (as in Toronto) was to be constructed and firmly affixed to the roof of the building. It was to have an approximately 6-8ft arm protruding out from the roof from which the abseiling rope was to be attached. The idea/plan was that each member of the team would line up, the first man would attach and abseil the 200ft to the pavement below. When he had detached the next man on the roof would slide down as number one made his way back up to the roof to repeat his initial drop. This routine was to continue all day.

A slightly irritating/concerning aspect of this routine was the fact that the route back to the roof involved entering the building's lift and ascending to the top floor of offices. Unfortunately this floor did not provide direct access to the roof area, which could only be reached by ascending a six section flight of stairs. As the exercise progressed and a degree of tiredness bordering on exhaustion began to creep in I could foresee those steps presenting quite a challenge.

On the 22nd of May 1993 the challenge began and as I attached my carabiner in readiness for the first descent I felt remarkably calm. Mind you I was a seasoned abseiler now and a world record holder to boot! The descents proved to be reasonably straight forward and the return to the roof area also fairly straight forward. Having said that I did manage to incur a nasty cut to my right arm by swinging into the wall of the building on one of my not so controlled descents. However, as expected as the hours passed those stairs covering the final stage of the ascent did indeed act as a major obstacle, especially for me, after all I wasn't a super fit, all rooting tooting, green beret awarded Royal Marine. No I was just a plain sailor who some thought had lost what little common sense he had. What I did have though was an absolute determination not to give up, even if I ended up crawling on my hands and knees, which towards the end I don't think I was very far away from.

The eight hour time limit finally arrived, as did the welcoming news that we had succeeded in beating the Parachute Regiment's standing record by a considerable amount. The number of abseils being 1382 which resulted in a total distance covered of 72.42km.(45 miles). Now I was a double world record holder, albeit a totally exhausted one. After the mandatory photograph session we all retired for a well earned drink, after which I could hardly walk. Not through consuming copious amounts of alcohol, but due to the fact that

I couldn't get my, admittedly meagre, muscles to work anymore. Still it was all so worthwhile and my sense of achievement was all consuming.

So, what next? - Alan, wherefore art thou!!!

True to form Mr Alan Darvill did indeed come up with yet another monumentous abseil challenge - the world's longest abseil. After a lengthy period of research Alan established that the standing world record could be broken by abseiling down the lift shaft of a fully operational potash mine situated just south-east of the village of Boulby on the north east coast of the North York Moors. Thereafter, the senior management of the mine were contacted and, after being subject to the outstanding negotiating skills of Mr. Darvill, agreed to allow our team to make the record attempt.

I was once again privileged to be present when the 'Recce' took place, which proved to be quite an eye opener with regard to what lay ahead. A senior representative gave us a tour around all the various operational areas of the mine. One particular aspect of the underground environment that really took me by surprise was the really high temperatures, which of course were due to the fact that we were so far below ground. The lift shaft identified as the most suitable for our record attempt was over three thousand feet deep. It was still very much an operational shaft and as such numerous temporary modifications would have to be made to accommodate our equipment and provide an acceptable level of safety.

Initially a complete side of the square shaped lift was removed, revealing an approximate six foot space stretching out to the wall of the circular lift shaft. The space revealed was the area in which the descent would be made. A strong metal platform was hastily constructed and affixed several feet below the open face of the lift. The prime purpose of this structure was to support the huge bundle of specially commissioned abseiling rope.

The big day arrived (yet another one!) - 2nd November 1993. The number of actual abseils involved in this record attempt unfortunately had to be restricted to four. This of course was understandable when taking into account the expected, relatively lengthy period of time to complete a single drop. To be followed by the re-setting up of equipment and the re-organising of supporting personnel prior to the next attempt. And of course Boulby was a fully operational, commercial mine, that could ill afford delays in production.

Once again I felt truly honoured to be selected as one of the four to take part - one of the perks of being a close friend of our intrepid organiser, Mr Darvill. I was to be the fourth man down (I didn't mind bringing up the rear!). The time waiting to be 'hooked-up' seemed never ending, mind you descending 3,627ft was never going to be a two minute job. To add to the occasion my new boss, Lt.Col. Paddy George OBE RM was in attendance. I think he found it quite intriguing that his new 2I/C, a mere sailor, was involving himself in such a physically challenging event.

Hooked up, thumbs up and off I went. The descent did seem never ending, but if I'm honest it was somewhat boring in comparison to say the CN Tower experience. Being enclosed in a lift shaft didn't induce the same adrenalin pumping excitement of plummeting down from the sky over the magnificent city of Toronto.

Job done, and another record broken. Could I really be a Triple World Record Holder? Who said I might find life boring in the Naval Careers Service. It goes without saying that the evening celebrations were memorable, leaving me to ponder how my life might have panned out if I'd opted to be a Royal Marine!

The influence of the Royal Marines during my time in the Careers Service was undoubtedly a major factor in making it more than just another office job. Lt. Col. Paddy George and I spent a lot of time travelling around the Region together and as two 'Falklands Veterans' we ended up good friends, with me really appreciating the advice and guidance he gave me over the years. This friendship was strengthened by the fact that we spent so much time together up in the Highlands of Scotland. Paddy joined the Region a week before an organised adventure training week walking The West Highland Way was scheduled. He was extremely keen to come along, which

I was all for. What better way to get to know your new boss. Thereafter, he took part in all the regularly organised adventure training exercises tackling the most challenging Munros in Scotland.

Another Royal Marine who really did end up an extremely close friend was Warrant Officer, come Major, Alec Maxwell. Alec relieved me when I retired from The Service, by which time we had climbed numerous mountains together. Alec was a well known and respected ex Corps Regimental Sergeant Major and a specialist 'Mountain Leader' to boot. It was an honour to go mountaineering with him and with his background I always felt safe and reassured whatever perilous situation we found ourselves in, and believe there were quite a few. Funnily enough Alec was in attendance when I was part of the R.M. Team that broke the world abseil endurance record from the Civic Centre Building in Plymouth. You've got to be part of something quite challenging if you want to impress these 'Bootnecks'!

Another Regional Adventure Training Week was planned, one that was to be far more challenging than anything that had taken place before. It involved spending a week on the Isle of Skye attempting to reach the summits of some of the most outstanding and precarious mountains in Scotland, not least the infamous 'In-Pinn'.

Unfortunately I was scheduled to attend a conference down south on the actual week of the expedition. However, all was not lost as

I was honoured to be invited to join the illustrious 'Recce Team' scheduled to plan out various routes the week before the actual event. It turned out to be a truly great time facing the extraordinary challenges presented by the mountains of Skye. The Cuillin Ridge proved to be formidable involving the requirement to abseil down a number of steep overhanging rock faces. I just loved it.

Sad to say, the weather was not always on our side and on the day we tackled the 'In-Pinn' on the summit of Sgurr Dearg there were high winds with heavy downpours of rain. Alec, who as always was leader of the group, assessed the conditions and came to the conclusion that there were far too many risks involved in attempting to scale and abseil down our final goal. Of course although extremely disappointing it was undoubtedly the right decision. A wonderful week with, for me, an unfortunate sting in the tail.

The following week, in gloriously sunny and ideal weather conditions, the planned adventure training week took place. All the fortunate friends and colleagues of mine had a memorable time which included successfully, under the professional guidance of Alec, scaling the 'In-Pinn'. I was of course extremely happy for them all, but at the same time gutted that I was now the only member of the Region's outdoor adventurers who could not claim to have conquered one of the extreme and hardest challenges in Scottish mountaineering.

With Alec now being a close personal friend of mine I made him promise to take me back to Skye to fulfil my dreams. I'm still waiting. Don't forget you owe me Alec!

The 11th of October 2000, my final day as a member of the Royal Navy. What better way to say farewell than a good old 'Tot-Time'. Annette and I were living in Bannerman Avenue, Inverkeithing at the time and diplomatically she agreed to go and visit a local friend. Six of my closest friends, including Alec, were invited to attend at 1145 when 'Up Spirits' would be piped. I had prepared well. A table was draped with a white ensign, a tot measure was on hand as was a 'rum fanny' and an adequate amount of glasses. Over the previous years I had managed to obtain quite a large amount of original naval rum and of course had saved more than an adequate measure for this special occasion.

The plan was to hold the Tot-Time, following all old naval traditions, sippers for the Bosun (me!) and the appointed 'Ticker Offerer' etc. All went extremely well and the assembled company were in fine form as we took off for the local Hillend Tavern for a follow up 'dinner time sesh'. Prior to our departure it had been agreed that as a one-off repeat dits would be allowed. Oh dear how those lanterns were swinging in the Hillend Tavern lounge!

It was an unforgettable and, for me, emotional day. Still time to move on. Let's see what the Police have to offer this time around.

FULL CIRCLE

At the tender age of 55 years I had resigned myself to the fact that retirement beckoned. My planning for this so called 'relaxing' period of my life did not extend much beyond the golf course and the Scottish Highlands. However, it was not to be. At this crucial time in my life my son Paul had resigned from the Royal Navy and was now a serving Officer with Lothian and Borders Police. He was stationed in Livingston as part of 'F' Division and noted one day that a support staff management job was being advertised. "I reckon this job has your name written all over it Dad," says he. I was not so sure myself, but half-heartedly completed an application form. Somewhat surprisingly I was invited for an interview. At this stage I decided to give it a real go and threw myself wholeheartedly into the all important preparations. I was reasonably satisfied at how the interview board, inclusive of a twenty minute presentation, went. That being said, I didn't allow myself to get too optimistic, after all I was the oldest of the candidates (all 95 of them!) which included a number of graduates and a serving Senior Police Officer.

It appears I must have impressed the board with stories of my naval background, varied sense of humour and ideas of how to transform the Scottish Police Service, which resulted in them, in all their infinite wisdom, offering me the position.

Once again serving with my son in a disciplined, uniformed organisation prompted him to compose a poem summarising my life up to that time. He had it framed and presented it to me on my final day in the Royal Navy. I think it to be an astute, amusing and accurate reflection of my colourful past. These are his words:

The Old Man Of The Sea

Through the back streets of Anfield ran a sixteen-year-old lad
Pursued by a copper for the crimes that he had
Committed in youth, he'd soon be doing time
But he gave them the slip on the Grey Funnel Line

The Penelope and Corunna too
He saw half the world as part of their crew
Until one fateful night in a ballroom in Fife
A wee Scots lass changed his whole life

A family man now with vows to keep
And a balance to strike between home and the deep

Loving husband and father of two
With a life at sea and a duty to do

So when the call came he went without hesitation
To a place where actions speak louder than chest decorations
And from the mist of battle, frightening and frantic
A quiet hero returned from the cold South Atlantic

Then the lad found a talent for finding folk willing
To sign on the line and take the Queen's shilling
So Constitute and Appoint said Elizabeth R
A Queen's Commission, the lad had come far

Therefore rest easy Blighty, your sea lanes are safe
With a new generation of sailors in place
Enticed by scouse tales of adventure on ships?
No, they promised to join if he'd stop telling them dits!

Now thirty eight years 'fore the mast has he
But what of the future for this old man of the sea
Perhaps he'll sail forever with the shore at his wake
Perhaps he's immortal like Nelson and Blake

Ah, but the law's long arm has crossed four decades
And caught up with its man in its own kind of way
No more life of adventure on the high seas for Phil
He's finally submitted and joined the Old Bill!

I think there is maybe a 'Poet' gene within the Armstrong Clan!

To be absolutely honest my time serving with Lothian & Borders Police, all of eleven years, did not really measure up to my expectations. The perceived similarities of the Royal Navy and Police organisations I was convinced would ensure a rewarding experience in the final years of my working life did not really materialise. This was made evident by the fact that sadly I developed an awful state of mind that revolved around me experiencing feelings of 'Yippee it's Friday' and 'Damn it's Monday'. Not something that had ever troubled me before, indeed, Falklands aside, I cannot recall many mornings of dreading to go to work - The Navy was a way of life. That being said, there were of course many aspects of my new working life that were both fascinating and fulfilling, leaving me with a detailed insight into the many and complex aspects of society.

The Business Manager Craig Hunter, who headed up the examining board for my new post, turned out to be an excellent boss and indeed a good and valued friend. We still meet up for the occasional game of golf and lunches over in Edinburgh, coming on nine years since my retirement. I learned a lot from Craig who was both demanding but fair when it came to dealing with the varied range of responsibilities associated with the post.

Operating as Craig's deputy, I acted as Line Manager (now there's a phrase I had not been familiar with in my naval past!) for a fair proportion of the civilian support staff. Also I was the Senior Administration Officer, Health and Safety Manager and Property Manager. In addition I found myself sitting on interview boards for applicants wishing to join our happy working team. Of course I wasn't allowed to take up this hallowed position until I had completed the all important Lothian & Borders 'Interview Technique' course. Needless to say I found this to be an almost uncomfortable experience as without a doubt, having just spent the past fifteen years in the field of interviewing and promotion boards, I was considerably more qualified than the instructors in front of me. Suppressing my urges to criticise some of the procedures being taught, I managed to hold my tongue and emerged with yet another interviewing course under my belt.

One aspect of my new challenging position that I truly welcomed was the fact that I was not forever deskbound, far from it. I regularly had to visit the police stations throughout the division, all eight of them.

Primarily these visits revolved around building upkeep and maintenance matters, but also involved speaking to the civilian support staff and dealing with any issues giving them cause for concern. In addition regular meetings were held with my fellow Admin Officers from the other five divisions that made up Lothian & Borders Police, which took me to Edinburgh city centre, the southern border with England and many more scenic areas throughout eastern Scotland.

On joining the Police Service one area I had difficulties coming to terms with was the fact that the majority of the civilian support staff were rigid with regard to what they considered to be their responsibilities. They were not prepared to be flexible if approached to help out when unforeseen problems arose. There were of course welcomed exceptions, whom I truly appreciated. These problematic situations were always difficult to resolve, even when I resorted to engaging in my most diplomatic and persuasive line of approach. In the background there was always the smug and quietly threatening option of getting 'Union' members involved.

What did amaze me a few years later was the complete change of staff attitude when the Scottish Police Service was being subject to a large scale thorough evaluation and the word 'redundancies' came to the fore. Co-operation was now the word of the day. All of a sudden when called upon to help out in areas not specific to their department, long awaited responses along the lines of "No problem Phil, just leave it with me" fell upon my disbelieving ears.

For all its highs and lows my time with Lothian & Borders Police was a period I do not regret and indeed consider myself fortunate to have experienced. As I approached my sixty fifth birthday and compulsory retirement I was asked if I would stay on for a further six months, which I agreed to, after all the salary I was receiving coupled with my generous naval pension was allowing Annette and I to enjoy a comfortable lifestyle.

My final departure from working life was a mixture of relief and apprehension. How would I deal with retirement? I certainly had a varied range of challenging plans in mind to keep myself occupied. My friends and colleagues within the Police Service really rose to the occasion with regard to my final farewell. Quite a number of social gatherings were arranged, which were extremely well attended. Gift presentations and associated speeches took me by surprise and were special in that they confirmed that over the years I had apparently gained the respect of many Senior Police Officers, normal 'Beat Cops' and, despite the occasional confrontation, the majority of civilian Support Staff.
Time to move on - active retirement here I come!

THE TWIGHLIGHT YEARS

As life progresses the invincibility of youth is gradually replaced by the realisation of mortality. The following thoughts, somewhat mixed and confused, I found scribbled on a scrap piece of paper. I recall composing these somewhat out of character words sometime in my mid sixties:

SELF PITY

Paying the price of years gone by
Adventurous, invincible, not afraid to die
Much to do and challenges to meet
Buoyant and happy with the world at your feet

Now vitality gone, tired and weak
Nothing to say, frightened to speak
Where is the man with life in his heart
Always up front, wanting to take part

The tiredness has come as the years role along
Time to ease back now, you are not so young

But life is still rich and full of wonder
Stick with it now, don't let yourself go under
You have it all, much more than most
So don't complain and give up the ghost

> Accept that the pattern of life is and will always be
> A source of wonder for all to see
> Feel blessed to be part of the human race
> Always keeping in mind that self pity is out of place

Strangely enough those thoughts which just manifested in my head, although initially depressing, served to spur me on with the determination to grasp and enjoy every day that came along.

Well past feeling sorry for myself, I eagerly looked forward to making sure that my optimistic plans for the years ahead were fulfilled. Travel with my good lady Annette was to be a priority, and although we had already travelled extensively to exotic places around the world there was so much more we longed to see. Next, which also had a travel element to it, was to crack on with climbing all the Munroe's throughout Scotland. Alec Maxwell and I were now very close friends and I couldn't think of anyone more suitable to keeping me right with regard to avoiding reckless behaviour when tackling remote peaks in the wilderness of the Scottish Highlands. Perhaps he could even improve my map reading and navigational skills? Now there's a challenge Alec! Finally, I had thoughts of writing my memoirs. Could I really get this done? I felt I had a good story to tell, but did I have the literacy skills to give a true and entertaining reflection of the interesting life I had so far led?

The wonder of the Scottish Highlands.

Paul, Philippa and the children had moved once again. This time not too far away from their riverside home in Helmsley. They had taken up residence in the small but quaint village of Oulston, set in rural North Yorkshire, approximately 20 miles outside York. Their new abode was a quite grand and formidable building in the form of 'Oulston Hall' no less. My son and his wife appeared to have taken on the personas of 'Lord and Lady of the Manor'.

Whilst Annette and I were staying one weekend an instance occurred that once again opened up the subject of my adoption, which in turn led to quite astounding revelations. After a most enjoyable but slightly exhausting day with the children, Paul, Philippa, Annette and myself settled down for what turned out to be a sumptuous evening meal and a most gratifying glass or three of quality wine. As the evening wore on our tongues were suitably loosened as we jovially moved on from one enlightening subject to another. By the time the malt whisky hit the table I was in full flow, relating all my old sea stories (once again!) before somehow lurching into the mysteries surrounding my adoption. Of course I had a captive audience, not least because of the potential hereditary health issues that could affect both my own children and precious grandchildren. After relaying all the known details I had of my birth mother and the steps I had taken to trace her, we all succumbed to a pleasant sort of weariness, said our goodnights and retired to bed after an extremely pleasant evening.

Coming downstairs in the morning to eagerly anticipated bacon rolls I was feeling quite contented with life and looking forward to another day with the children. Paul entered the kitchen looking a little apprehensive. "Good morning Dad, take it you enjoyed last night?".
"I certainly did," came my honest reply.
It was then that Paul came out with "Dad I hope you don't mind and I can well understand if you get a little annoyed". Oh dear what's coming here I thought.
"But after we went to bed last night Philippa was so intrigued with regard to your adoption recollections that she went 'online' and

carried out some searches into your background."
"I don't mind at all," came my honest reply, "How did she get on?".
"Really quite well Dad. Do you want to take a seat before we call Mum down".
What came next absolutely stunned me. Computer savvy Philippa had managed to come up with all my birth mother's personal details via a 'Births, Deaths and Marriages' website. She placed in front of me her laptop which displayed a copy/record of the children born to Eileen Vivyan, my mother. It appears I was the eldest of her five children. I had two sisters and two brothers.

I was the first born to my mother Eileen in 1946. In 1949 she gave birth to a girl, Dorothy. In the early 'fifties' another girl, Joanne and two boys Alan and David arrived. This information opened many doors, not least as access to the relatively new digital age phenomenon known as 'Facebook'. Dorothy we discovered had an active and well subscribed 'Facebook page' containing an array of photographs, details of friends and relations and general background history. Looking at photographs of my siblings was a strange experience, with the inevitable comparison in facial looks leaving all my immediate family somewhat bewildered.

As before the temptation to rush off and make contact with my birth mother and step-brothers and sisters was difficult to control.

I now had details such as addresses, telephone numbers and Facebook to allow me finally to get in touch with my 'other family'. This led to me finding out various facts. Apparently my brother Alan died at a relatively early age. My sister Joanne married and moved from Merseyside to live in southern/central England. Dorothy still lives in Liverpool and brother David has a home in St Helens. Also I managed to find out that my Mother was now living with my brother David.

So once again the question is 'Have I made contact?' The answer, which at times I find hard to believe myself, is no. Which of course leads to yet another question. Do I have a duty to my offspring to investigate if there are any hereditary medical issues relating to my 'Vivyan' line? To their credit not one of my family has ever put me under any sort of pressure to follow that route.

Unfortunately and sadly I am now aware that my Mother Eileen has died, having lived into her late eighties. Has that closed the door to me ever finding out who my natural Father was, or did she divulge her heartbreaking past to any of her children? Whatever, 'Mum' please rest peacefully and be assured that your son Michael has had the most fulfilling and rewarding of lives. Perhaps we'll meet again someday.

Number one grandson Andrew was always destined to follow a career involving adventure and physical challenges, as opposed to an academic based working life. Not that he is more than an above average intelligent young man, but the thought of an office based job is far from appealing to him. Now who does that sound like, surely not his old grandad! Perhaps the Armed Services might benefit from his presence? Royal Marines here he comes.

His doting grandmother Annette was not impressed when Andrew announced he was going to apply to join the Royal Marines. I of course could fully understand her concerns. It was a troubled world we lived in at the time with the British Armed Forces deeply involved in high casualty conflicts in both Iraq and Afghanistan. As opposed to when I joined up, when 'going to war' was not part of my thought process, there was a certain inevitability that the present day recruits would find themselves amongst the action in one of the world's numerous conflict zones. Although well aware of what may lie ahead it did not deter Andrew in the slightest and as with everything he commits to he threw his heart and soul into being awarded the coveted Royal Marine 'Green Beret'. Of course he was successful in his application to join up and subject himself to the longest and most gruelling infantry training in the world.

Let's talk about motivation. Andrew was born to be a Royal Marine, and believe me the Royal Marines are lucky to have him. Always excelling in sports and physical pursuits, he deservedly played rugby at international level, representing Scotland at the relatively early age of 17 years. His preparation with regard to selection to join the Royal Marines was nothing short of inspiring.

His introduction to commando training was as brutal and challenging as it always has been for past generations of 'Bootnecks'. The first major hurdle was to pass the week eight 'fitness test', an arduous and almost body breaking experience designed to really sort the men from the boys. If anyone was prepared for this challenge it was Andrew. He had done everything he could to ensure he would progress to the next phase of training. Even then he thought of one final factor. The evening before, Andrew whose family are Christian but not obsessively religious, faced this major milestone, he left the comfort of his mates in the mess and quietly made his way to the camp chapel to pray for strength and support in his efforts to succeed - that's motivation.

Almost a year after joining, Andrew was to pass out of training having been awarded his hard-earned green beret. He also managed to achieve his goal as one of the few 'Originals'. These are recruits who manage to progress through training without having been back-classed through injury or not meeting the standards required at various stages of the physical and mentally demanding course.

A large family contingent gathered to make the trip down to the Commando Training Centre Royal Marines (CTCRM) in Lympstone, Devon. The ceremonial passing out parade, during which Green Berets are officially awarded, was to be conducted by Her Royal Highness Princess Anne. We all departed for C.T.C.R.M. excited at the prospect of seeing Andrew's passing out parade, none more so than his mum, Julie. As a small memento of the occasion I had compiled a poem which was framed along with a small photograph of Andrew proudly wearing his hard earned green beret. The poem is as follows:

A COMMANDO

A baby born to give us pride and joy
A spirited character, a precious boy
Full of adventure, courage and a strength unseen
He was destined to be one of the best - a Royal Marine

Climbing trees, back-flipping off walls
Respectfully not hearing his Mother's calls
The signs were there right from the start
Always giving of his best, straight from the heart

A true Scot is he, tall and proud
Knowing what's needed and never too loud
Whatever the goal one thing is for sure
He'll give one hundred percent and a little bit more

In a troubled world danger lurks in many a land
Threatening our beliefs and requiring a stand

Our country is grateful for we have the best you could meet
The men with a green beret, the highly trained elite

A wondrous life awaits you, grasp it and know without doubt
Your comrades in arms will always be there to help you out
Be bold and commit as you always do
Take care my boy - God bless you Andrew

Seventy-two years old and still enjoying life to the full. As I lay in bed one night with my seventy third birthday fast approaching, I found myself reflecting on all the experiences I had been blessed with throughout my eventful time on earth. Inevitably the Falklands War entered my thought process. How many years had passed since that life changing event? It then dawned on me that in 1982 I was thirty-six years old, the exact time period as had passed since the end of the conflict to my present age. I clearly remember the days of going to early morning action stations wondering if I would still be alive at the end of the day. It's as if I have been given two lives. My gratitude and wonder is immense. To whoever determines the progress of human life I say thank you, I wouldn't have changed any part of mine, both of them!

An aspect of life I've always been saddened about is the almost unavoidable ways in which we lose touch with close friends. In my case

it has never been purposely planned or arranged, but it has happened.
Dave Watson - Close childhood friend, adventurer and partner in crime.
Graham Major - We experienced so much together, from the horrors of war to the joy of returning home enriched with a great appreciation of the value of family, friends and life in general.
Alan Darvill - Truly one of life's characters who brought adventure back into my life. We hailed from somewhat different backgrounds, but developed a respect for each other that ensured we both enjoyed some memorable moments together.
Then of course there were all the many friends and colleagues I got to know so very well whilst serving in the Naval Careers Service and Lothian and Borders Police. As I've said losing touch was never intentional, however, circumstances change and close family will always be the priority. Thank you sincerely for the good times and never to be forgotten memories. You have all enriched my life.

As I sign off, reflecting on all the amazing aspects of my life, I glow with pride at the early achievements of the wonderful grandchildren this book is dedicated to: Andrew, a quietly confident adventurous young man (so similar to my good self!) with an astute business head on his shoulders. Mikey, a qualified Doctor at the relatively young age of twenty-three years. Robbie, a third year medical student. William a second year medical student. John, an aspiring medical student.

Stephen, a potential professor (watch this space!), and the delightful Katie, a young lady who doesn't know how to stop smiling. Her personality will take her far - I love you all.

Well, that's it then. A life I couldn't have scripted any better. Travel and adventure. Meeting the absolute love of my life at such an early age. Being blessed with two wonderful children and seven exceptional grandchildren. Thank you all for making every day special.

Cheerio for now guys. Have a wonderful life - maybe see you on the other side!!

TA-RA !

In summary:

HAVE YOU?

Experienced the wonder of being raised in Liverpool during the forties, fifties and sixties.

Stood less than 2ft away from John Lennon as he sung 'Twist & Shout'.

Met the absolute love of your life at the tender age of 19 years.

Stood on the summit of a Scottish mountain and gazed at the splendour and wonder of the Highlands.

Been diagnosed with cancer.

Been awarded 'Prize Money' as a member of the crew of a Royal Navy ship.

Over a sustained period of time woke up every morning praying that you would still be alive at the end of the day.

Appeared in the Guinness Book of Records as a triple world record holder.

Had to leave your Father in the certainty that you would never see him alive again.

Felt a sense of overwhelming pride as you watched both your Son and Daughter graduate.

Played a round of golf at The Old Course St. Andrews.

Attended Prime Minister's Question Time.

Rounded Cape Horn in storm conditions.

Received a Commission from Her Majesty the Queen.

Faced the prospect of your wife losing her sight.

Been to war.

Dined with the Prime Minister of the United Kingdom.

Had a 'hole-in-one' during a game of golf.

Dived in close proximity to a great white shark.

Written a book and had it published.

ANNEX

POEMS & THOUGHTS

1. OUR SON

In the heart of Scotland one cold and wintry morn
A wondrous event took place - our precious son was born
Over forty years from boy to man
He has moulded and developed the Armstrong Clan

With a Father away and a Mother on her own
He never gave cause for concern if the truth be known
Always a joy and never downcast
He looked to the future, never blaming the past
He excelled in school without a Father's support
Both academically and in the field of sport

There have been times of worry, sorrow and bereavement
But life is reality inclusive of pride and achievement
Now on reflection and considering it all
We could not have been more blessed with someone so unique as our son Paul

2. LIFE (written on a train from Kings Cross 18 Dec 77)

Life is strange in many ways
It's full meaning never unfurled even at the end of our days
One day of joy another of sorrow
Never knowing what's coming tomorrow

I can laugh, cry and experience pain
Fall flat on my back and pick myself up again
And through it all that pestering doubt
Of how it began and just what's it about

I try to reason and ask myself why
But the answer evades me the harder I try
Where it began and when will it end?
On what source of wonder does my race depend?

If I could imagine infinity I could confidently say
That the mystery could be solved in some far off day
But is the human brain able to cope?
Do we need the answers or can we survive on hope?

3. Letter to my wife: (written on the dining room table with Annette in the same room, 11 Sep 78)

My dearest, darling, adorable Annette,

At this very moment in time I feel an overwhelming need to somehow express my infinite love for you. If I were merely to say from my position at this table that "I love you" you would surely pass it off as one of my boring daily duties which you have come to expect, without really stopping to think of all the true feeling behind that simple statement. Through circumstance life has cast me in the role of a 'silly sailor', but if by some magical means I could be transformed into a writer or poet I feel my love for you could inspire me to give the world some of the greatest and immortal works of literature as of yet has not been seen. Still I am immeasurably happy and content in my role as a doting husband, it's just that I know my love deserves a better form of expression than I will ever be able to give it. Enough my darling, I will now casually stroll over to offer you my simple "I love you" and feel that wonderful glow as I tenderly kiss your cheek.

Yours for all time

Phil

4. Reflection on the Falklands: (written 05 Mar 83)

I'm quite content and happy once more
To be back home with all I adore
The year gone by has made me see
The true value of my wife and family

To leave home not knowing what's ahead
To dwell on coming events with an awful dread

Please lord let me return
To the precious people for whom I will always yearn

Dark days of death and pain
Comrades lost, never to see home again
The cause was right, the price was high
To live in freedom young men must die

5. Reality: (date - late 70's, early 80's) - Unfinished.

Reality is war, sudden death and unthinkable injury. We go through life in the safe cocoon of suburbia reading and hearing news reports of distant and not so distant conflicts. With sincere feelings over social gatherings we express opinions without ever giving deep and serious thought to the reality of fellow human beings acting to destroy each other. Life is a wonderful gift, but we should never lose touch with reality if only to keep in perspective that .... (and so my wife calls me to bed!) - Frustration!!!

6. A passing thought: (1970/80's)

Who is sane, who is well?
Who lives in peace and who lives in hell?
Who has it right and who has it wrong?
On which side of the divide do any of us belong?

7. To My Wife: (Our apartment, Naples, November 1977)

My wife is sad and I try in vain
To bring the smile back to her face again

I love her so, me it hurts as well
Just how much words will never tell

And yet I know in days ahead to be
Our joy will be there for all the world to see

It's ten years now that we have been together
And I pray so that the Lord will make it forever

He's given us so much, and more
With Paul and Julie who we both adore

Life is sad in many ways
But I know now happiness is going to fill the rest of our days

8. Short poem: (1970/80s)

A woman is a woman and needs a man
A man is a man and lives as he can
A wife needs love and the comfort of home
A husband needs to provide and not live alone

9. Another passing thought: (1980's)

Unless it's spontaneous, trying to write inspired lines through boredom is an uphill struggle. At moments, in a great need to express oneself, words can magically flow onto paper. To try and recreate those moments when at a loss for a way to amuse oneself is a hopeless task. Simple words can be made great words when the time and inspiration are right. Alas that time is not to be tonight!!

10. A grovelling apology: (Tesco car park - 16 Jan 15)

A few harsh words that never should have been said
Causing anguish and pain before going to bed
I think and wonder how this can be
How can I hurt someone who means so much to me

Forgive me dear and let us stay
Close to each other in our own special way
One thing is certain and I know it's true
There is no one in this world more loving and caring than you

11. Valentine's day - never!

ANNETTE - MY LIFE

No flowers, no cards, no roses on the vine
But a deeply held gratitude that you are, and always will be - mine
Gifts are not needed on this commercial day
We express our love in gestures and what we say

The day we met my life changed forever
And through the highs and lows we have remained together
How else could it be for two that were meant to be
As one in life for all eternity

Our children are our gift and source of pride
I've watched them develop with you by my side
It's your values and love that has made them so
Now we watch as their children grow

Annette, the joy you give is beyond my powers to express
You've made my life, given me contentment and deep rooted happiness
Your kindness and spirit are there for all to see
And I thank the Lord that he gave you to me

12. Composed as my dear wife Annette contrived to change my nature in the 70th year of my life! (16 Nov 15)

I AM ME

We are what we are and that will always be
Developed through life to make you and me
There are good, clever, well-meaning and those with disdain
But however close we are not quite the same

My friend John was a wonderful person I'm sure you'll agree
But John was John and I am me

Iain is sincere and the love for his wife is plain to see
But Iain is Iain and I am me

No man is perfect, we all have our faults that's for sure
But being understanding and compassionate is what we should strive for
Don't aim to cause pain, that's not what it's about
Life is for living, without constraint or self-doubt

The people I know both colourful and plain
Have various qualities, but not all the same
That's life and exactly as it should be
I don't need to be someone else, my name is Phil and I am me

13. A few words for my good friend John on the occasion of his 60th birthday.

MY FRIEND JOHN

It was back in the 70s' that we first met
As neighbours then friends, as strong as you get
There is no man I know as true as he
Well, I suppose if you think about it, there's always me.

English by birth but both Scots at heart
There was an affinity with John right from the start
We two came north and couldn't find fault
Both with our wives and the quality malt

The Navy connection was always there
John in the dockyard and me elsewhere
He knew his trade, all the technical bits
Whilst I got along with flannel and well-worn dits

John has now reached that magical age and should not despair
There are good times ahead with plenty to share
But if feeling sad he should perhaps recall
Amongst many of his friends he is the youngest of all

Welcome to the club of bus passes and dentures
When going up town is one of many wild adventures
It was only last week, what a time we had and how
I'd tell you about it, but I can't remember now

Always ready to help when he can
There's not many like John - a sort of special man
He listens to my stories, patiently and to the end
Who could ask for more from a grand old friend.

Sadly John did not make the grand old age of 70.

14. Composed for the spreading of the ashes of our dear friends. 29 Jun 16

HELEN AND JOHN

Their laughter, their style, their sheer enjoyment of life
Moulded a couple into a special man and wife
Forever thoughtful with others always in mind
They knew no other way than being generous and kind

Our times together brought nothing but joy and cheer
Their sincerity and truth we will always hold dear
How do you adequately express how good they were
A couple who enriched our lives, a precious pair

Farewell my friends you are together again
Embraced by love and devoid of pain
Life will never be the same now that you're gone
Thank you for the treasured memories - forever remembered
Helen and John

15. Yet another 'Date of writing unknown'. Suspect it was composed not too long after re-engaging to complete service to the age of 40 years within the Royal Navy.

My family gives me the strength I need
To see me through all that in which I have to succeed

The days apart seem a high price to pay
For the security and happiness that will be ours one day

Not being together invokes a tremendous strain
How can such love involve so much pain?
The years I've chosen ahead, is that wise?
Surely so, with complete love and happiness as our prize

16. Written (scribbled!) in Traders Hotel, Singapore during mid 1990's.

If you had knees and legs like mine
You'd feel your creator had committed a crime
Still they get me around, I don't need a staff
And what is more they give my friends a good laugh

Acknowledgements

My heartfelt, sincere and everlasting thanks to my amazing grandson (and Agent!), Stephen, whose foresight and belief paved the way to getting this book published. Your cheery smile warms my heart.

To Gary Sutherland, an established author and family member, for his excellent advice and guidance. The beers are on me.

To Paul Warriner, an artist with outstanding skills. Thank you sincerely for the depiction of a Royal Navy Frigate crashing through the waves and for your approval to have it incorporated on this book cover.

To all my close friends and colleagues who gave approval for their names to be used when describing various exploits and events. Much appreciated.

And of course, mention must go to my beloved wife Annette, without whom the events described would never have happened. Take care dear. You are, and always will be, the centre of my life.

CPSIA information can be obtained
at www.ICGtesting.com
Printed in the USA
BVHW031156300421
R12177800001B/R121778PG606023BVX00004B/4

9 781839 754616